MAKING WOMEN PAY

MAKING WOMEN PAY

MICROFINANCE IN URBAN INDIA   Smitha Radhakrishnan

Duke University Press   *Durham and London*   2022

COVER ART: Ganesh
Ramachandran

© 2022 DUKE UNIVERSITY PRESS
All rights reserved
Printed in the United States of America on acid-free paper ∞
Text designed by Courtney Leigh Richardson
Cover designed by Drew Sisk
Typeset in Minion Pro and Trade Gothic by Westchester
Publishing Services

Library of Congress Cataloging-in-Publication Data
Names: Radhakrishnan, Smitha, [date] author.
Title: Making women pay: microfinance in urban India /
Smitha Radhakrishnan.
Description: Durham: Duke University Press, 2021. | Includes
bibliographical references and index.
Identifiers: LCCN 2021002649 (print) | LCCN 2021002650 (ebook)
ISBN 9781478013938 (hardcover)
ISBN 9781478014874 (paperback)
ISBN 9781478022169 (ebook)
Subjects: LCSH: Microfinance—Social aspects—India. | Women
in economic development—Government policy—India. |
Discrimination in banking—India. | Income distribution—India.
| Women—India—Economic conditions—21st century. | BISAC:
SOCIAL SCIENCE / Sociology / General | HISTORY / Asia / India &
South Asia
Classification: LCC HG178.33. I4 R335 2021 (print) |
LCC HG178.33. I4 (ebook) | DDC 332.0954—dc23
LC record available at https: //lccn.loc.gov/2021002649
LC ebook record available at https: //lccn.loc.gov/2021002650

For the women of the world who take on exploitative debt in order to survive

Abbreviations and Acronyms · ix
Acknowledgments · xi

Introduction · 1

1   The Invisible State of Gender and Credit · 25

2   Men and Women of the MFI · 47

3   Making Women Creditworthy · 70

4   Social Work · 100

5   Empowerment, Declined · 124

6   Distortions of Distance · 148

7   Impact Revisited · 177

Conclusion · 197

Methodological Appendix · 211
Notes · 219
Bibliography · 233
Index · 245

CEO   Chief Executive Officer

CGAP   Consultative Group to Assist the Poor (World Bank)

CSR   Corporate Social Responsibility

MFI   Microfinance institution

MFIN   Microfinance Institutions Network

NBFC   nonbankiing financial companies

NGO   Nongovernmental Organization

RBI   Reserve Bank of India

SHG   Self-help group

SKS   Swayam Krushi Sangh, a prominent MFI

When I embarked on this project in 2011, I wanted it to be small and contained and focused on microfinance training programs. I wanted to get it out into the world as quickly as possible so that my research could engage with the exploding literature on microfinance that I saw growing around me. But that did not come to pass. This project took nine years. Because as with any interesting project, the more I learned, the less I felt I knew, and the context of the project—what I thought it was—kept expanding. By the time I finished this book, I had not just researched training programs or a more obvious expansion to commercial microfinance in urban India. I had also examined self-help group (SHG) programs, the Indian rural banking infrastructure, Reserve Bank of India policies around financial inclusion, Kiva.org data, and a complex burgeoning literature on financialization. The kind of time and commitment required to get the project to feel like it was approaching "done" far exceeded anything I could have imagined, and thus required far more support than I would have expected. I have been extremely privileged to have gotten all that I needed and then some.

At the outset, I thank the companies I call Kanchan, Sowbagya, and Prosperity. Their willingness to work with me, introduce me to the worlds they operate in, and speak candidly to me about their work lies at the essence of this book. I also thank the many field-workers and clients who made room in their hectic lives to chat with me and allow me to interview them. I am grateful to all my interviewees and informal interlocutors I met along the way. Special thanks to Kim Wilson for the introductions she provided for my 2016 research, and to Priya Surya for providing me with my first orienting interview early in this project.

I extend my deep gratitude to Wellesley College and especially the Sociology Department. My colleagues have been particularly supportive and encouraging over the course of this lengthy path and have always believed that I had something important to say, even when I doubted it. I am particularly grateful for the heartfelt and continuous support from Peggy Levitt, Markella Rutherford, and Lee Cuba. At every step of the way, the college has also been exceptionally generous in providing me with leave from teaching and research support through faculty awards, and later, through the LuElla LaMer Slaner chair.

I have had wonderful research assistance over the years for this project. In the field, Bagyalakshmi Thyagarajan and M. R. Mamatha provided able support for Tamil and Kannada respectively. I enjoyed the time we spent together and the supportive presence they each provided in sometimes difficult conditions. Both Bagya and Mamatha also helped with the translation and transcription of the interviews and fieldwork they helped conduct. I am eternally grateful to Elango Minnoor and Darshana Minnoor for making my family's stay in Bengaluru in 2012 smooth and memorable. Thank you also to Sarada Krishnamurthy for hosting Bagya and I in Coimbatore. At Wellesley, Ana Plascensia Casillas and Mariam Saifullah provided particularly critical support analyzing my data in the early stages. Emily Eck provided able research assistance while I was in residence at Boston College. Meredyth Grange provided outstanding transcription services. In the final stages, expert editing by Debi Osnowitz got the manuscript out the door in record time.

A project of this scope is impossible without strong funding over many years. My gratitude goes to the American Association of University Women (AAUW)'s American Fellowship, for funding for my 2011–2012 fieldwork. Later in the process, a Frederick Burkhardt Fellowship from the American Council of Learned Societies (ACLS) funded a year of writing at the wonderfully supportive Boston College Sociology Department, where I was surrounded by outstanding colleagues and interlocutors. The Burkhardt also funded a second round of research in India in 2016 as well as much-needed support for transcription and research assistance. I am extremely grateful to have been a part of this remarkable program.

Slices of this book in various iterations have been presented at dozens of talks and conferences. The book you have before you benefited tremendously from all these interactions. I am particularly grateful for opportunities to present this research at the re:Work International Research Center at Humboldt University in Berlin, the Fletcher School of Law and Diplomacy's Gender and International Affairs Conference, and the Dhar India Studies Speaker Series at Indiana University, Bloomington. Sessions at the American Sociological Association conferences in 2017–20 as well as the Society for the Advancement of Socio-Economics' invited panel on "Zelizer around the world" proved extremely useful as well. In addition, the Society for Economic Anthropology's workshop on Financialization in 2017 in Iowa City was an intellectual turning point for me. In 2019, I was grateful to speak about this work in Ahmedabad at the ICT4D conference, an audience that gave me much confidence and critical feedback. Shortly thereafter, I benefitted from an engaged and generous audience as a part of Brown University's South Asia Speaker Series.

Outside formal institutional spaces, I have been lucky to be surrounded by colleagues who are also friends, and many of them have conversed with me, read chapters, and helped me in some fundamental way to make this book happen. Cinzia Solari is always by my side as a ready sounding board and supportive voice. Nina Sylvanus read early drafts of my introduction and always encourages me to keep going with unparalleled kindness and admiration. Sarah Babb has been a strong support for this project from the start, hosting me at Boston College during my fellowship year and, later, reading drafts, an early version of the prospectus, and more steps along the way than I can remember. A writing group she formed along with Alya Guseva, Emily Barman, and Michel Anteby was hugely helpful in articulating and shoring up the connection between this project and the field of economic sociology. My thanks also to my fellow sociologists of South Asia for feedback at various stages: Michael Levien, Fareen Parvez, Gowri Vijayakumar, and Poulami Roychowdury. Thank you to Patrick Inglis for timely and useful feedback on my introduction during the pandemic.

An earlier version of chapter 4 appeared in *Economic Anthropology* as "Of Loans and Livelihoods: Gendered 'Social Work' in Urban India." A previous version of chapter 5 was published in *Signs: Journal for Women in Culture and Society* as "Empowerment, Declined: Paradoxes of Microfinance and Gendered Subjectivity." Many of the core ideas that organize this book emerged from working with Erin Beck on the *Sociology of Development* article we coauthored, "Tracing Microfinancial Value Chains: Beyond the Impasse of Debt and Development." I am grateful for the anonymous reviewers of all these articles for helping me shore up key parts of my argument.

A huge thank you to Ken Wissoker at Duke University Press for once again having faith in my work, to editor-extraordinaire Gisela Fosado for shepherding the manuscript through the process with efficiency and care, and Ale Mejía for able editorial assistance throughout the process. A special thank you to the anonymous reviewers who gave me amazing feedback that greatly improved the final product.

I would not be who I am or where I am without my parents, Sharada and B. D. Radhakrishnan, or my brother, Prasant Radhakrishnan. Their love and support for me lies at my core, integral to this work and all my life's work.

The labor of writing a book is ultimately underwritten by those who share the everyday fabric of the writer's life, and this was especially true for this book. My deepest gratitude goes to Medha, who grew up along with this book, and Abhigyaan, who was born along the way somehow. You both keep me grounded and remind me that we all need a fairer future. Your intelligence, curiosity, and love mean the world to me. And most of all, I thank my nurturer and unconditional source of support, Ganesh, who never doubted for a second that I would get this done, and was willing to do whatever it took to make sure that was true.

On a temperate spring day in Bengaluru, India, twenty women ascended the stairs of a dark but airy concrete building in a dense working-class neighborhood. They were filled with anticipation and they chatted excitedly among themselves. On this day, they would each receive ten thousand rupees (about two hundred dollars at the time) from a commercial microfinance institution (MFI) called Samudra.[1] I had learned from my interviews with other borrowers like them that they were likely to pay school fees, pay off more expensive loans, and meet medical expenses with these funds. They had promised Samudra that they would repay this loan monthly at an annual interest rate of 22 percent, and that they would show up in person every month at a center meeting in their neighborhood to repay the required amount. This group consisted of migrant women, who spoke Urdu and Tamil, not the local Kannada language of the region. Many were garment workers and most were mothers.

Two Samudra staff members, a woman and a man, both in their twenties, oversaw the disbursement that followed. Sandhya, the young woman, cheerfully helped seat the women in rows on the polished concrete floor as they awaited their disbursement. She had recruited and organized this group, and this was her moment of triumph, when her customers would receive their funds. When the customers were settled, she leaned casually against a wall, smiling. Her work was, for the moment, complete. Her bright yellow salwar kameez,[2] printed with florescent blue boats, remained bright in the dim room. In the festive atmosphere, Sanjay, the young man, began reviewing the rules and regulations regarding the loans. Wearing a button-down shirt with slacks, he looked like an office worker with some authority, but like Sandhya, he smiled broadly at the women gathered, even as he read out rules that sounded boring and routine, as protocols required. "Will everyone come to meetings on time?" "Does everyone understand that for each rupee we lend you, you will pay back one rupee and twenty-two paisa? Plus our service fees?" Everyone agreed, again, nodding and smiling. After a few minutes of announcements, Sanjay called their names, one by one, and each woman rose to accept their ten thousand rupees in cash from Sanjay, which they quickly whisked away into purses, blouses, cloaks, and envelopes. Each woman thanked Sanjay, nodded thank-you and goodbye to Sandhya, and departed to their homes, some in groups and some alone. As I witnessed the scene, I noticed a palpable collective joy.

This typical disbursement scene in the world of commercial microfinance in India appears to confirm a prevailing understanding of small loans for vulnerable women in India and other parts of the global South: that women happily receive loans from generous lenders and can be counted on to reliably repay. It is easy to believe that the joy of disbursement signals real opportunity for the women borrowers I witnessed receiving funds. But the optics of this scene are deceiving. By disbursing the funds, Samudra initiated loans that will profit their company on terms that the women gathered can ill afford. The cash is expensive—at least two to three times more expensive than the prevailing rate of interest at public and private banks, despite the fact that these borrowers are likely to repay at a near-perfect rate. Like payday lenders in the US, Samudra specifically targeted this group of working-class women, most of whom regularly experience economic distress, and would profit substantially.[3] Sandhya and Sanjay felt pleased to be disbursing ten thousand rupees each to this group of customers because they believed it would serve their customers well. But they also knew that the group's timely repayment would be required for their own salaries and promotions.

India constitutes the world's largest market for financial services. There, 465 million adults still lack access to basic services for credit and savings.[4] In the last two decades, however, commercial microfinance has come to saturate the everyday lives of women in both rural and urban contexts in India in the name of state-led efforts to promote "financial inclusion" and "women's empowerment." I argue in this book that these efforts appear to help women borrowers, but in fact extract value from them through exploitative relationships that benefit more privileged groups. Commercial microfinance in India thus relies upon and strengthens gendered and class inequalities, undermining working-class women's entitlements while shoring up the positions of especially class-privileged men, who appear to be helping them by providing financial services.

The Bengaluru disbursement scene reveals that microfinance involves women borrowers receiving money. But it also shows that loan officers, branch staff, and corporate leaders together facilitate the group formation, the timing of the loan, and the terms on which customers receive and repay loans. Sandhya did the work of recruiting this group and getting them all to the branch office at the right time with all the proper approvals in place. To accomplish this, she had developed a personal bond with each client that now also connected them to Samudra. Sanjay, in contrast, a member of the staff at the local branch office, did his job at arm's length from the customers. He followed proper protocols around disbursement put in place by regulators and enforced by corporate leadership. Many other players indirectly influenced the mood and script of the disbursement event. Outside the Samudra branch office, dozens of other MFIS competed for the same borrowers in an increasingly crowded financial ecosystem targeting working-class women. Every day, all these actors, along with many others outside the frame of this scene, make Indian microfinance work.

This book explores the inner workings of India's profit-oriented microfinance sector during a period of relative stability after a phase of rapid growth and crisis. I examine the chain of actors, institutions, interests, and policies that continue to make the high-interest loans offered by Indian MFIS appealing to millions of vulnerable borrowers. I investigate how such loan programs actually work, who benefits, and what the long-term effects are on women borrowers and the MFI employees who serve them. Studying this chain of interconnected actors, I argue that commercial microfinance is best understood as an extractive industry. Instead of serving poor women, commercial microfinance exploits social inequalities to extract value away from those women, in service of more privileged groups who believe that they are helping the marginalized.

The Structural Context of Microfinance in Millennial India

The gendered value extraction of microfinance occurs within the context of economic liberalization, an increased concentration of wealth among India's most privileged, and a profound lack of basic services for most Indian citizens. Within this broad context, those who engage with the microfinance industry, whether as borrowers, employees, policy makers, or remote actors, all occupy divergent social locations, constrained by class and livelihood, gender identities, and state-driven regulatory environments.

Microfinance can be considered a hallmark of neoliberal India; its rise to prominence has emerged in lockstep with liberalization policies since the 1990s, which have dramatically privatized India's economy and brought unprecedented levels of wealth to India's most privileged citizens.[5] Liberalization in the Indian economy took place over two decades and in many sectors, from industry to banking to infrastructure. In all these areas, policies pivoted the nation away from a partly socialistic economy oriented toward poverty reduction, which had been conceived of in the postwar era of the 1940s and 1950s, and toward a globalized economy oriented toward economic growth." This pivot has served the purpose of accelerating economic growth and, by some measures, has reduced absolute levels of poverty. But it has greatly accelerated both urbanization and inequality.

According to a 2016 report, India is the second-most unequal country in the world, after South Africa, with millionaires controlling 54 percent of the country's wealth.[6] Economic indicators suggest that these staggering levels of inequality have been accompanied by rising unemployment since the early 2000s, with a spike in 2018, especially among urban women.[7] The turn to liberalization has done little to provide the majority of India's citizens access to basic health care, education, housing, or sanitation. In this context, it should come as no surprise that small loans are often used to meet expenses that most Indian citizens require, but they receive no public subsidy to access.

Although the Indian government started rolling out large programs of small loans targeting women in the early 1980s, the new millennium brought an influx of billions of dollars in foreign equity capital that helped Indian MFIS "scale up."[8] Venture capitalists from the US especially started viewing Indian microfinance as a promising investment opportunity and sought to funnel dollars toward profitable business models in the global South that would also serve development aims. I initially believed that this influx signaled just how much power foreign investors wielded in the Indian microfinance industry. But later I discovered that the Indian government's regulatory frameworks had consistently limited that influence in order to prioritize the expansion of domestic banks and investors. Banking regulations did not allow Indian companies receiving investments to include those funds for the purposes of lending. Funds from outside India could only be used to expand infrastructure, improve technology, build branches, or buy equipment. As a result, the huge influx of equity capital into the Indian financial sector did not directly translate into increased funds for MFI lending. Instead, it was a 2005 policy change incentivizing Indian banks to channel funding toward MFIS that profoundly changed India's financial ecosystem for the poor.[9] Almost overnight, Indian MFIS became beholden to Indian banks, many of them public. Flush with funding for the first time, from 2005 onward, Indian MFIS started aggressively finding new clients, expanding to new neighborhoods and regions, and improving their organizational capacities.

neoliberalism

The new regulatory environment reflected nationwide plans to promote "financial inclusion," a policy package also launched in 2005. These policies allocated responsibility to private financial companies for the financial aspects of "women's empowerment" programs. In parallel, the state curtailed substantive "empowerment" projects for women. They instead shored up "thrift and microcredit" programs that were lean and required little oversight or accountability.[10] As a result of these poverty policies, shaped by new logics and fewer regulations, a new financial ecosystem crystallized in millennial India, one in which women in both rural and urban areas were encouraged to acquire loans, brought literally to their doorsteps, with high economic and social costs.

Class and gender inequalities structure the everyday functioning of this new financial ecosystem. Most microfinance borrowers are women (96 percent in India), but the industry is controlled and financed almost exclusively by men. These organizational dynamics unfold in a context governed by state mandates for financial inclusion and women's empowerment. In this new financial ecosystem, the state is able to mandate multiple competing financial institutions to serve the poor, while also incentivizing them to disburse expensive debt with little regard to whether those loans serve their borrowers' own interests.

Beyond Treatment or Consequence

The existing fulsome body of research on microfinance has tended to approach the practice as either an apolitical treatment that must be assessed according to its "impact" on the borrower or as an inevitable consequence of neoliberalism. The most sophisticated studies combine these approaches, addressing borrower impact and political economic context. But I argue that both paradigms miss how microfinance exploits structures of gender and class to facilitate the extraction of value from those at the bottom in service of those at the top. Understanding microfinance as an industry not only highlights and offers a framework through which to understand the extraction of value, it also highlights the importance of the regulatory environment and competition in constraining and incentivizing the actions of financial institutions in the context of market-oriented development.

Impact has been arguably the primary optic through which microfinance has been studied and evaluated.[11] Despite divergent conclusions, early studies overwhelmingly focused on whether or not a small group loan would be good or bad for women, an economistic framing that avoided political and social context. When scholars did emphasize context, institutions, and interactions, the purpose was to understand and improve implementation.[12]

Responding to this framing, scholars from multiple disciplines and methodologies have put forth compelling research about microfinance's positive or negative impacts on borrowers. This approach has produced invaluable insights about the everyday workings of microfinance in the lives of borrowers. Lamia Karim's path-breaking work in rural Bangladesh, for example, showed that, for many women, loans from the Grameen Bank and BRAC caused financial and social ruin, collateralizing the social ties that have kept rural women afloat in the past.[13] In contrast, Paromita Sanyal's research in West Bengal, India, showed that, in the context of state-run self-help groups (SHGs) linking groups of rural women to bank loans, there were important positive impacts on women's empowerment due to the collective character of meetings and increased physical mobility among women. Incentivized to emerge from the domestic sphere by the promise of cash, women forged ties with one another that carried over to other contexts of collective action.[14] Other scholars, including development economist Naila Kabeer, have been more circumspect about both microfinance's potential and its pitfalls.[15]

These studies exposed the limitations of microfinance while also discovering its successes. Along the way, these same studies provided clues about the broader political economy from which the logic and everyday practice of microfinance emerged. Karim's ethnography, for example, highlighted the dilemmas of loan officers in rural Bangladesh who had to force vulnerable families to repay. She revealed the high-level political deals that made the widespread rollout of microfinance appear to be a good rural development strategy for the state from the 1990s onward, when neoliberal reforms were underway around the world.[16] Expanding upon these insights, Ananya Roy identified new, elite actors who saw microfinance as an opportunity for a double bottom line that could enrich their coffers while also enhancing their reputation. Examining microfinance as an apparatus of neoliberal development, Roy's work revealed that the focus on impact was misguided. Roy showed that, through neoliberal discourses, banking elites had constructed racialized women in the global South as saviors, while promoting the notion of self-sufficiency.[17]

Melding treatment and consequence approaches, recent work on microfinance has argued that the global expansion of microfinance is exemplary of a broader political economic phenomenon: the *financialization of poverty.* "As global financial markets for credit have become saturated, excess financial capital has sought out new markets for investment, increasingly turning to subprime markets outside the financial system. Commercial microfinance is the consequence of this global transformation; even poverty has become a financial product that can be bought and sold. The financialization of poverty, a phenomenon spearheaded by bankers but supported by policy makers and even nonprofit organizations, helps construct poverty as a condition that can be addressed through cash loans, even though studies show that poverty is rooted in relations of power.[18]

Women borrowers in particular experience the financialization of poverty as an everyday, embodied experience of marginalization. Sohini Kar has shown that in India, the poor become "enfolded" in finance through commercial MFIS. Women borrowers come to construct their lives so that they may abide by the strict rules and requirements of loans, even as they demonstrate resourcefulness that maneuvers outside official rules. Kar reveals also that loan officers, an understudied group in the existing literature, expend significant emotional and physical labor to extract debt from vulnerable borrowers.[19] Understanding microfinance as the financialization of poverty, then, helps advance us beyond the too-narrow framing of "impact" and the too-expansive framing of "consequence" by illuminating political economic dynamics.

MICROFINANCE AS AN INDUSTRY OF GENDERED EXTRACTION

As microfinance continues to expand and become further entrenched around the world, I build upon these perspectives to further specify the core ingredients that are needed to conceptualize microfinance in a way that takes seriously structures of social inequality and the discourses that legitimate and naturalize those structures. I engage the situated perspectives and motivations of actors and institutions who are interconnected with one another, including women borrowers, loan officers, program managers, branch staff, corporate staff, and C-suite executives. Centering unpaid and underpaid gendered labor as the primary source of value in extractive microfinancial chains, I find that in the Indian microfinance industry, men in finance, privileged in their existing social positions and endowed with political and economic power, extract value from women in debt.[20]

An "extractive industry" paradigm helps us understand exactly how microfinance allows privileged men in finance to profit from vulnerable women in debt while appearing to help them. In the current literature, the term *extractive* refers descriptively to industries that extract natural resources from the earth and turn them into valuable commodities in local and global markets.

Without the value-adding process of "extraction," natural resources would remain "untapped," and thus, valueless.[21] I turn this descriptive usage into an analytical usage by building upon existing constructions of women's labor, time, and intellect as "untapped resources," a framing advanced in global development discourses.[22] Microfinance extracts the unpaid labor of women to organize themselves and their neighbors in order to repay expensive, restrictive debt in a timely manner. In addition to their unpaid labor, women's images, stories, and experiences with education lend symbolic value to more powerful actors in the microfinance industry, almost exclusively men. Once connected to financial institutions through relationships of trust, and later, through credit scores, the labor and symbols of women borrowers bring value to local and global financial markets, but not necessarily to women borrowers themselves. Instead, the extracted value gets funneled toward more privileged groups, who experienced enhanced financial and reputational gains. Within MFIs, class-privileged men (and a few women) ride an escalator to the upper echelons of the industry, leaving working-class and poor men and women behind on a "sticky floor." When we understand microfinance as an extractive industry, we turn on its head the notion that microfinance is an intervention aiming to empower and enrich poor women. Instead, we begin to see how microfinance extracts labor and honor from poor women for the benefit of primarily men employed by financial companies and their allies.

To unpack the paradigm of extractive industry in detail, I rely upon three theoretical traditions: feminist commodity chains, actor-oriented sociology, and relational work. When synthesized, these perspectives help clarify and illuminate the structure and form of microfinance as it operates in India and likely in other parts of the world as well.

Drawing on ethnographic observation and interviews in southern India, I triangulate the perspectives of clients, trainers, and frontline loan officers, as well as other MFI staff, leaders, and investors. I situate my analysis within the history of Indian banking policy, the changing regulatory state, and the broader context of financialization. I also situate key actors in the global North who engage with commercial microfinance in India and elsewhere: online lenders on peer-to-peer platforms such as Kiva.org and employees of global companies engaged in repayment and marketing. These actors provide ideological cover for the commercial microfinance industry, allowing the situated practices and effects of MFIs to escape scrutiny. Together, these actors in diverse social locations help MFIs and similar financial institutions efficiently extract value and wealth from poor and working-class women,

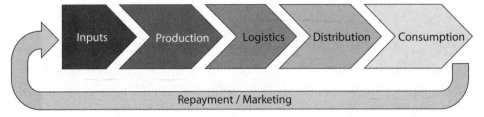

FIGURE I.1. Michael Porter's (1985) classic value chain.

supported by state and global institutions, and organized by gender and class inequality.

FEMINIST COMMODITY CHAINS

This critical theory emphasizes women's unpaid labor within a macro-structural context of inequality and provides the foundation for the extractive paradigm for microfinance I propose.[23] Commodity chains analysis, *out.* emerging from world-systems theory, posits that the various steps involved in the production of a commodity, whether a T-shirt or a television, reveal geopolitical, social, and institutional inequalities. Each step along the formal points of production in the life cycle of a commodity adds value to commodities that circulate within a global political economy.[24] Feminist commodity chains research uncovers the informal forms of labor—paid and unpaid—through which women produce commodities and reproduce the labor force. Once we see Indian microfinance driven by women's work, and situated within a broader chain, we start to recognize how women's labor enhances profits enjoyed by those higher up the chain.

What might feminist commodity chains look like for microfinance? Michael Porter's classic chain examines sequential processes through which commodities in a capitalist system gain value.[25] Specifying these processes to improve efficiency and enhance profits, Porter's model has informed myriad adaptations, one of which appears in figure I.1. Represented horizontally, this model depicts a cyclical process, with each step adding value to previous links in the chain. Marketing and repayment fuel its continuation, although in practice, commodity chains also depend on people and places, which are geographically dispersed and organized according to historical patterns of *Context* inequality.[26] *Comm. chains themselves not enough*

The processes associated with microfinance are carried out by individuals with gender and class identities that are geographically defined and constrained. Figure 1.2, therefore, presents my adaptation of Porter's model, depicting a hierarchical commodity chain organized through class, gender, and geography. This chain is immersed in a financial ecosystem structured by a state-driven regulatory environment that constrains the practices of actors, and it is flooded by competing products targeting working-class and poor women.[27] Organized hierarchically, with mostly men at the top and mostly women at the bottom, figure 1.2 includes the social actors, institutions, and environments that constitute India's microfinance industry. The hierarchies in this model more or less mirror global social and economic structures, but with local actors and the financial ecosystem setting boundaries for capital inputs moving through the system. While power within this system is exerted top-down, value is extracted from the bottom-up, fueled by a feminine base of labor and the consumption of financial products that are used to make ends meet within households.[28] This conceptualization of microfinance as an industry helps expose the regulatory

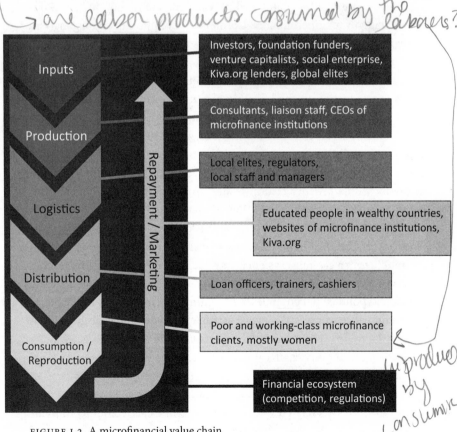

FIGURE 1.2. A microfinancial value chain.

environment and real conditions of production in order to push for transparency and accountability.

While a feminist commodity chains perspective reveals hidden dynamics of gendered labor, hierarchy, and organization, we must probe further to examine the situated interests of the individuals whose work extracts financial profits. Actor-oriented sociology has been used to great advantage in studies of global development organizations, aid, and the implementation of global development programs in local contexts to study human agency in context.[29] Actor-oriented sociology "locates individuals in the specific life-worlds in which they manage their daily affairs"[30] and recognizes that individuals and social groups are capable and knowledgeable within their given context, actively solving the problems most relevant to their lives. Furthermore, this approach acknowledges that, often, the motivations of actors in a similar social location conflict with those in another location, and may also conflict with the goals of the organization that employs them. By highlighting human agency, an actor-oriented approach helps us see how the financialization of poverty is produced on the ground, while explaining the huge gap between formal mandates and on-the-ground practices.

Several recent studies have adopted actor-oriented approaches to understand how women borrowers navigate microfinance and make it useful in their own lives.[31] These scholars emphasize the details of how women borrowers use microfinance within the particular economic, social, and political constraints of their lives. Erin Beck argues, in fact, that microfinance has persisted not because it is helping, but because of women's creative usage and transformation of the possibilities that microfinance presents, especially in impoverished contexts where there are few alternatives for pursuing a livelihood. Extending these insights, I show in this book that women borrowers in southern India come from more diverse class backgrounds than we might expect and take out loans for a surprising variety of economic, social, and political purposes.

Microfinance workers also juggle multiple identities and goals in addition to their professional and organizational mandates. The work of frontline MFI workers is pressing and immediate, and often sits uneasily alongside industry mandates for financial inclusivity or women's empowerment imposed by the government. Microfinance workers try to meet client needs, secure promotions, support their families, and meet quotas for customer outreach. Apart from frontline MFI workers, leaders and regulators also juggle multiple goals and identities; they must address the needs of diverse stakeholders with divergent priorities while also attending to their own personal reputation, career goals, and family priorities.

An actor-oriented perspective invites us not only into the experiences of many interconnected actors within the industry but also into organizational dynamics, incentive structures within the industry, and the interface between the financial industry and state policies.

RELATIONAL WORK

Feminist commodity chains and actor-oriented perspectives help balance macrostructural understandings with agency. But in order to conceptualize how the different parts of the extractive industry work together, we require an understanding of relationships, particularly those between women borrowers and the MFIS. How and why do women borrowers, often stratified within their own communities along lines of caste and class, come to trust one another, their loan officers, and the MFI? These relationships cannot be taken for granted. Between borrowers and loan officers, these relationships are forged by sharing intimate information about assets, housing, occupation, health, childbearing, and family. When borrowers share information with one another and with MFI staff, they establish relationships of trust that are reinforced through the rituals of loan-taking. This mutual trust forms the basis of the gendered financial ecosystem that has emerged from financial inclusion initiatives and the expansion of microfinance in India, and pushes MFIS to create creditworthy women through loan officers, who must cover up default when it happens and help produce high repayment rates for MFIS operating in vulnerable neighborhoods. Through relationality, women and loan officers, trainers, and other frontline MFI staff establish both social and economic ties.

Drawing upon Viviana Zelizer's concept of *relational work*, I suggest that, to understand the financialization of poverty, we must recognize the relationships—simultaneously economic and social—that make profitable finance for the poor possible.[32] India's MFIS and the policies that support them rely upon relational work, particularly at the bottom of the chain, where working-class women join a lending group and forge relationships with each other as well as with their loan officers, usually men. These ties of trust, intimacy, and mutual reciprocity help bring MFIS legitimacy in a context where communities are often suspicious of financial companies that are not formal banks.

This book explores two distinct realms of relational work. First, I explore the essential but invisible relational work between loan officers and women borrowers and between women within neighborhoods. These relationships are labor intensive, often fraught, and constitute the foundation upon which the financialization of poverty rests. Without women organized into specific kinds of groups that comply with particular risk-adverse regulatory frameworks who also trust one another enough to repeatedly take loans together, commercial microfinance cannot continue to expand. And if those women do not develop reliable relationships with MFI staff who can work with them to produce near-perfect repayment rates, even when times are tough, MFIS cannot function at all, much less with the financial and reputational success they currently enjoy. *rely on relationships*

I contrast this type of relational work with a highly visible but artificial and nonessential relational work between women borrowers and remote global North actors who appear to be engaged in microfinance, whether through employment in a large international MFI or by lending on Kiva.org. I show that while many of these remote microfinancial actors express commitment to the values of self-sufficiency and empowerment upon which microfinance is ideally based, the connection that they experience in relation to borrowers, when experienced, is almost entirely fictional. Based on anecdotes, personal experiences in a particular region of the world, or presumptions about virtuous and less virtuous businesses for poor women to be engaged in, the relational work of remote microfinance actors disguises the more complex and troubling variety of financial products in the world dubbed as "microfinance." The high visibility of remote actors in microfinance misleads publics around the world and distracts from the extractive character of the commercial microfinance industry. *fake : disguise*

The Gendered Chain of Value Extraction from Bottom to Top

A) WOMEN BORROWERS AND THE SATURATED LOAN ENVIRONMENT

Microfinance targets women successfully in urban India because women borrowers are both needy and exceedingly resourceful. They navigate complex social and economic environments from constrained positions and manage to get by and often thrive despite overwhelming constraints. In urban neighborhoods, the gendered financial ecosystem consists of loans that vary in their level of predation. Informal moneylenders, commercial MFIs, self-help groups, chit funds, and family loans together make up a complex web of

strategic targeting of women

obligations and labor that increasingly rely upon women for repayment. The MFI clients I met used their loans for a variety of expenses that they could not meet through other means: school fees or college fees for their children, medical bills for necessary procedures, improvements on their homes, wedding expenses, or paying off more expensive debt obtained from pawnbrokers or neighborhood moneylenders. Although microfinance thus offers borrowers access to financial products at lower costs than those of neighborhood money lenders, these loans have simply not addressed the vulnerability of working-class families, who are in a constant struggle to meet the immediate health, educational, and social needs of their families.

Women borrowers, who are almost always married to men, are overwhelmingly engaged in informal work, which by some estimates makes up as much as 90 percent of all employment in India.[33] They face a combination of class, caste, and gender disadvantage that largely prevents them from moving out of slum neighborhoods. Many have husbands or sons earning stable incomes, but others struggle to make ends meet monthly. Borrowers living in urban areas are most often domestic workers or stay-at-home mothers who run temporary businesses that bring in a supplementary income. Many are factory workers, earning paltry, unstable wages. A few are true micro-entrepreneuers. There are, indeed, success stories of entrepreneurial women who have grown their own small businesses that sustain a livelihood for their families. I met one Bengaluru woman from the neighborhood of Kadugondanahalli, for example, who ran a flour mill out of a rented shop space. She employed other women from her neighborhood in her small shop. This was a rare success because the capital needed to come up with a flour mill costs at least twenty times the amount of a typical microfinance loan. Most women could never access the kind of capital needed to start a sustainable business. Indeed, the MFIs I studied did not expect their borrowers to have their own businesses. Instead, they wished to lend to "working women," who were employed, usually as domestic workers. The approach that MFIs had to borrowers reveals the vulnerable structural position of women borrowers within the context of India's economy as a whole and the inability for MFI loans to improve that structural position for most customers.

Most women I met were fully engaged in what Sohini Kar has termed credit-work: "the everyday set of practices that women engage in to access, maintain, and repay loans." Kar argues, "[Credit-work] highlights the multiplying demands on women's time, while—as with much of women's unpaid work—[it] goes unrecognized as labor."[34] To meet monthly consumption

loans show lack of soc. services

and medical expenses, many borrowers I met required a constant influx of loans to compensate for their lack of access to basic social supports. Women participate in lending groups to come up with a lump sum in order to pay school fees for their children, to repair their homes, or pay off more expensive debts. But there are significant inequalities between women borrowers living in slum neighborhoods that the presence of MFIs exacerbates. Better-off women living in slum neighborhoods leverage their class stature and their connections to organizations and political parties to organize other women into loan groups and lead those lending groups, even if they do not need the loans themselves. They may then loan the money out to other women in the neighborhood that do not qualify for loans from MFIs at a profit (a practice that is not permitted by official rules). Other powerful women partake in expensive loans simply to accrue prestige and goodwill among women in their communities, which can be used for political or social purposes when needed. *soc capital*

For all women borrowers, regardless of relative privilege, MFI loans are just one source of credit in a complex financial ecosystem crowded with competing financial products and services from both governmental, nongovernmental, and private sources. I delve into the origins and development of the financial ecosystem in which microfinance exists in chapter 1, while I focus on the pressures, strategies, and responses of indebted women in chapters 4, 5, and 7.

B) MFI WORKERS AND THE PRESSURE OF TARGETS AND MOBILITY

MFI loan officers and trainers often come from working-class backgrounds similar to the women they lend to and view their MFI jobs as valued pathways toward upward mobility in the context of widespread unemployment for young workers with modest levels of education. Those from rural areas may have degrees from small or less prestigious institutions. Most speak little or no English, and many I met had migrated from small towns or rural areas in Karnataka, Tamil Nadu, or Andhra Pradesh. Others came from working-class urban neighborhoods. At least two out of the eighteen customer-facing staff I interviewed came from families in which their own mothers had taken microfinance loans, which had introduced them to the microfinance industry and later led to employment.[35] Most were referred by relatives or recruited at college employment fairs. *MLM lenda who*

Sohini Kar regards MFI workers as the primary agents of microfinance, carrying out the physical and emotional labor of bringing the poor into financial systems.[36] In this study, I primarily focus on two kinds of MFI field-workers:

loan officers, who work directly with customers in the work of organizing groups, verifying them, and then collecting loans, and trainers, who offer optional, supplementary programming to MFI clients. Some of these workers are women, but most are men. Loan officers I met had to serve large customer bases of five hundred to six hundred customers in dense, vulnerable neighborhoods. Trainers occupy a slightly more prestigious role within the MFIs I studied. Like loan officers, they must meet quotas for training women on topics such as entrepreneurship or financial literacy. Organizations demand that trainers and loan officers alike extract good attendance numbers and inspiring success stories from their work, even when those outcomes can feel almost impossible to attain. Whether in loan officer or training roles, frontline MFI work is grueling and emotionally demanding. As a result, the turnover within these positions is high. Those MFI workers who stay within the industry are motivated by the financial rewards and the chance for true upward mobility, which some of them achieve. Very often, however, the outcomes their organization demands are at odds with workers' intentions to help their clients.

Company cultures within MFIs perpetuate gender and class inequalities, while relying on them to do their work. Within these organizations, privileged men sit at the top and less privileged men at the bottom as loan officers. Women may gain employment in corporations, but they encounter a sticky floor and far fewer opportunities to advance careers within the industry. Nonetheless, these masculinist companies—oriented toward scale, profit, and efficiency—go to great lengths to maintain their legitimacy in the face of serious challenges to the high moral ground they seek to occupy. Sustained by macroeconomic policies, their practices eclipse social concerns and instead support the goals of private finance.[37] I focus on the experiences and context of MFI workers in chapters 2, 3, and 7.

C) MFI LEADERS AND THE PRESSURES OF PROFIT AND SOCIAL GOOD

MFI leaders and banking regulators come from privileged class and caste backgrounds and are almost all men. This layer of the industry strategizes about how to make their companies profitable while also considering how they can maintain the high moral standing of their companies in the face of public challenges to their credibility. These leaders interact very little with borrowers, but local and global publics, as well as borrowers themselves, hold leaders in high esteem because they are seen as helping the poor. MFI leaders and regulators are motivated by what has been termed the double bottom line. They endeavor to build profitable organizations that serve shareholders and grow in value every year, but they also want the public to view that growth in a virtuous light. In order to do that, they must comply with regulations, foster positive work environments within their organizations, minimize the risk of scandal, and emphasize the benefits they provide to borrowers and workers. They must carefully document stories of customer success, ensure that their customers are sufficiently poor to meet the target criteria for their segment of the industry, and produce a near-perfect repayment rate. Together, these outcomes generate legitimacy and an ethos of charitability toward MFI leaders and the government policies that support them, even as MFIS expand in scale and profitability. Analyses of MFI leaders and their roles appear in chapters 1 and 2. *begin. → future expansion*

D) ARCHITECTS OF THE FINANCIALIZED GLOBAL ORDER

I did not directly study financial executives, venture capitalists, managers of social impact index funds, or national-level policy makers, but they do play influential roles in the microfinancial chain, sitting right at the top. These architects establish the global rules by which financial markets abide and the global supply of money in which Indian banks and financial institutions are situated. I went into this project believing that this group would have the most influence in the Indian financial sphere. I discovered instead that government policies and banking regulations laid down by the Indian state and corporate sectors control the dynamics of extraction that structure Indian microfinance. Global financial actors indeed benefit from the industry and undeniably help set up the environment in which the other actors I identify do their work. But these actors do not necessarily establish the terms upon which gendered and class-based extraction processes actually take place. My research thus suggests that, even though the financialized global economy indeed sets the context within which extraction through financial companies takes place, many of the most exploitative aspects of microfinance are carried out by state, local, and corporate actors. I touch upon the roles of these actors in chapter 1.

E) REMOTE MICROFINANCE ACTORS AND THE WORK OF LEGITIMIZATION

Just outside the chain, contributing to what I call "reproduction/marketing" are employees of major global microfinance companies, and everyday people, mostly located in the global North, who lend through peer-to-peer lending platforms such as Kiva.org. These actors are removed from the actual dynamics of gendered value extraction within the industry and serve *"sponsor" programs??*

the valuable role of funding and representing microfinance as benevolent to the rest of the world. In particular, remote microfinance actors help sustain the link between microfinance and women's empowerment. Like other global financial actors, these actors are also instrumental in providing funding, albeit to a far lesser extent. They are more important, however, in *what the culture* helping project a favorable reputation for microfinance companies that help those companies avoid scrutiny from the international arena. While other extractive industries have "greenwashing" campaigns that make oil companies look like they care for the environment, remote microfinance actors produce a rosy image of microfinance that conceals its real work. This is not only because of the marketing, as in the case of oil companies, but also because of the knowledge they rely on.

actively removed

Kiva lenders and international MFI employees experience lives that are far removed from the real interactions and products through which value is extracted from women borrowers. As a result, they have relatively abstract understandings of the everyday lives of borrowers, and they tend to generalize the experiences of women, of poverty, and of what it means to be self-sufficient. Whether lending on Kiva or actively working in the global MFI industry, remote microfinancial actors circulate simplistic understandings about the direct relationships between women, loans, and economic self-sufficiency and empowerment. In interviews and ethnographic observation, I found that that these remote MFI actors ignore or obscure information that conflicts with work they are doing in order to protect the perceived integrity of their own jobs and actions. Chapter 6 focuses on this remote set of actors.

Uncovering the Invisible Labor of Financialization

As the opening anecdote of this book makes clear, observing commercial microfinance, even in detail, does not reveal the dynamics that lie beneath the surface. I quickly learned direct observation and interview data provided a limited, and sometimes misleading, understanding of industry dynamics and of the financialization of poverty as a whole. I addressed this challenge by triangulating individual accounts, reports created by MFIs and other relevant organizations, and historical research. My research centered the non-elite actors who constitute the financialization of poverty in India, but I also engaged deeply with the many elite actors who create and sustain the front-facing dynamics I observed.

This study draws from eight months of ethnographic research in New York City and south India, most of it in 2012, and from 138 interviews conducted between 2011 and 2016. My interviews include fifty-five microfinance clients from two competing for-profit MFIs in the south Indian states of Tamil Nadu and Karnataka, sixty-nine interviews with MFI professionals from all levels of the industry, and fifteen interviews with lenders who supported entrepreneurs on the microlending platform Kiva.org. As I had no previous contacts with microfinance companies in India, I began by reaching out to a large MFI that I call Prosperity International (henceforth, Prosperity), a major multinational corporation based in New York.

Through Prosperity, I learned about entrepreneurial training for MFI clients in south India and especially about its Shaktisri program, one of the company's prime client education offerings. I thus began to research the relationships between Prosperity and its Indian partners. I spent two months attending meetings on Indian programming at Prosperity's head offices in New York City. There, I observed discussions and spoke with staff directly involved in the program's strategic planning and implementation. Through Prosperity's New York office, I gained an introduction to the company's office in Bengaluru, and through employees there, I connected with MFI clients and staff at multiple levels of the organization.

In Bengaluru, Chennai, and Coimbatore's outlying towns, I closely observed the everyday operations of the Shaktisri program, conducted in partnership with a relatively small, up-and-coming MFI that I call Kanchan (see figure 1.3). Shaktisri's entrepreneurial training for clients was part of Kanchan's corporate social responsibility (CSR) initiative. I attended Shaktisri trainings, interviewed clients afterward when possible, and interacted with trainers and other staff multiple times before asking for interviews with them. I also attended several internal Prosperity events and gatherings, including a six-day annual training for trainers. These sessions illuminated the tensions between Prosperity and Kanchan, together with the various divisions between their respective staffs.

Because my position within Kanchan did not permit a full view of lending operations, I reached out to a competing MFI working in the same neighborhoods and lending to the same clients. This large, nationally reputed MFI, which I call Sowbagya, offered a logical comparison. I approached Sowbagya's managing director, and he invited me to observe home visits, training sessions, center meetings, and events at local branches. I thus witnessed many different types of urban neighborhoods, varying dynamics among borrower groups, and varied interpersonal dynamics within branch offices. I also witnessed the launch of a new financial literacy program, Vriddhi, just rolled out for Sowbagya clients. I attended pilot trainings with clients

FIGURE I.3. Author with Bagya (research assistant and sister-in-law) and Nandini, a Kanchan trainer during Coimbatore fieldwork in 2012.

and staff trainings with managers in charge of implementing the program in their respective regions. When appropriate, I used these opportunities to recruit clients and MFI workers, including staff involved in Vriddhi, for interviews.

In the years following my fieldwork in India, I recruited US-based microfinance professionals who had worked in India, as well as Kiva lenders. These busy professionals could be interviewed only remotely, by phone or online. I was unable to conduct ethnographic observation of daily life at investor firms or even at large MFIS with global operations. Through continued conversations with MFI professionals, however, my understanding of the industry deepened, and in 2016 I returned to Chennai and Bengaluru for interviews with high-level MFI leaders. Expanding beyond Kanchan and Sowbagya, I interviewed founding directors and corporate-level staff at several more MFIS. I also followed up with Sowbagya leadership to update my knowledge of the Vriddhi financial literacy program, which was by then four years old and had reached tens of thousands of Sowbagya clients.

Ethnographic access is always difficult to secure, but I found the MFI landscape particularly sensitive. Because the industry is often in the public spotlight, companies and interlocutors expressed wariness of long-term research. The MFIS I approached were happy to host me for a day or two, but when I asked to attend training sessions or branch events regularly, over a long period, access became unreliable. As my research continued, therefore, I relied more heavily on private interviews rather than ethnography. One-on-one interviews were more easily facilitated through contacts, and less subject to organizational surveillance. The methodological appendix recounts these interpersonal challenges and opportunities.

As a sociologist, I always have to ask, "What is this a case of?" As I dove more deeply into this project, I realized that it was inadequate to assume that India's microfinance industry was a local case of the global phenomenon of financialization. I also realized that it was not necessarily just the latest in a line of gender and development programs coming out of the Indian state. It was, I learned, a case of banking policy being used as a development tool at M.C, a time when that tool conveniently benefitted financial elites and gender and development agendas. I dove into the history of financial inclusion in India and found startling parallels between current microfinance policies and efforts by the British to expand banking to rural populations in the nineteenth century. The minutiae of Reserve Bank of India circulars since 2000 were also crucial for understanding how MFIS became so powerful in the contemporary financial landscape for the poor.

Triangulating data from all these sources provides a detailed, but nonetheless partial, view of the everyday workings of India's microfinance industry as well as its embeddedness in local and global institutions and financial networks. My ethnographic observations early in the timeline of this project revealed the everyday work of microfinance unfolding between MFI borrowers and workers, as well as within lending groups. My interview data in the later years of my research revealed institutional dynamics that molded those everyday interactions and ongoing relationships. I thus sought not only to identify everyday processes at multiple sites within India's microfinance industry but also to contextualize those processes within practices, institutions, and the broader ideologies through which microfinance continues to maintain its legitimacy.

Outline of the Book

The book explores the extractive industry of microfinance from multiple angles. Chapter 1 constructs a history of gendered finance in India, from colonial times to the current era of financial inclusion, to illuminate the workings of state policies that the commercial microfinance industry obscures. I explain why and how national policies helped constitute the current gendered financial ecosystem in which poor and working-class women became responsible for restrictive debt. Chapter 2 examines MFIS as gendered organizations. Jobs with MFIS are prized and offer social mobility where unemployment is extremely high, but working-class men have greater access to these opportunities. Women, in contrast, tend to experience a sticky floor. Men who do move up within organizations, however, often hit a class ceiling, as MFI leaders come directly from the most privileged classes in Indian society.

The next three chapters examine the everyday work of microfinance that unfolds between MFI workers and their clients, drawing together attention to relational work, value extraction, and the importance of symbols of women's success. Chapter 3 examines how relational work between MFI workers and clients generates creditworthiness for working-class women. Through a combination of scripted and ad hoc interactions, MFIS lead clients through processes of loan verification, training, and repayment, all the while creating social ties that sustain repayment, even in difficult times. Working-class women can thus acquire a digital credit identity and access to larger loans, while loan officers, mostly men, receive promotions. Turning to relational work between women, chapter 4 focuses on the unpaid work of women volunteers who organize groups for loans. Within these groups, more powerful women can deepen vulnerability for needier, less powerful women, while drawing others who may not wish to take loans reluctantly into gendered finance. Chapter 5 examines microfinance's conjoined twin: training, to which working-class women often respond with polite indifference. The disconnect again exposes the divide between women's everyday lives and the social programs meant to empower them. Training programs allow for the extraction of success stories and the production of goodwill toward MFIS.

Chapter 6 continues with an analysis of relational work by turning to microfinance in the global North, the part of the microfinancial chain that offers reproduction/marketing to fuel the extractive chain. Although highly visible, I show that these remote actors undertake artificial relational work that distorts the on-the-ground relationships of inequality that make microfinance run in India. Drawing from research with lenders on Kiva.org and MFI professionals designing programs for clients in the global South, I reveal a decontextualized understanding of Third World women's poverty through which development actors in the global North help provide effective ideological cover for commercial microfinance in India and around the world. In my last empirical chapter, I review key links of the extractive microfinancial chain in class perspective: MFI clients, mid-level MFI workers, MFI leaders, and remote global actors. Taking on the impact literature from a new angle, I examine the biographies of individuals to show how the microfinance industry disproportionately benefits the most privileged in the chain. In my conclusion, I synthesize my arguments throughout the book to explain how an invisibilized state facilitates the continued reliance of MFIS on class and gender inequalities. I suggest policy changes within the industry and within MFIS that may lead to a more equitable future for the financialization of poverty in India. Specifically, I argue for more women as workers and industry leaders, an elimination of the class ceiling, and increased attention to programming that promotes the physical and social mobility of clients. Finally, I explore the generalizability of the extractive paradigm of microfinance I set up here to other parts of the world.

1. THE INVISIBLE STATE OF GENDER AND CREDIT

How did urban slum neighborhoods and most rural areas in India become saturated in expensive debt? And why do MFIs in India lend almost exclusively to women? Are MFI loans different from the financial offerings of India's state-run microfinance program of SHGS, which has been expanding for three decades?

When I began my research in India in 2012, I found it extremely difficult to even formulate these critical questions. Microfinance was already so saturated in the urban slum communities I studied that neither MFI employees nor industry leaders questioned the core guiding practice of lending exclusively to women in groups. The MFI workers I spoke to took for granted the idea that women were virtuous and reliable borrowers, while men were not. They believed that offering loans and services to women was the best way to serve the poor. Several MFIs also believed that providing clients with educational programs about incurring debt responsibly would help them move up in the world. But where did these beliefs come from?

I argue in this chapter that the present state of the gendered financial ecosystem is a product of a multilayered colonial and postcolonial history in which successive governments have attempted to provide banking and financial services to marginalized groups, most recently to women. The position of women in relation to India's banking system gradually shifted, from a position of exclusion to one of extraction. While in the colonial era women were invisible as objects of financial inclusion, mirroring the absence of women in colonial Britain's banking policy, postcolonial era banking policies heightened women's visibility and started identifying women and lowered-caste groups as targets. Liberalization policies from the 1990s onward accelerated this transformation, culminating in a 2004–5 policy change that drove a massive transfer of funds from state-run banks to the MFIS sector. This policy change has enmeshed the nationalized banking system in the profit-oriented logics of financial companies, while endowing them with the essential function of providing fair access to credit to historically excluded groups. The result has been a significant transfer of the moral and political imperative to include women in the financial system from the state to commercial financial companies, supported by essential funding streams. This transfer produced the gendered financial ecosystem I witnessed during my research.

When Ramya, the director of a new financial literacy program, Vriddhi, shared with me her opening lesson, I gained my initial understanding of the complex financial ecosystem women borrowers navigate. In her Bengaluru office one afternoon, she propped up a colorful poster, the content of Vriddhi's first lesson for new MFI clients who had just taken a loan with their partner MFI. The chart, designed as a pictorial table, outlined the pros and cons of financial options for women MFI clients who needed to save money or take a loan. For saving, the table identified four choices: 1) hide it at your house, 2) contribute to an SHG, 3) deposit it at the post office, or 4) deposit it at the bank. If you are in need of money, loans were available from 1) moneylenders, 2) friends and family, 3) SHGS, 4) MFIS, and 5) banks. Together, these options formed an uneven spectrum, with a progressive tradeoff between convenience and access for savings, on the one hand, and security and fair terms for loans, on the other hand.

The spectrum for saving money put the mattress at one end and the bank at the other. If you were to save your money at home, you would have it when you needed it, but it might be stolen or damaged. At the other end of the spectrum, if you put your money in a bank, it would be safe, but you would have to retrieve it from the bank, which could be difficult. The more accessible option for saving money compromises on safety, but safer options are less convenient. You may find it logistically difficult to withdraw cash from an ATM, or you may experience limits on withdrawal that make it difficult to use your money when you have a lumpy expense.[1]

The spectrum for loans, on the other hand, were a matter of trading convenience for exploitation. The most convenient loans, from neighborhood moneylenders, charged exorbitant interest rates. These can be acquired in a hurry, arrive at your doorstep when you need them, and you can summon a large amount if you need it. But in a matter of weeks, these moneylenders exert huge pressure to repay. At interest rates that can exceed 10 percent per month, the debts become unsustainable very quickly, putting the safety of your family potentially at risk. On the opposite end of the spectrum, banks offer fair interest rates for smaller amounts of money but require a long verification process. Thus, banks may not offer you the amount of money you need at a time when you really need it.

SHGS, the post office (to be discussed below in more detail), and MFIS were in-between options on Ramya's chart. SHGs offer options both for savings and loans, depending on the design of the specific group, and meet in your neighborhood. Interest rates are low and cooperatively managed, benefitting everyone. But because the pool rotates, funds may not be available when you need them. MFIS, in contrast, do not allow savings[2] but may provide a more convenient option for loans than banks. MFIS are still less exploitative than the neighborhood moneylender. The post office offers a simple, no-frills savings account and in 2017 rolled out loan options as well. Although the post office appears to be a critical institution in the financial ecosystem for the poor, how women in marginalized communities use it requires further study.

The environment that Ramya captured on her chart emerged from four historical moments, each of which left behind legacies that shape the contemporary financial ecosystem for marginalized groups in both rural and urban India. Viewed together, these four moments each helped transform the orientation of the banking system in relation to women. In the new millennium, the state-led banking system has turned the project of inclusion over to private companies; poor and working-class women have become objects of extraction. Privatization in the system at large and extraction from marginalized women by new financial companies led to the crisis of 2010. In the postcrisis period, as I will show, MFIS reconcile the imperative of inclusion with the practice of extraction by regulating themselves in collaboration with the government and by promoting a vision of livelihood that preserves intrahousehold inequalities. All these moments expose how and why commercial finance today functions as an industry of gendered extraction, highlighting in particular the importance of the evolving financial ecosystem, shaped through state regulations. In relation to figure 1.2, which laid out the structure of gendered extraction, this chapter lays out the history of the constraining environment in which microfinancial chains are immersed.

I begin in the nineteenth century, when failed colonial attempts to include rural Indians in the financial system left behind a stratified system for formal banking that excluded women. This time period further strengthened local moneylenders, while also supporting family-run banks based on familial and caste identities. The second moment, during the 1960s and 1970s, was a period of active government intervention that we might today call financial inclusion. These interventions attempted, albeit inadequately, to give attention to women borrowers in rural areas. The aggressive disbursal of loans during this period created a culture of unreliable men, while also creating a priority sector rule that later would be used to support MFIS. Liberalization starting in the 1990s is the third moment I analyze. During this time, women become visible as agents of development through SHGS and MFIS. Policy changes in 2004–5 accelerated this shift and established the practice of gendered financial extraction. Finally, I examine the period after the 2010 crisis. This postcrisis environment set up the need for MFIS to establish a socially oriented image that remedied the obviously extractive practices of the most recent period. MFIS had to make extra efforts to make the public believe that they had their clients' best interests at heart, and state agencies had to appear to be regulating MFIS in order to regain public trust that had been lost during the crisis. The state accomplished this by establishing new regulations around MFI lending, including a digital credit bureau of sorts and new norms around the relationships they would establish with borrowers in order to make them creditworthy, the topic of chapter 4.

Despite the fact that this study focuses on urban settings, I primarily pay attention to histories of rural financing in this chapter. This is because rural populations have long been the explicit focus of various efforts to expand access to the formal financial system. The existing literature makes the implicit assumption that those living in urban areas have access to fair finance as a result of their proximity to banks, which are concentrated in urban areas. I could not locate policy histories that specifically aimed to address the financial needs of the urban poor. Rather, I found that commercial MFIS working in urban areas were actively adapting existing understandings of rural experiences of financial exclusion to apply to their own programs, as in the case of Ramya's chart. Based on the existing literature on rural microfinance in India, it appears that there may be some shared structural features of urban and rural poverty in terms of access to financial services and experiences of financial exclusion.[3] The targeting of poor women for both SHG and commercial microfinance appears to be just as aggressive in rural areas as in the urban areas I observed.[4]

This chapter foregrounds the significant influence of the state in setting up the constraints within which MFIS operate. As I claim throughout this book, government regulations and policies constitute MFI operations to a much larger extent than we might expect from claims about MFIS as commercial entities separate from the state. The MFI staff and leaders I interviewed were familiar with state efforts to improve the financial conditions of the poor and viewed themselves as private, market-based actors compelled to work with and around the state. Here, I argue that their very existence is a result of state policies, failed strategies, and a new approach to regulation that allowed the state to abdicate its responsibility to directly provide fair financing to India's majority. This context helps us better understand the varied efforts that MFIS have made to promote a social ethos and educate clients, all while continuing to scale up their operations locally and across the country. The significance of this history also underscores a broader point I make in this book: that the specific conditions that microfinance borrowers experience are determined largely by local and national government policies and institutions, with foreign capital playing an indirect role. Specifically, the passive regulatory actions of the Reserve Bank of India in recent decades, has had the effect of deepening women's subordination within the realm of the domestic, even as it appears to be empowering them.

Moment 1: British Experiments with Social Banking

Colonial records show that the unpredictability of peasants' livelihoods made them vulnerable to accumulated debt, forcing them to take on new debt to pay off old loans. Ironically, colonial officials were particularly concerned with high levels of exploitation experienced by peasants at the hands of local moneylenders and made several attempts at providing land mortgages at low rates, including the Land Improvement Loans Act of 1883 and the Agriculturalists Loan Act of 1884. These and similar laws were neither comprehensive nor effective, as farmers continued to experience unsustainable levels of indebtedness to local moneylenders.[5]

During the same period, the colonial state also decided to incorporate banking facilities within the rapidly expanding imperial post office system, which started offering savings accounts in 1882. This postal banking system provided minimal banking to Indians in remote areas and continues to be a key institution in the country's banking infrastructure, having been expanded dramatically in 2017. I found no accounts indicating whether during colonial times women had access to these facilities or whether they were

designed and assumed to be for men alone. The question of women's relation to finance and banking in colonial India thus remains unanswered by
historians.

By the turn of the twentieth century, cooperative societies had become
better established in Germany and Britain, accelerating efforts to expand
cooperative banking institutions in British India. The imperial state rolled
out thousands of credit societies with an evangelical fervor, aiming to free a
"country literally devoured by usury."[6] Remarkably, a familiar dimension of
this expansion continues to haunt credit today: an ideology of self-help as a
solution to exploitative moneylending. And even though the state was the
agent of expansion, the cooperative society movement ushered in a rhetoric
that emphasized member ownership and operation, an early articulation of
self-help. But the colonial state's formal banking systems never penetrated
rural areas or reached out to women, and levels of rural indebtedness continued to climb as moneylenders remained entrenched. Moneylenders often
doubled as landlords and exploited peasant tenants excessively. Landowners
forced peasants to pay rent at a fixed time, sell their crops immediately after
the harvest at low prices, and then buy back grain at higher prices to plant
again. Peasants were thus trapped in perpetual debt cycles that the cooperative banking system failed to interrupt.

Alongside imperial institutions, indigenous banks provided more affordable financing to agriculturalists, as recent historical scholarship has shown,
but only within caste networks, which ensured self-regulation and trust. According to Malavika Nair, the Chettiar banking system comprised a network
of interconnected but separate family-based banks, each of which could
take deposits, issue bills, and offer loans.[7] By the late 1920s, this system
controlled between \$3.2 and \$5.2 billion (in 2008 US dollars) and had also
gained prominence in Burma, Ceylon, and Malaya. The Great Depression
of the 1930s, however, destabilized these banks' operations, as many of their
agricultural holdings fell into foreclosure and more and more families decided not to continue with their businesses.

By the 1930s, the colonial government had set up a network of over 100,000
rural cooperative banks, a number that exceeded even the peak of postcolonial efforts to enhance rural banking.[8] These cooperative banks were to protect
rural groups from the grip of notorious moneylenders. This massive outreach was seemingly successful at first, but eventually efforts were stymied by
longstanding social divisions. Local elites dominated the cooperatives and
became embroiled in political struggles that such institutions were supposed
to undercut, or at least avoid.[9] Sean Turnell finds these financial institutions

were poorly equipped, particularly in their oversight and record keeping, and the elaborate system failed in its most basic charge: simplicity.[10] The downfall of the imperial cooperatives also suggests that, at their core, these institutions were unable to extend credit successfully to rural populations because they could not adequately establish trust in the formal transactions they were providing.

Early efforts by the colonial state to address financial vulnerability in rural areas involved more than regulation. They involved the active creation and expansion of new institutions that at least outwardly aimed to redress the exploitative systems of credit that dispossessed vulnerable groups. These colonial efforts viewed peasants as a relatively undifferentiated group and did not, at least in official policy, create provisions for women. Rather, they established a stratified banking system that has persisted to this day, where formal banks, originally designed for European men, were out of reach for most rural Indians. State efforts to establish more affordable, cooperative banking failed to dislodge entrenched social hierarchies, while indigenous banking institutions, such as the caste-based Chettiar banking system, operated on principles of exclusion, funneling credit to some agricultural communities while locking most out. This landscape of intertwined state and private institutions set the stage for postcolonial efforts to establish social banking and eventually led to the liberalization that opened the door for microfinance. It left behind a strengthened system of usurious moneylending in rural areas especially and a highly stratified system of finance that left women out altogether.

Moment 2: Postcolonial Community Banking and Its Decline

After Indian independence, a massive focus on rural cooperatives created unprecedented outreach for what remained the world's largest rural credit system. Yet poor governance and lack of mutuality between state governments and cooperative members left penetration of rural credit paltry at best. Those served were primarily agri-businesses and large landowners. As late as 1954, the all-India rural credit survey found that formal finance was meeting less than 9 percent of rural credit needs.[11] Through the 1950s and 1960s, aggressive new laws encouraged banks to open in rural and semirural areas, but these laws were largely ignored, and rural financing available was only for plantations and large commercial operations. For the first two decades of Indian independence, therefore, the stratified colonial banking system remained intact despite aggressive government efforts, with most of the borrowing occurring among better-off urban borrowers seeking larger loans.

Dramatic changes began in 1969. Following other newly postcolonial countries, the Indian state nationalized the banking system, starting with the takeover of fourteen of the largest commercial banks. Supported by development economics, the state claimed that commercial banking entities, driven by profit, were unreliable for promoting equity. From 1969 to 1990, the state pursued active policies that dramatically expanded banking in a way that emphasized equity. For example, new licensing laws required that, for every urban branch opened, a bank had to open four branches in an unbanked area. As a result, thousands of bank branches opened, many in remote areas, dramatically expanding the provision of cooperative credit to rural households—albeit always through men.

Banks came forward with specific programs, such as the Integrated Rural Development Program (henceforth, Integrated Program), to handle small loans and began disbursing them liberally to male heads of households. Significantly, even during this period of rapid expansion, although women were named as a target group, there was significant leakage to nontargeted groups, and the loans did not effectively reach women-headed households. Most often, the funds allocated to women were used for household businesses rather than capital investment, as was intended.[12] However, the rapid expansion of banking facilities reduced deprivation in what was considered the "most backward" regions of the "most backward" states in India, providing some cushion against extreme deprivation in drought-prone agricultural regions.[13] Here, aggressive government action countered the tendency for banks to cluster within cities and serve the rich, practices more beneficial to financial institutions. Nationalization thus expanded state capacity and forced banks to serve populations for the sake of providing a vital service, rather than earning a profit.

In parallel, starting in 1974, banking nationalization efforts culminated in several consecutive initiatives to establish a priority sector lending requirement. Emerging from the same interventionist politics that fueled nationalization, the Reserve Bank's priority sector requirement by 1979 established that 40 percent of bank portfolios be reserved for lending to the disadvantaged. Banks targeted loans for specific purposes, including education, agriculture, minority groups, and small and medium-sized businesses. The priority sector requirement also mandated banks to earmark part of their debt capital for direct lending to priority populations.[14] Despite the mandate, most banks lacked the human resources or technical expertise to reach out to these groups, and the patterns of financial exclusion that the priority sector requirement aimed to fight largely remained intact. As I will show later, however, the priority sector requirement became a crucial legacy of this interventionist period of banking expansion, and eventually helped fuel the rapid expansion that MFIs experienced in the early 2000s.

The rural expansion of banking services in the 1970s and 1980s brought problems that further differentiated women and men borrowers. The policies' focus on disbursement to the poor meant that the banks doing the disbursal often lacked operations systems or infrastructure to collect loan repayments. Mass dissemination of loans became popular, as politicians leveraged their expansion by sponsoring "loan *melas*," or large gatherings where loans were distributed en masse to rural men with no provision for collection.[15] Through these practices, rural men became socialized into a culture of debt in which there were no real consequences for nonpayment. Loan *melas* and other generous disbursement programs, which largely excluded women, ended up supporting middle-class images of rural men as irresponsible. This gendered view continues to inform the microfinance industry, but with amnesia about the context in which the banking sector engaged marginalized rural men in the mass disbursement of loans.

The policies of the decades immediately following independence sought aggressively to expand fair rural banking through nationalization, strict policies, and disbursement. While there was evidence that these policies did in fact decrease vulnerability in some of the most marginalized regions of the country, it also created a crisis of loan nonpayment for banks and a culture of debt in which men were constructed as irresponsible. These shortcomings, due largely to poor operations systems and a lack of infrastructure, appear to have sustained the stratified banking system of the late colonial period. As new banking policies came into force in the 1990s, however, the priority sector requirement remained in place, creating a policy space in which MFIs could later collaborate with the state for expansion.

Moment 3: Liberalization and the Pivot to Gendered Extraction

In 1990, a massive loan write-off cost the banks and the state the equivalent of $2 million (USD) to make up for the excesses of the preceding two decades, signaling the end of the Integrated Program as well as an end to aggressive rural banking policies. Despite dramatic expansion, banking was failing to reach the neediest, and the system was rife with inefficiencies and poor service. The massive write-off of rural loans then precipitated another dramatic change, which transformed the banking sector once again: liberalization. During the 1990s, the Reserve Bank changed the strict licensing requirements for banks to open rural branches and welcomed new private banks to the financial landscape. Thousands of rural cooperatives were closed, and some were purchased by private banks who later sought to intervene in the burgeoning rural market for microfinance. In many areas, these changes brought the moneylender back to the center of rural life. As in many countries, liberalization in India meant not just scaling back the state but also reorganizing state programs. Between 1990 and 2005, India reorganized its outreach to rural households, for the first time calling upon rural women to act as agents, not just beneficiaries of national development.

The systematic exclusion of women, particularly rural women, until economic liberalization in the 1990s, lay the groundwork for the gendered financial ecosystem in which microfinance is situated in today. The historical record suggests that, whether financial services were expanding or contracting since colonial rule, women were never viewed as agents of development. This taken-for-granted perspective effectively wrote them out of Indian finance. This third moment, then, was not only an expansion of financial services to women but also a pivot from longstanding practices of exclusion in relation to women to a form of inclusion that in practice has functioned as extraction.[16] Primarily men, working within NGOs and state agencies, spearheaded this pivot. In contrast, women's efforts within activist movements were co-opted by the new state programs that leveraged the language of empowerment meant to challenge patriarchal structures on a systemic level. During this third moment, then, we see the state identifying women as agents of development and aggressively bringing them into the sphere of finance through SHGs, and later, MFIs, but with few protections against excessive exploitation. This confluence of factors turned an inclusion and empowerment project into one of extraction and exploitation.

A small pilot program in southern India in 1992, led by the National Agricultural Bank for Rural Development (henceforth, National Agricultural Bank),[17] launched the SHG bank linkage. Informed by the success of programs in Bangladesh, India's national-level banking institution for the rural majority decided to implement a program that built upon the demonstrated successes of Bangladesh's joint liability group model, in which women take out a loan in a group, leveraging their social obligations to one another as collateral. But the National Agricultural Bank carried the program out differently. Working in cooperation with village-level women's groups and organizations, the program provided groups of women in rural areas with linkages to established banks. Through these linkages, women in the group could take a loan from the bank and could also save together. Without the linkage, rural woman did not have the creditworthiness to take a loan from a bank, and indeed had never been offered any kind of options for formal financing. Savings options were also virtually nonexistent.

The new program fulfilled the goals of multiple stakeholders. From the banks' perspectives, the backing of local NGOS and the National Agricultural Bank meant that they could, through SHGS, fulfill their legally mandated obligations to lend to priority sector consumers, an obligation that most banks had not met. From the perspectives of rural women, who had long been indebted to local moneylenders, SHGS at the very least brought in an additional avenue for access to cash, and on better terms. Furthermore, these loans might be used to support small businesses to reduce seasonal vulnerabilities experienced by rural households. Studies conducted during the early years of this new SHG program suggested that apart from cash, loans for rural women could be used for nonfarm enterprises. Microenterprise, these studies suggested, might provide better insurance for bank loans than seasonal agriculture. These studies, carried out by Vijay Mahajan, also provided the basis for the nongovernmental and later, commercial, microfinance industries.[18] Unlike previous programs, both the SHG linkage program and the nascent NGOS that imitated their template explicitly targeted women, overturning a century of banking policies that regarded men as the most important agents of development.

The timing of India's national SHG program in 1992, inspired by Bangladesh's women-focused lending programs, also reflected two decades of research and advocacy around the importance of women as development agents around the world. As early as 1970, Esther Boserup had argued that efforts to promote industrial production in developing countries had excluded women in ways that were ultimately detrimental to development as a whole, and that women needed to be included in development, particularly in the shift to mechanized agricultural production. By the 1990s, however, scholarship and activism had shifted beyond inclusion/exclusion frameworks to advocate for engaging both women and men in community-oriented development more broadly, a focus reflected in the 1995 UN Conference on Women.[19] Critical perspectives on gender and development came from feminist scholars in India who were critical of both state-led socialism and neoliberalism. These scholars leveraged feminist perspectives to push for alternatives to capitalist development, pushing back against earlier "add women and stir" perspectives that they viewed as inadequate and potentially harmful for women.[20] These feminist engagements with development policy largely failed to gain traction within state institutions; in contrast, efforts to promote women-focused microcredit[21] programs became linked to women's empowerment, and became popular in India and around the world. Despite their focus on women, emerging microcredit programs, led primarily by men, ignored the idea that transforming gendered relationships between men and women was fundamental to development efforts, instead adopting simplistic inclusion models that feminist scholars had long rejected.

The self-help movement continued growing, but starting in the late 1990s, these bank linkages faced new competition: commercial microfinance institutions (MFIs). Starting out as cooperative women's NGOs, organizations such as BASIX, SHARE, and Swayam Krushi Sangh (SKS) reached out to women clients in rural areas, many of whom were already accessing SHG groups, and provided them with another option for loans to support nonfarm enterprises. Rather than a bank linkage, these organizations would finance the loans themselves. They charged higher interest rates, albeit still lower than neighborhood moneylenders. MFIs also offered training programs of various kinds, geared toward improving women's livelihoods, in competition with similar offerings to SHG members. In the southern state of Andhra Pradesh, MFIs and SHGs competed for the same clients, and often, clients took loans from both sources, a situation that ended up fueling a disaster that shook the burgeoning MFI industry to its core in the crisis of 2010, a situation that I will explore below.

Scholars have evaluated the expansion of SHG microfinance in divergent ways that appear contradictory at first glance. Paromita Sanyal's work shows that women in SHGs establish social ties with other women and that these ties become useful in other contexts, from domestic conflicts to village assemblies.[22] In contrast, Kalpana Karunakaran emphasizes that the expansion of SHGs allowed the state to abdicate its responsibility for women's livelihoods.[23] I find both arguments compelling and consider them compatible and supportive of the view I present here, that the shift to SHGs en masse turned a women's empowerment effort into one of gendered extraction. Women participating in SHGs may be more likely than other women to acquire newfound capabilities; these capabilities advance the agenda of the neoliberal state and the goals of state developmentalism without shoring up women's entitlements to better jobs or access to property.[24]

By 2000, SHG linkage programs were well established, but new, largely unregulated MFIs, which, under Reserve Bank regulations, were termed "nonbanking financial companies" were competing with one another for women clients, especially in the southern state of Andhra Pradesh. In the short term, these developments may have benefited rural women, who had become recognized agents of credit and debt in their households. In addition, the expansion of both SHGS and MFIS created a workforce of mostly men who learned to organize women into groups and lend them money. Many of the MFI employees I interviewed had previously worked in SHG programs. As both SHG programs and MFIS aimed to "scale up," their competition became intense, and some analysts predicted a crisis.[25] At this point, however, the state began offloading the burden of making women creditworthy onto MFIS and their clients, many of whom were already members of SHGS.

The pivot to gendered extraction solidified between 2001 and 2006. During this time, the World Bank provided a $110 million (USD) loan to support the large-scale rollout of SHG-based loans in the southern state of Andhra Pradesh.[26] By the end of 2006, this state-sponsored program, Velugu, had organized 2.29 million households into 171,618 SHGS. These groups were backed by a number of local-level structures, training programs, and efforts to develop technical expertise, all meant to be "a one-time infusion of equity capital" to establish the program on sure footing.[27] On the heels of Velugu, the government of Andhra Pradesh followed up with a new program, the Indira Kranti Patham, which by 2010 had established another 1 million SHGS.[28]

Between April 2007 and July 2010, private MFIS attracted an astonishing $646.9 million (USD) in foreign equity, ballooning India's MFI loan portfolios to over $2 billion (USD) by 2010.[29] Ironically, the concurrent global financial crisis led to the establishment of microfinance as its own asset class, as global financial investors searched for new products in which to invest. In 2008 and 2009, respectively, microfinance portfolios of the global top ten funds grew by 31 and 23 percent.[30] These assets looked like better investments precisely because they were lent to women in noncyclical trades—the very nonfarm activities that Mahajan had identified as the backbone of rural livelihoods in the early 1990s. But these influxes alone cannot explain why MFIS could expand their lending so dramatically.

Financial institutions need two kinds of capital: equity and debt. Equity financing expands the company and can be used for training staff, opening new branches, or improving technical capacities like information systems. According to Indian regulations, however, financial companies can only accept equity financing from foreign donors or investors. Debt financing, in contrast, must be domestic. In this regard, India is virtually unique in the world: its expansion of credit among MFIs had to be driven by domestic money. As a result, MFI leaders and investors explained to me, raising debt capital from Indian banks was extremely difficult in the early 2000s.

As Anjali, one of the few women in MFI leadership, explained, "At that time [lending money to MFIS] was radical because ultimately microfinance is unsecured lending to poor women, no collateral. And the idea that formal banks would back that was, at that point, quite unthinkable." Nonetheless, Gopal, a cofounder of an MFI I call Grama Valachi, cited a change in the lending environment for MFI startups around 2005:

[In the early 2000s, you had to] run behind the banks and go and beg them for money, and they used to say, "Who the hell are you? Get lost!" (laughing). And then you have to call back again and show your face and say, "No, no, no come see this report; come and see this; come and see this." . . . It took a lot of effort because they didn't trust us in the beginning. And later on, when we showed that we are there with a full [proposition], then they started giving slowly more and more. It took lot of time. It took years. And once they started believing that this whole system worked, and they were happy they could kick off their priority sector, and their portfolio was performing at like 100% on-time repayment. Which other sector has this kind of thing? [Then] all the eyes started opening up. And that's when all the bankers started saying, "This looks like a fantastic business."

Gopal and other leaders I interviewed believed that their persistence in convincing banks to invest with them led to a substantial uptick in funding, but I discovered that a small regulatory change may have been what made all the difference. In 2004 and 2005, Reserve Bank revisions to the priority sector lending requirement allowed nationalized banks to meet their priority sector quotas by lending to MFIs, categorized as non-banking financial companies (NBFCS). With this change, public banks could use MFIS as intermediaries to meet their obligation to provide funds to excluded segments of the population.[31] In the 2005–6 Union Budget, the finance minister stated explicit support for MFIS, requesting additional favorable policies and earmarked funds:

At present, micro finance institutions (MFIS) obtain finance from banks according to guidelines issued by RBI. MFIS seek to provide small scale credit and other financial services to low income households and small informal businesses. Government intends to promote MFIS in a big way. The way forward, I believe, is to identify MFIS, classify and rate such institutions, and empower them to intermediate between the lending banks and the beneficiaries. Commercial banks may appoint MFIS as "banking correspondents" to provide transaction services on their behalf. Since MFIS require infusion of new capital, I propose to re-designate the existing Rs.100 crore Micro Finance Development Fund as the "Micro Finance Development and Equity Fund," and increase the corpus to Rs.200 crore.[32]

All of my interviewees who were in positions of leadership in MFIS during this time period reported a dramatic uptick in bank funding after 2005. Furthermore, at least two of the firms I studied were founded after this period, perhaps motivated by the new availability of debt capital from banks. Both these new firms targeted a section of the population previously excluded from state-led microfinance: urban working-class women. None of the MFI leaders I interviewed, however, expressed recognition that this regulatory tweak might have transformed the entire landscape of debt capital flows in the MFI sector. Once foreign equity began flowing in alongside domestic debt capital, MFIS could strategically allocate their portfolios to show greater growth in loans, even when debt and equity funding were not perfectly aligned.[33]

This triangulation of new ambitions for MFIS and the state, together with a policy environment that supported the expansion of credit to the weaker sections of society, left poor rural families in Andhra Pradesh operating in a financial ecosystem in which many loans were chasing the same clients. Rural Andhra Pradesh, then, may have been the first context in which a financial ecosystem operating centrally on the logic of gendered financial extraction came into being. That environment, like those that followed, was created in large part by state agencies and regulations, from the Reserve Bank at the top to the government of Andhra Pradesh at the intermediate level to the specific districts in which this mix of both SHGs and MFIS were rolled out. While mass dissemination of loans in rural India had a precedent in the 1970s and 1980s, this context was different because the loans were directed almost exclusively to women, and at a volume that was staggering, having been shored up by financialized capital markets both in India and abroad. After 2005, working class urban women joined rural women as agents of development who could be activated through debt relations.

On the ground, these loans precipitated a transformation in everyday understandings of gender and finance. Where before rural women were all but invisible in rural households, they were now solely, not just equally, responsible for the household's finances. Urban working-class women, many of them migrants from rural areas, were starting to not only be workers but also borrowers. Targeting women served two causes at once. It promoted the cause of women's empowerment and appeared both to compensate for historic exclusions and to elevate the position of women in society, even as substantive programs shoring up women's empowerment were curtailed.[34] But this focus was also self-serving for financial institutions and built upon gendered presumptions. Whether rural or urban, women were viewed by both financial institutions and the government as better credit risks than men, a set of holdover assumptions from an earlier time, when rural men had been socialized into a culture of irresponsibility with credit. Women were deemed better credit risks because research had shown that women's nonfarm microenterprises provided a last recourse for agricultural families whose destinies were otherwise tied to erratic and unstable markets.[35] Furthermore, a view of poor and working-class men as irresponsible fit with prevailing tropes of men in the global South as abusive alcoholics, while women were hardworking and resourceful.[36] These tropes resonate in India and in global development circuits.

By creating a financial infrastructure oriented toward such microenterprise, both commercial and SHG microfinance reinforced, rather than transformed, women's subordinate positions. Existing legal and labor market structures that disadvantaged poor and working-class women remained intact, while women's access to property rights remained insecure at best. Both the state and the new financial corporations started lending to Andhra Pradesh women en masse in an effort to transform women into creditworthy financial subjects. But their logics were at cross purposes, at least in part. Women who failed to qualify for either kind of loan, perhaps because of poverty or social alienation, remained uncreditworthy. Thus, this moment may have accelerated class differentiation among rural and urban working-class women.

Women's involvement in self-help not only imposed the discipline of loan repayment on women borrowers, it also introduced a range of trainings and organizational structures, including the women's groups, village organizations, and *mandals* (administrative centers). Many women involved in SHGS received technical training in accounts and bookkeeping. As a result, when MFIS started to challenge the hegemony of SHG bank linkage programs, they found that women borrowers already had some experience with loans, and many had specific skills that could help MFIS minimize their risk and ensure repayment. The introduction of MFIS also meant that women had options to take loans from multiple sources with similar group-based structures that were now familiar. And they did. They also continued taking loans from moneylenders and informal sources, even though part of the argument for MFIS was to reduce reliance on moneylenders. Households borrowing from both MFIS and SHGs averaged more than ten loans in Andhra Pradesh by 2009.[37] With this deluge of debt, the media linked a string of farmer suicides to MFIS and so created a public relations nightmare for these institutions.[38] Central to this crisis was the outsized ambition of Swayam Krushi Sangh (SKS), the MFI that had grown most rapidly through foreign equity capital and had even held an astonishingly successful IPO in 2010, generating ninety-eight times the face value of the stock.[39]

In October 2010, the Andhra Pradesh government passed an ordinance aiming to regulate MFIS to prevent exploitation of vulnerable clients, an act that brought the situation to a head. The ordinance established new requirements, including a transparent display of a loan's interest rate and a fast-track option for MFIS to collect against defaulters in court. Other aspects of the ordinance were stringent—for example, requiring permission from local leaders before lending to an SHG member.[40] The chief minister of Andhra Pradesh characterized MFIS as moneylenders and announced that clients in the state should not repay their loans. Within weeks, collections dropped from 98 to 10 percent, and inflows of capital from banks and foreign equity investors dried up. Dubbed "the AP crisis" or simply "the crisis" by my interviewees in the industry, this mass nonpayment shook the industry to its foundations. Many small MFIS folded, and the captains of the industry were forced to gather, regroup, and recoup to save the largest institutions. They appealed to the Reserve Bank.

This third moment, then, witnessed the expansion of MFIS both in terms of infrastructure and lending capacity, facilitated by a regulatory rule change by the national Reserve Bank. Once MFIS started to threaten the hegemony of government SHG programs, however, the local state clamped down hard, and the combination of exploitative lending and government pushback sent the industry into a tailspin. But what was most important about the two decades of liberalization leading up to the Andhra Pradesh crisis was the pivot to gendered extraction focused on women borrowers, who suddenly became subjects of debt and objects of empowerment. In the most recent moment, MFIS responded by rebuilding their public image and collaborating with the Reserve Bank but maintaining the gendered norms established since the 1990s.

Moment 4: A Regulated MFI Sector

Soon after the unprecedented nonpayment of over 9.2 million borrowers—the largest recorded nonpayment in history—the Reserve Bank formed a national commission headed by Y. H. Malegam, a veteran of the Indian Central Bank. In 2011, the influential Malegam Committee released a report concluding that MFIs had neglected the poor. The Malegam Report laid out a national regulatory framework, including a cap on interest rates, a cap on compensation for leaders, restrictions on multiple lending, and the establishment of a credit bureau.

MFI ambitions had been chastened by the crisis and the Malegam Report's findings, but my review of the documents and interviews with MFI leaders suggest that, in practice, MFIs had significant influence over the regulations suggested in the report. For example, Narayan, an MFI leader, explained that he and his organization had devised a formula for maintaining a slightly lower interest rate than their competitors. Capping the return on equity (ROE) at 20 percent, Narayan explained, ensured that any improvements in efficiency would be passed on to borrowers rather than returned to investors. This philosophy may seem admirable, but it also justifies interest significantly higher than the market rate. Narayan brought legitimacy and rationality to his banking business. When speaking with the regulators on the Malegam Committee, Narayan recalled,

> I said [we charge] twenty-five and a half [percent interest]. . . . So, he said, "Okay, but when everybody is lending at much higher rate, how is it that you're lending at twenty-five and a half?" And then I explained the philosophy. And he noted it down. I saw him noting it down and then later in the committee recommendation he actually produced this [philosophy] verbatim. This policy of ours is produced verbatim in the committee report. So, I had a logic. I mean somebody can still say charging twenty-five and a half percent from the poor is very high. Okay, fine you can have your views; everybody is entitled to their views. But if somebody deems to ask me, "Well how is it that you're charging so much," I have a logic.

Narayan was one of the key architects of the Microfinance Institutions Network (MFIN), formed in 2008. Composed of the top CEOS and founders of the largest MFIS, MFIN began sharing data, tracking multiple borrowing, and drafting its own code of conduct. Some of the network's leaders and chief architects had anticipated a crisis, recalling a smaller crisis in 2005–6 that had led to little change in the industry.[41] When the crisis transpired in 2010, therefore, MFIN had a code of conduct and self-regulatory measures drawn up and at the ready. Vijay Mahajan, the network's chair, wrote letters to the chairman of the State Bank of India and the governor of the RBI, proposing the code of conduct and beseeching them for "help to convert the crisis into an opportunity," with the code and other measures as the "basis for collective alignment" between regulators in Mumbai and policy makers in New Delhi and Andhra Pradesh.[42] Several commentators objected to the close collaboration of government regulators and MFI leaders in crafting these regulations, calling instead for state-specific regulations or more elaborate, microfinance-specific regulations that would address the unique features of group loans.[43]

Missing from these critiques, however, is recognition of the positions of working-class women, and questions of whether they have been transformed by the vicissitudes of state regulations and financial corporations remain unaddressed. Given what Christa Wichterich calls, the "feminization of indebtedness,"[44] any recognition of women at the center of microfinance had been notably dropped from the conversation. Instead, MFIS renewed efforts to present their programming as empowering for women, establishing new training programs on financial literacy and empowerment, and adopting new modes of conduct in employee interactions with clients, a topic to be explored thoroughly in later chapters. But at the macrolevel, the regulations put into place aimed to protect poor and marginalized families in general, ignoring the fact that this new form of debt rested upon the collateral of women's reliability, vulnerability, and rootedness in their neighborhoods. Thus, the new regulations did not fundamentally alter the extractive character of gendered debt that was introduced in the 1990s and deepened with the mass expansion of MFIS after 2005. MFIS themselves ignored issues of gender equity, resulting in a loss of support, seemingly once and for all, for the transformation of relationships between men and women in the household, a notion introduced by feminist critiques of development as early as the 1990s.

In a 2016 interview with longtime microfinance policy-maker Sundaram, he emphasized that the driving vision behind the simultaneous expansion of commercial and state-run microfinance initiatives was to view men and women together as part of a cohesive household. In his narrative, the notion of addressing gender inequities by providing more stable livelihoods for women *and* men is replaced by an effort to bring cash into the household by both parties. As he explained why it is always necessary to draw men into any development scenario, he reflected upon the patriarchal space of home:

> Eventually when everything is done, the project goes home. The banker goes home. The microfinance fellow goes home. The borrower goes home. So, you have borrowed money. If she [the client] says, "I have given the money to my husband, he is running his auto rickshaw," then *it is* empowering gender. Look, finally the food has to come to the table . . . The woman becomes functional for getting that done. She gains her space, her respect. Food comes to the table for everybody. This is not a feminist agenda we are driving here. It is a livelihood agenda where both of them have a contribution to make, and the household feels better off comparatively . . . the livelihood that they have and the household they have needs to be considered.

Sundaram's understanding of a livelihood agenda, which he sees as opposed to a straw man feminist agenda, suggests that at the end of the day, women need to get along with their husbands so everyone can go home, conceived here as a hetero-patriarchal space. With loans at home, men and women can have food on the table. Sundaram draws from assumptions about women as a cohesive group based on benevolent patriarch assumptions, the foundation of household economics of the 1970s. In this conceptualization, men and women pool resources within a household and the patriarch decides how these resources will be divided according to everyone's best interests. This concept has been shown to be empirically false, since such benevolent pooling does not reflect household dynamics, particularly in vulnerable households.[45] Yet this conceptual apparatus sustains and justifies the continued expansion of gendered debt, stabilizing and legitimating the saturated financial ecosystem in which women are included, but as objects of extraction.

Conclusion

Concern with providing rural and poor Indians access to fair credit has been on the national agenda for more than a century. Each successive effort has attempted to address deep social divisions, divergent financial landscapes across the country, and the tendency for local elites to monopolize moneylending and thus tighten their control of the poor. In this chapter, I have highlighted four moments that I argue have helped produce the gendered financial ecosystem that prevailed during the time of my study. First, in the early twentieth century, the colonial state recognized the need for fair banking for the rural majority in the colonial economy, but the policies and institutions created during that period had the effect of deepening the embeddedness of moneylenders and set up a stratified financial system that persists today. The poor was conceived of as a rural population, and peasants were men; women could not be subjects of their own loans, an assumption imported from colonial Britain. After independence, the postcolonial state sought to deepen and expand banking access in the twentieth century, with a mix of successes and failures. Yet even during India's most progressive periods, efforts to reach rural clients had consistently excluded women, even when there were de jure efforts to reach out to them. During the times of greatest expansion, banks socialized rural men into a culture of debt in which repayment was not expected, a situation that created an unsustainable level of unpaid loans within the nationalized banking system. The crisis was resolved in the 1990s with the implementation of liberalization policies that refocused lending practices on urban and wealthier borrowers.

But this third moment also signaled the emergence of the rural woman as an agent of development in her own right, a result of global policy trends and the success of Bangladesh's state-led microcredit programs. As explicit programs to promote sustainable livelihoods and better job prospects for women were cut, India piloted and then expanded the SHG bank linkage program, moving women increasingly to the center of India's financial inclusion strategy. MFIS, strengthened by an inflow of cash due to a policy tweak in 2005, started to compete with SHGs to offer rural and marginalized urban women highly profitable loan products. The outpouring of loans to the poor, in competition with state programs from 2005–10, created a crisis of nonpayment that forced MFIS to organize as an industry and collaborate with the national Reserve Bank to sustain them. In the fourth moment I discuss, since 2010, MFIS continue to scale up. But they are now regulated, legitimate actors seen to be helping poor women. While they must operate by different rules and interact with women clients differently than they used to, they must also constantly burnish their public image in order to maintain legitimacy in a context where most clients continue to be suspicious of financial companies.

This history reveals three crucial points that influence my argument in the rest of the book. First, it provides an account of commercial microfinance in India that reveals the extent to which domestic policies and capital flows have set up the current saturated loan environment that vulnerable women borrowers find themselves in. The huge inflow of global equity capital in the early 2000s is indeed an important part of the story of commercial microfinance in India, but it is modest relative to the many other factors that have made microfinance the industry of gendered extraction it is today. Relatedly, this history highlights the extent to which so many aspects of state policy—whether from the Reserve Bank or from district or state-level governments—have shaped the conditions under which commercial MFIS do business. Finally, this history reveals that rural and marginalized urban women experienced a dramatic pivot during liberalization; they went from being excluded from financial services altogether to being at the center of financial inclusion policy precisely because they could be made into subjects of effective extraction. In the realm of microfinance, a livelihoods agenda is one that aims to shore up the hetero-patriarchal household, rather than one that enhances women's and men's entitlements.

2. MEN AND WOMEN OF THE MFI

When Santosh left a lucrative career in commercial banking to start a microfinance company, he faced ridicule from many skeptical colleagues in commercial banking. Santosh recognized, however, that it was an opportune time in the early 2000s, when urban markets were still untapped. New Reserve Bank changes in priority sector lending rules were allowing inflows of debt capital that were previously unavailable. Foreign investors were also interested in the microfinance business. On the ground, self-help groups were well established. At the time of our interview in 2012, Santosh was the founder and CEO of Sowbagya, which had grown from a tiny startup to become one of India's largest MFIs. Santosh expressed humility about the remarkable success of his company, which became profitable after running at a loss for the first few years of its existence. In an interview, Santosh also emphasized his commitment to the people he serves. He left his previous career out of a sense of responsibility to serve the underprivileged. He spoke at length about the mission-driven nature of his organization, which he was most proud of, but he also emphasized that personal interactions with clients sustained him. He narrated a recent incident: "I went to visit our branch in New Mumbai last week . . . and a group of women were there with a thali [ceremonial plate] with *arathi* (ceremonial fire) with lamp with *sindhoor* (vermillion powder) and all that. It was very embarrassing for me. In the middle of the street, these women were doing this [circling the fire around me] as if I am some god-man or something. And then they of course bend down and touch your feet and this and that. But that is the way they show [their appreciation]." Santosh experienced a ritual for honoring a guest or esteemed person, carried out by repeat customers outside a branch office of his company in Mumbai. The common ritual would be carried out for a god at a temple, a revered politician, a religious leader, or for a newlywed couple. Santosh felt, with embarrassment but also pride, that he was being treated like a god-man.

At the same time, as the leader of a prominent MFI that rode out the crisis and had to be accountable to investors, he admitted that at times the mission to serve the underprivileged was compromised in order to improve valuations of the company. "When we first started, we had this mission, this vision," he reflected.

> And we stuck to it. And in the middle this whole thing about valuation— how fast you grow in terms of customers, in terms of your loan assets, how valuable your company is from a company valuation angle, that sort of thing—took importance [sic]. Within the industry, that became the number-one objective. That diluted the mission, but you know, we also grew fast, and we did all kinds of things. We also made mistakes, but generally, we kept at the mission. And at the end of the day, we are today valued as one of the best, whether by winning awards or people wanting to invest in us, people wanting to put money with us, people wanting to give us loans, people wanting to work with us. Today we are very highly regarded in the industry, and that, of course, gives you lot[s] of satisfaction.

Here, Santosh reveals that although a sense of responsibility drew him to the people he served, once in a leadership position, the drive toward increasing the value of the company strongly influenced his actions. Since his company is now highly regarded and successful, his customers' spontaneous ritual ceremony in his honor, although embarrassing, confirms for him that he was now doing both: serving his customers and keeping up the profits.

The Indian microfinance industry, geared toward gendered extraction, operates through individual MFIs that combine state and corporate logics. Because of their dependence on government policies and regulations, as well as the state-sanctioned responsibility they have taken on to provide financial services to the marginalized, frontline MFI workers must prioritize customers who are predominantly poor and working-class women. But at the upper echelons of the MFI, leaders abide by the logics of financial corporations, with the motivation to scale up, extract more profits, and pass on those profits to investors. A considerable literature has shown that both states and financial corporations operate according to andocentric norms.[1] These organizations view men as default employees and as a result devalue characteristics and work defined as feminine. Indian MFIS are what Joan Acker identified as gendered organizations, in which jobs, bodies, and hierarchies establish and reinforce class-specific articulations of masculinity and femininity.[2] But to understand gendered dynamics within MFIS, we require an even more specific understanding of gender in organizations involved in the work of governance, the "process of implementing modern state power, of putting the program of those who govern into place."[3] Lisa D. Brush suggests two frames for understanding gender and governance that are helpful for uncovering the gendered dynamics at Indian MFIS: the *governance of gender* and the *gender of governance* (see chart 2.1).

The *governance of gender* frame draws our attention to how MFI interactions with women clients within communities "construct and instruct women and men in properly gendered identities, behaviors, expectations, opportunities, and realms of social life." Brush asserts that organizations involved in governing do not simply reflect a culture or society steeped in masculine domination but rather actively perpetuate this domination while subordinating women and femininity. I elaborate on Brush's framework by showing how the practice of governance that unfolds between clients and MFI employees is simultaneously steeped in gender, class, caste, and regional distinctions. Interactions between loan officers and trainers teach groups of women to honor men who represent the MFI. Clients also come to admire women MFI workers, who embody a caring, capable femininity that clients can relate to. This is because MFI women often combine wage earning with mothering and thus become aspirational figures for some clients. As I show in chapter 5, client educational training programs, another dimension of governance, expose women clients to similar ideals, encouraging women to identify both as workers and as mothers. The gendered performances of MFI workers, both men and women, help crystallize the dominant organizing principle through which frontline MFI work is carried out: *benevolent protectionism*. Through benevolent protectionism, frontline MFI workers provide the financial services that allow for women's access to high-interest loans, as well as other services that MFIS may provide for clients' welfare and improvement. These appear to clients as services for their marginalized communities that aim to protect them from illicit or unethical lending practices.

But within the workplace, women and men are tightly organized along lines of gender and class in which motherhood and work are in fact not compatible at all, revealing that the *gender of governance*—who actually *is* in power

Chart 2.1. Brush's framework in relation to MFIs

| Governance of gender (outward facing) | Benevolent protectionism |
| Gender of governance (inward facing) | Corporate masculinity |

within these state-like organizations—remains rigidly male dominated. Within the organization, men who are successful at performing benevolent protectionism experience job satisfaction and upward mobility, while similarly employed women face a sticky floor. Those who hire and fire workers in their MFIs express a preference for men, justified by the needs of clients for reliable and consistent service.

At the upper levels of MFIs, benevolent protectionism yields to organizing principles of *corporate masculinity*, which privileges profit making as the primary aim. But MFI leaders like Santosh must moderate expressions of corporate masculinity to reflect the altruistic image of the microfinance industry. Powerful men in the sector thus seek legitimacy from the principles of benevolent protectionism that operate on the ground with clients. Women at the top, in contrast, tend to be concentrated in the soft work of philanthropy and client education, where they exist at all. When women in MFIs strive to adopt the norms of corporate masculinity, a phenomenon scholars have long observed in corporate contexts,[4] they are often viewed negatively by their peers.

We saw in chapter 1 that the Indian state outsourced to MFIs its responsibility for providing financial services to India's most marginalized. As a result, the state involves MFIs in the work of governance without transforming the profit-maximizing logic of extraction that drives financial companies. As government-regulated private institutions oriented toward marginalized women, MFIs must appear at all times to be protecting the best interests of their clients. That outward appearance organizes their frontline work, necessitating benevolent protectionism. But as financial companies, they are organized to extract the maximum value from clients allowable by the legal frameworks they abide by. To accomplish this balancing act between legitimacy and with profitability, MFIs leverage gendered modes of governance, between their employees and clients as well as within their own organizations. Both benevolent protectionism and corporate masculinity shore up and extend masculine privilege and domination within the MFI and in the communities where they work, all the while consolidating patterns of gendered extraction.

Indian MFIS employ diverse actors, from people with twelfth-grade educations to those with PhDs and extensive consulting experience in institutions like the World Bank. From the earliest days of commercialization, the industry was exciting for Indians, both in India and abroad. In the early 2000s, the burgeoning Indian microfinance sector inspired an educated workforce of men and women from around the world. I interviewed four finance professionals located in the US, three of them women, who had moved to India right after college or graduate school to work in microfinance. They had secured positions at companies like SKS, Unitus, and BASIX, and by their accounts, they were not alone. These professionals established new programs and products, charted new markets in rural areas, and helped raise equity from major investors. That early period of expansion became the blueprint for the diverse workforce the industry would attract in the years that followed.

Employees within India often move long distances to take positions with MFIS. Many of those I interviewed in urban areas had moved from rural areas, where they had been working in government development programs or NGOS. They had moved seeking better pay and working conditions. Employees from rural areas bring to urban MFIS a deep familiarity with the circumstances of families who manage persistent or seasonal poverty. This experience allows them to connect with working class urban clients on a personal level. Employees working in the upper levels of the industry, in contrast, come from highly privileged social locations and have little firsthand understanding of clients' struggles. Professionals in IT, finance, and banking leave their elite occupations to enter the microfinance industry, driven by the ideal of making a broad social impact. They bring with them neoliberal logics of self-sufficiency, financial sustainability, and profit maximization. Still another group comes from mid-level government positions, bringing with them attention to processes and an orientation to social service. In new MFIS in the early 2000s, men and women from all these backgrounds created new organizations, each with their own rules and standards, and often competed mightily against one another.

MFIS developed distinct organizational cultures, each depending on the background of the founder and his immediate networks. An MFI founded by IT professionals built leading-edge infrastructure and established a meritocratic, profit-oriented culture similar to that of Indian IT firms. An MFI founded by the leader of a state banking system drew significant capital from state banks and recruited colleagues who developed strong procedures and systems for audits. An MFI founded by a private banker applied a norm of customer respect to its working-class clients and drew from the world of international finance for strategic personnel and startup capital. A founder with a background in education recruited educators and NGO workers, building an organization that bundled loans with social messages about health care, hygiene, and parenting. As these MFIS competed, often seeking the same clients, however, they became increasingly similar. Frontline staff began moving from one to another, causing companies to prevent poaching by promulgating no-compete rules. Those who survived the 2010 crisis also streamlined their operations significantly.

When I started my fieldwork in Tamil Nadu and Karnataka in early 2012, the crisis was still fresh. Some organizations in Andhra Pradesh had seen their operations crippled in other southern states, but Sowbagya and Kanchan had been less exposed and had experienced minimal losses. Leaders in these companies were focused on renewing capital investments and shoring up internal procedures to ensure that their reputations and financial flows could keep their businesses growing. Employees I spoke with at all levels of the industry expressed optimism about their chances for upward mobility and satisfaction that their work was serving a social cause. But workers also faced great pressure to meet specific targets for training or loan recruitment, and they were eager to have forms filled, target numbers met, and their managers' expectations fulfilled. The work was grueling, and workers were haunted by the possibility of failing to meet targets, especially for training. Serving vulnerable clients while also achieving scale and efficiency was an ongoing challenge. Good customer relations were imperative for expansion, but constant capital inflows from investors were also crucial. This balance—between state-like requirements for service to beneficiaries and corporate requirements for profit—were articulated through gendered organizational principles that affected the experiences and career trajectories of MFI employees.

Benevolent Protectionism: Performing Authority and Care

How do MFI workers govern gender in their interactions with women clients who are always already constructed as requiring assistance? I found patterns among both men and women alike that suggest that MFI workers emulate the state in their interactions with clients. Employees take pride in their ability to offer them assistance in tough times and act as an ally in good times. Men and women alike enact this benevolent protectionism, but do so in gender-specific ways that elicit divergent responses from clients.

After many meetings with leaders at the main office, I was invited to a Sowbagya branch office in a dense Bengaluru neighborhood in one of the oldest parts of the city. The office was on the third floor of a yellow concrete building so easy to miss that I walked past it three times before calling someone on my cell phone to lead me inside. Met by the branch manager, Vinay, I found other businesses occupying the lower floors of a building that appeared to have been residential, with internal layouts typical of urban apartments. At the door of Sowbagya's office, a cluster of sandals waited at the door, and I deposited mine alongside. Vinay met me, along with Mamatha, my research assistant, at the door and invited us inside the bright, open-air office. Soon after we arrived, he gathered the branch staff for a morning meeting.

We introduced ourselves, and Vinay asked employees to introduce themselves as well. In the circle of fifteen employees, I noticed two women; the rest were men. They introduced themselves by first name and told us how long they had been with the organization and how many customers they handled. Most had been with Sowbagya for two to three years and handled between five hundred and six hundred customers. Two of the men were field staff previously but now worked at the branch office. When introductions were over, Vinay invited Mamatha and me to pose questions. Mamatha asked those assembled to narrate a time they felt especially satisfied with their jobs. This proved to be a generative opening question, as almost every employee had a story. These stories, shared in front of superiors, conveyed an image publicly presentable to a foreign researcher but were often distinct from accounts I heard privately in interviews. Publicizing Sowbagya's programs for customers, field staff described themselves as borrowers' helpmates who could channel resources in times of need.

Aditya, a cashier who had previously been a field-worker, narrated a typical story. A customer's mother had been suffering with an eye problem, and he had been able to connect the family to Sowbagya's eye camp, through which she qualified for free cataract surgery. Aditya had felt happy with this outcome and, he reported, the woman's family had as well. Suresh, another employee, related in great detail the plight of a client whose husband had recently met with an accident and died, leaving her with a nine-month-old baby. A delay at the police station had then postponed issuance of the death certificate, a document necessary for the thirty-thousand-rupee life insurance policy that comes with a Sowbagya loan. Because this death was accidental (not suicidal), this customer was entitled to life insurance money from Sowbagya, but the death certificate was required. Working for weeks with the customer and local police, Suresh had just seen the issue resolved. The customer would be receiving the money.[5]

In Suresh and Aditya's narratives, Sowbagya provided vital services that poor customers badly needed but were unable to access on their own. Sowbagya staff acted as mediators, offering clients a liaison to government services. Important to staff was a sense of duty, blended with empathy, toward customers who seemed especially needy or deserving. Field staff often reported a sense of purpose in which they went the extra mile. Suresh's story also exemplifies Sohini Kar's analysis of "bundled" life insurance for microfinance customers, which ensures "a way to recover outstanding debts in case of the borrower's or her guarantor's death . . . life insurance is another mechanism by which to account for the riskiness of lending to the poor."[6] In Suresh's narrative, he underplayed the financial benefit to Sowbagya of the life insurance policy, emphasizing instead how he helped a worthy client obtain the payout. Similarly, Aditya's account of the eye surgery served the company by drawing attention to its social responsibility programs.

By fulfilling the role of state-like care providers, the men of microfinance derive a sense of purpose and respect from directly serving vulnerable women. Naren, a young loan officer of twenty-three, had been working at Sowbagya for three years, following a brother and uncle employed by the company, and had come to handle a portfolio of 550 customers. Explaining that he loved the job, Naren elaborated, "The joy is that customers give us a lot of respect when we meet them on road. . . . For example, one customer had a green vegetable business. Our company had provided her the first loan. She was doing business on the footpath. Since she [and her husband] were doing well, we gave her seventy-thousand-rupee loans. Now, they have a big shop. That customer, even now, greets us when there are so many people around. I feel that they pay me that respect. I feel very happy."

Naren's narrative underscores the benefit of a position that makes him the face of a reliable organization helping families improve their lot in life. This customer, now paying him respect as proprietor of a large shop, reinforced his status as a respectable young man doing good work. Such affirming interactions are particularly important for MFI workers in a city like Bengaluru, where upwardly mobile information technology (IT) workers earn salaries that might be more than ten times those of entry-level MFI workers, and flaunt those salaries through high-end consumption. In Bengaluru, as in other cities, IT workers travel rapidly past dense areas where Naren and his colleagues work. For an MFI worker, therefore, a greeting by a neighborhood customer offers a sense of purpose while also helping lift up the company.

As I accompanied Rajiv to a training session on the outskirts of Chennai on a blazing March day, a group of twenty-five women gathered in a living room had been waiting, they claimed, for over an hour. Rajiv had much work to do to keep the group focused. As always, he was sharply dressed in a tie, dress shoes, formal dark pants, and a formal button-down shirt in a stylish pastel tone. The fraying edges of his pants and the thin layer of dust that covered his shoes, however, betrayed his having driven a two-wheeler to the training. At any of the IT or business process outsourcing (BPO) companies nearby, dusty shoes and fraying pants might have raised an eyebrow or two, but here Rajiv's formality was impressive. A thick mustache and careful shave, typical for Tamil Nadu men, topped off his stylized respectability. Rajiv was not just a loan officer but a trainer. In some companies that offer specialized training in entrepreneurialism or financial literacy, trainers occupied a tier slightly higher than loan officers in the hierarchy of customer-facing staff. Trainers tended to have college degrees and sometimes graduate educations as well. In Kanchan's Shaktisri program, the trainers were highly skilled and leveraged their knowledge in varied ways to engage clients, but always through gendered performances that articulated authority and care.

At over six feet tall with a figure that hinted at his former life as a body-builder, Rajiv stood head and shoulders above most of the assembled women borrowers and commanded an authority beyond his age. But his ready smile was inviting. As he unfurled a large sheet of white paper and taped it to the concrete wall, making a portable chalkboard of sorts, Rajiv asked the group, "How old do you think I am?" They all giggled. "Twenty-five," said one woman. "Thirty," said another. "Not more than thirty," said a third. Rajiv affirmed that he was twenty-five. "I believe that you are all older than me, right?" he added. Everyone agreed. "Is there anyone here younger than me?" he asked. One woman raised her hand. "Okay, fine," responded Rajiv. "You treat me with respect. Everyone else can call me Little Brother [*Thambi*]." A wave of laughter passed over the group.

Throughout the training session, Rajiv corrected borrowers who addressed him as "Sir [*Sar*]," the default term of respect for any official man, interjecting "Thambi" whenever possible. A few women who addressed him as Thambi were clearly uncomfortable and followed with either a demand or a nervous giggle, as if testing his willingness to be like their little brother. Rajiv, in contrast, was at ease. He had lived in communities like this one all his life. Still, he had managed to acquire a postgraduate education and a fancy job, a rare accomplishment in such neighborhoods. He could be impressive, authoritative, and a little brother all at once.

Rajiv relied upon his own brand of charisma to attract participation in the trainings he conducted. He opened sessions with a simple game, like charades or a tangram, to make clients comfortable, a step officially required but carried out by only two of the eight trainers I observed. Rajiv invited clients to solve problems together, whether articulating their strengths in the module "Who am I?" or augmenting the lecture on time management with a live demonstration using a bucket of water. In trainings on budgeting, he bet on having one or two members of a large group with enough education to do simple math. In all his interactions, Rajiv emphasized that the assistance was free. Even if the trainings seemed inapplicable, he would frequently say, their utility would become clear in the future. Unlike competing MFIs who were only after their money, he claimed that Kanchan was offering them something valuable that company leaders thought would help them in life. Rajiv's style and message thus helped to legitimize Kanchan as a company serving society in a state-like capacity.

Rajiv's performance of masculinity was just as important as his message. His clothing, his alternating formal and casual manner, and his on-the-spot adaptation of company materials impressed clients. Countless gestures conveyed not only his down-to-earth accessibility but also his status. He avoided sitting on the floor with clients (perhaps to avoid making his dress slacks even dustier) and instead stood upright, above them. When he once sat down because another trainer, a woman, insisted, several clients rose spontaneously to their feet to fetch him a chair, an impulse that he quelled immediately, insisting that he was fine on the floor. He was self-deprecating at times. He also often stepped outside during the training to make seemingly important calls.

Even though he was not particularly effective in explaining why the training was helpful or what clients were expected to learn, Rajiv convinced clients that Kanchan was in their neighborhoods for their own benefit. Rajiv successfully used his youth and charisma to establish engaging relationships. His regional, class-specific performance of masculinity helped keep an audience of busy urban women attentive while also burnishing his own reputation and that of his organization.

In contrast, Ranjan, a trainer in his late forties with a long career in state development agencies, deployed a more authoritative, paternalistic style that emulated the state. Ranjan, who had recently joined the microfinance industry, felt that Shaktisri's vetting for women entrepreneurs was insufficient and that most were unsuited for the company's "advanced" training. Still, Ranjan was able to effectively perform benevolent protectionism, drawing respect and admiration from clients for himself and the MFI, even when he was not offering them information they found useful.

When he walked into a training, Ranjan expected the women to respect him. Rather than drumming up interest with inviting quips, he was didactic. He often substituted his own, abbreviated versions of Shaktisri's participatory pedagogy, presuming that clients lacked math skills to calculate income and expenses or discuss strategies if expenses exceeded income. In my observations of his trainings, this approach often did not go well. Clients were fidgety and, in one training, repeatedly asked when the meeting would be over, to which Ranjan responded that the material could not be taught in a hurry. Yet his paternalism did not jeopardize the company's legitimacy. Paternalism may have been a poor pedagogical strategy, but it conveyed benevolent protectionism effectively. He was (at least theoretically) offering help, even if clients lacked the patience, education, or intelligence to learn his lessons. This masculine mode of governance was familiar to clients and did the work of legitimizing Kanchan and its program.

Men employed in MFI social programs assume a masculine performance of benevolent protectionism that is saturated in the hierarchies of class and caste. These leaders also tend to come from careers in state programs, where they are accustomed to respect from the vulnerable groups they aim to help. John, the head of Bhavishya's CSR division, exemplifies this masculine articulation of benevolent protectionism. Neither a banker nor a company board member, John is a former state employee from a privileged background who got his start managing his state's self-help group program in its early days. During a field visit to check in on Bhavishya clients, he lectured clients about the importance of educating their children, rhetorically asking a group of clients in a Chennai slum about why he was different from them. Answering his own question, he then cited his education and, seeking to inspire, encouraged them to save and make sure their children studied so they could rise to positions like his. The clients performed the gendered and class-specific responses John expected from them, outwardly indicating their belief in the company, as well as in the false notions of upward mobility John laid out. Perhaps some truly believed that their children could be like him; most had taken loans for their children's education.[7] Whatever their motivation, they smiled, nodded, and pressed their hands together respectfully.

Women in similar front-facing roles also did their best to emulate benevolent protectionism toward clients, emulating the authority of care of the state through a femininity that invited aspiration and relationality. Even though MFI employees are predominantly men, women are employed at every level of the organizations I studied and comprise 19 percent of frontline industry staff.

Woman loan officers model a socially oriented womanhood that requires care, uplift, and understanding of the community beyond their own homes and families. This powerful message is sometimes at odds with the more individualistic, family-centered models provided in the trainings (see chapter 6). Yet by carrying out the everyday labor of connecting with clients, women MFI workers demonstrate community uplift for other women. Clients admired women MFI workers and, in some cases, found them aspirational for their daughters. Women on the front lines of MFI work share many of the same responsibilities as their male counterparts, but the women I interviewed seemed more effective at building and sustaining relationships with clients and, especially, at resolving repayment issues (see chapter 4).

Nandini, a star trainer employed by Kanchan, approached her clients very differently from the men I encountered. With a mix of sophistication, educational privilege, and ability to operate in clients' cultural milieu, she articulated benevolent protectionism through her class-specific performance of femininity. Nandini was twenty-six when we met and had been a trainer with Kanchan for three years. She served the semi-urban communities outside the metropolis of Coimbatore, in Tamil Nadu, but traveled frequently to Chennai to help train new trainers. As a woman speaking to other women about entrepreneurship, even across divisions of class and educational privilege, she could appeal more effectively than Rajiv or Ranjan for clients' time and attention.

During the first training session I observed, in an especially dense slum on the outskirts of Chennai, we sat in the dusty verandah of a home owned by a wealthier member of the community, not a client. As was often the case, the woman who owned the house sat apart in a chair, observing us from a distance. Behind us were rows of parked motorcycles, part of an adjacent business, and over four hours sitting on the concrete floor, we often rubbed shoulders with motorcycle wheels. And yet when Nandini stood in front of the group of eighteen, these clients expressed excitement about the training they were about to receive (see figure 2.1).

Nandini explained that this training would be different from anything they had experienced because they would learn to run a business and make

FIGURE 2.1. Clients gather with interest for Nandini's training.

money for their families. Rather than the expressions of skepticism from clients so many of the male trainers I observed experienced, Nandini elicited appeals. One woman pleaded, "We're simply sitting at home. I want to do something; please tell us what do. I want to do something. I don't want to just sit at home. Please help us." Distaste for "sitting at home," which referred to domestic and care-providing tasks, came up frequently in training sessions. Clients expressed ambitions to "do something," which always meant earning extra money for their families. They expressed admiration for Nandini and other women MFI workers for doing something and felt that these women could guide them better than a man.

Benevolent protectionism, whether articulated by men or women facing clients with knowledge and products, helps us understand, in part, how MFIS govern gender. As I will show in chapter 5, the specific teachings they offer call into being particular kinds "gendered citizen subjects,"[8] namely, working mothers. Here, however, I have drawn attention to another understudied aspect of the governance of gender: how agents of governance perform gender in class-specific ways in order to elicit loyalty, respect, and legitimacy from beneficiaries. I now turn to how these performances with clients are linked to the gendered and class-specific opportunities MFI workers have within their organizations.

"I Would Rather Have a Guy": The Masculine Logic of MFI Fieldwork

Turning from the governance of gender, I pivot to examine the dynamics of inequality within MFIS. Brush argues that the gender of governance "consists of men's general monopolization of, and women's exclusion from, otherwise neutral state institutions and social policy practices."[9] Analysis of the gender of governance in Indian MFIS shows that even in these organizations, supposedly oriented toward the empowerment of women, women are themselves marginalized from the most important work, whether in the field or in the corporation. While corporate masculinity explicitly dominates the strategic aspects of MFI leadership, to be discussed in the next section, profit-maximizing logics require masculinity among field-workers. Even though the gendered performances of women staff like Nandini and other women MFI workers I observed conveyed to clients the idea that women and mothers can and should combine work and motherhood for the benefit of themselves and the family, but such ideals were nearly impossible to attain within MFIS. As I show in chapter 5, MFIS also promote this ideal of combining work and motherhood in their teachings. But within their own organizations, the sticky floor that women employees encounter as well as explicit preference for workers who are not mothers shows that it is almost impossible for mothers to thrive in most MFIS.

I met several men who had experienced significant mobility within MFIS, like Naren. Men from working-class or small-town backgrounds with a twelfth-grade education were satisfied with the opportunity and mobility the industry provided.[10] In contrast, women with similar backgrounds experienced a sticky floor, which impeded their rise.[11] Some women loan officers I met or interviewed had been in the same position for many years, despite excellent records.

While women often indicated that they had chosen not to rise up the ranks, this was not always the case. Janaki had been a loan officer at Sowbagya for eleven years and reported enjoying her work. Family reasons, she explained, had kept her from moving on to other positions. Sundari, another loan officer, had been working for Sowbagya for six years and had been named top performer several times. She had been offered a promotion but wanted to avoid additional responsibility. In contrast, Nadia, a young MFI employee who had worked with Sowbagya for two years, had used MFI employment to move beyond her experience of marginalization and had accepted her role as primary breadwinner in her family. She was poised to move ahead in the company, but as I will discuss in greater depth below, Nadia essentially gave up being a primary caregiver for her daughter in order to put herself in a position to do so. I was unable to follow up with her to learn about her subsequent trajectory.

There appeared to be at least some opportunity for women who were not yet mothers. Nandini, introduced above, was a single woman enjoying success as a trainer, a position that she was directly recruited into from her university. The only woman I met who had risen through a few levels within an MFI firm was Jyoti, another single woman. At age twenty-seven, Jyoti had worked for Sowbagya for over six years and had become an individual loan officer, one of the firm's most prestigious field positions. Since joining the company as frontline field staff for group loans, she had enjoyed three promotions and oversaw several of Sowbagya's products, including housing loans. Unlike other urban field officers, who tended to stay in the same neighborhood, Jyoti zoomed all over Bengaluru on a two-wheeler, working with clients who took one to two-lakh loans (up to five thousand dollars). Like the men I interviewed, she found the job satisfying and not too stressful, and she felt confident that she could resolve any customer's problem.

The experiences of the women I studied in the lower tiers of microfinance help explain why clients identify with women loan officers and view them as models: these women are navigating structures of opportunity and exclusion familiar to clients. Whether they remained in the same position for years or advanced through the organization, women in MFIS need not necessarily adhere to middle-class ideals of professional femininity in which women fulfill their obligations as mothers and cultural transmitters before pursuing career advancement.[12] Rather, lower-tier MFI workers labored to serve their community as well as they could while still earning a wage for their families. However, Indian MFIS, I found, do not value this labor because they construct it as unreliable.

Ritu had been a financial analyst for a large private bank but had taken a long break from her career to raise her children and support her husband, a successful businessman. At the time of our interview, she directed social programs for Bhavishya. Ritu explained that managers and MFI leaders, regardless of gender, are likely to avoid hiring, promoting, or advancing women, who were inherently unreliable. She added that she personally avoided hiring mothers. Despite working in an environment saturated with the discourse of women's empowerment, Ritu offered many reasons to employ only men or, if required, women without children. "When you talk about gender issues, I am thinking about myself. How good I am in giving equal opportunity to guys as I do to women?" She explained,

> I know my boys [men employees] will never go on maternity leave; we have to accept that women do these things; however good the reasons may be, the fact is that they do it. From the organization's perspective, and from where I am sitting today, do I really need one of my community workers going on four months' maternity leave? When the rural women are desperately in need of their service, do I need some female employee calling me early in the morning when we have urgent work that should have been done yesterday—a beneficiary in a slum getting a medical intervention, and she says, "Oh, my child is sick. I cannot come for work today"? Do I need all these when I can run an organization without these? When an employer says "all things are equal," I would rather have a guy, which is already happening from time immemorial. I do not blame women. Equal opportunity should apply at home as well. Why can't the man be at home and take care of the sick child and let the mum go to work, since she has an emergency? Unfortunately, no, that does not happen, and that is a reality. It will not

change for the next 100 years. . . . No, I cannot practice gender equality, much as I would love to. I recognize and realize the shortcomings of a woman in the workplace. . . . [When a woman comes for an interview] the first question I ask is "Are you married?" They say, "Yes." The next question I ask is whether they have children. They say no, and I am more than happy to give them the job. The moment they have a child, they become a liability and are no longer available.

Ritu's views on women in her organization display the interplay among individual attitudes, organizational practices, and cultures of class and gender inequality. Her strongly worded criticism of programs that aim for women's empowerment reflect a mix of disappointment in the women she has hired and dismay at the exclusion of poor men from India's development projects. Having moved repeatedly with her husband, she had also experienced the challenge of a second-place career, despite her ambition, intelligence, and ability.

Without an intersectional frame that incorporated the interaction of class and gender, Ritu had come to lead a workplace in which men could advance and women with children would remain excluded. Her commitment to serving the poor and destitute conflicted strongly with efforts to build a gender-equitable organization in which women from all class backgrounds could forge careers. Ritu's frank statements reveal that for MFIs and their partners helping poor beneficiaries came at the cost of careers for women in her own organization. Perhaps because she was a woman in a prominent position, she could assert views that she knew were controversial, voicing her challenges and frustrations to me. None of the men in similar positions whom I interviewed commented in this way about gender within their organizations. Since the time of my research, however, gender inclusivity has been recognized in the industry as an issue, indicating that even now women seldom, if ever, rise to positions of greater responsibility in their organizations.[13]

Corporate Masculinity: Profit Extraction as an Ethic of Care

At the upper echelons of MFI leadership, the expression of masculinity from higher-up MFI men aligns closely with what Raewyn Connell terms hegemonic masculinity, the "institutionalized pattern of masculinity in the milieu of corporate management [that] involves a focus on competitive achievement and a certain ruthlessness in achieving personal and corporate goals." This pattern of masculinity, Connell argues, reflects a managerial culture that "defines business success as the highest good for the society as well as the individual."[14] India's microfinance sector supports this hegemonic pattern of masculinity, which I modify for the corporate context and name *corporate masculinity*.[15] For MFI leaders, however, corporate masculinity must be moderated to reflect the outwardly altruistic character of microfinance. Powerful men in the sector thus seek legitimacy from the benevolent protectionism performed by lower-level staff members. They receive support as well from upper-class women, who at the corporate level tend to be concentrated in the soft work of philanthropy and client education.

In the context of this corporate culture, even privileged women face marginalization. At the time of this writing, none of India's top MFIs or small finance banks have women CEOs, although at the dawn of Indian microfinance many women were involved in launching microfinance and microcredit NGOs.[16] The industry has no official statistics on how women are concentrated in different areas of the industry beyond the field staff and total staff distinction (where women make up 19 percent of field staff and 12 percent of staff overall).[17] But I noticed higher concentrations of women in back-end support, human resources, and roles related to firms' corporate social responsibility programs.

Many of the women I interviewed had strong academic backgrounds in management, economics, engineering, or development and had been recruited directly into prominent roles, but these roles did not seem to serve as a springboard to more significant leadership positions due to a combination of gender, class, and caste norms at home and at work. As Ritu's narrative and life trajectory suggests, in the industry's higher echelons, even highly educated women with ambitions for career advancement often had to navigate class and gender norms for supporting their breadwinning husbands. While it might be tempting to attribute this orientation to middle-class Indian cultural norms, researchers have repeatedly shown that the same norms are part of managerial cultures in the US, Europe, and Australia.[18] In the Indian microfinance industry, the norms of middle-class Indian patriarchy converge with those of Western-style corporations. As a result, normative internal cultures consistently reproduce the binary between breadwinning and caretaking, even when women are breadwinners or could be.

Deepa started working at Sowbagya after finishing a graduate degree in rural management from an esteemed institution in India, following a rigorous engineering degree. When she joined Sowbagya, she underwent a management development program in house, where she was trained on every vertical within the company. She then had her choice of vertical and chose field operations because, as she put it, "I thought I am a field person." But exploring north Indian urban slums to set up field operations, she soon found resistance to women both in the organization and in the field. She also felt unsafe. The conditions seemed different from those in Bengaluru or Chennai, where microfinance products, along with self-help groups, have a long history. "The very nature of slums [there], it's really difficult, you know, I mean, it's really hard," she noted. "So they [the leadership team] said it's not possible for us, you know, to put all the females out there," she recalled.

Deepa then sought to change positions within Sowbagya. "The next closest for me to get my hands dirty and understand was the operations department." Yet even there, she had to be out in the slums of Delhi, interacting with clients and branch staff and devising ways to engage them through new products, programs, and services, even as she tried to achieve operational efficiency. She had found the diverse set of people from varying educational backgrounds in the organizations challenging, though she avoided reporting specific instances:

RITU: I learned a lot. The kind of people I worked with, you know, they were probably not as educated as, you know, I am, but it was a totally different challenge to kind of, you know, work with them. In probably a good way as well because they can, I mean, they are nice, they are very nice people. But if they are mean, then you really don't want to get into that kind of you know—[pauses, hesitates]

SR: You can't even, there's a communication—

RITU: Exactly, there's always a, you know, I just cannot, because I come from that type of background, I cannot, but you really have to, as a manager, or as, you know, the person in charge, you have to ensure that you first learn from them because I'm of course new . . . You really have to kind of have to get in and make that kind of rapport with them.

Deepa's hesitating account indicates the distance she perceived between herself and the other workers in Sowbagya's middle management, as well as a divide between the experiential understanding of less-educated field-workers and her academic understanding of the same issues. As a manager, she sought a balance, but as a young woman from a privileged background, she found it difficult to be as confrontational as she felt she probably needed to be for that context. Words escape her to describe the limitation she experienced, but her mention of her background suggests that it had to do with a class divide she felt.

After a brief stint at Sowbagya, Deepa moved to the US because of her husband's job. When she returned to India, she continued working in microfinance but joined a consultancy firm that provided financing for development of small, medium, and microenterprises. The focus on small businesses distinguishes these firms from microfinance companies. Deepa, unlike many of the professional women I met in microfinance, had accepted the premise that the microfinance industry provided a service, not necessarily a tool for alleviating poverty or empowering women. As an engineer who had internalized at least some of the cultural norms of corporate masculinity, she expressed support for the idea that development goals could be advanced through what she termed a sustainable financial model. Notably, however, she saw no future for herself in microfinance, nor did she discuss any aspect of gender oppression in her interview.

In contrast, Maya, the director of a client education program at a major international MFI, had climbed to a position of significant leadership but was still kept out of strategic roles within her company. As an Indian woman leading an education effort, often considered the soft side of microfinance, she was determined prove herself. She made every effort to scale up the program and meet the quantitative criteria for expansion set by her international bosses and local partners. Outwardly, Maya expressed support for the women she served and for the cause of microenterprise more broadly. Unlike Ritu, Maya portrayed herself as an advocate for empowering women. Previously a World Bank consultant, she was committed to expanding women's microenterprises to increase incomes for their families, and she hoped to leverage her position between Prosperity and Kanchan to create a new, sustainable institution, a hope that did not, to my knowledge, materialize (see chapter 6). Maya wished to have various institutions, including the US-based company Prosperity, invest jointly to train women, first in basic entrepreneurship and later in skills for making profitable products, gradually scaling up the training business. She also envisioned training for trainers, with an accreditation that would be profitable and, eventually, provide skilled trainers for the burgeoning training industry.

Maya was particularly well positioned to act on these ideas. She had pioneered the India-wide rollout of the Shaktisri entrepreneurial trainings, to be discussed in chapter 5, with Kanchan as a local partner. She also worked well under pressure, leveraging her contacts to adapt training materials when requested, and she could organize large events on a dime. Maya emphasized having the entrepreneurs take the lead with her initiatives. Like other women leaders I interviewed, she was invested in an understanding of women's empowerment that viewed marginalized women as equally capable as she, a highly educated leader in an international company.

Yet Maya's ambition to move into a more strategic role with her employer was constantly thwarted by the daily trials and tribulations of running a training program. In her view, her trainers were not empowered enough, did not pursue numbers enough, and did not take it upon themselves to figure out the best ways to get their materials to clients. "As soon as you give them the task, there's a disconnect," she lamented,

> You know, I need someone I'm not finding, and I'm not shy to say it—I need a second Maya to release me so I can go and really do stuff. . . . You know, my team members come up and every morning say, "Can you take a look at this?" And I can't tell them, look, I'm playing a strategic role [and thus don't have time to provide this hands-on support]. So, I look at it. I'm trying very hard to say it [that hands-on support is not my role] so that they get empowered and take on more responsibility, but they require support. It's not like microfinance, where once you have your lending methodology, credit check, and risk management in place, you are all set. . . . You can't compromise on the training quality. If I find somewhere that entrepreneurs are complaining that they've not understood anything, then I will pack my bags and reach them.

Maya claimed solidarity with the entrepreneurs she trained, but she sometimes alienated her own colleagues, team members, and employees. Moreover, her role, in implementation rather than strategy, did not directly yield profits. So Maya was less valued within Prosperity than she would have liked. Her situation had concrete implications for her employees. In a training session for trainers, I observed participants frequently criticizing Maya, in hushed tones, both for being too authoritative and for blaming them for failing to deliver their programs appropriately to enough people. Maya's position in the company, along with her gender, kept her from being able to emulate corporate masculinity. At the same time, her privileged status, which created distance from the benevolent protectionist ethos on the front lines of MFIs, made it difficult to foster a sense of solidarity with those who worked for her.

Because of the areas in which women are concentrated in Indian microfinance and how their class and gender identities coalesce, women on the front lines can leverage a feminine version of benevolent protectionism to forge relationships with clients. Class-privileged women are recruited directly into the upper echelons of these firms but, like frontline workers, may be held back from fieldwork positions. These women, while better off in the industry on the whole, still are unable to forge pathways to power in a corporation that internally valued a focus on valuation and profits legitimated by breadwinning men. As a result, ambitious women are trapped in areas of service and philanthropy. They must help their clients but often lack the power of their male colleagues. This fraught position can undermine their legitimacy and lead to ideological positions that undermine gender equity in both their organizations and the programs they design and administer.

Conclusion

To begin to understand how gendered power works at Indian MFIS, I have focused in this chapter on two distinct, but interconnected, areas: the *governance of gender*, or how MFIS articulate gendered norms and aspirations to their clients in the context of providing state-like services, and the *gender of governance*, or the conditions that women and men face within specific MFI workplaces. I have shown that in each of these areas, MFIS balance two competing imperatives: the imperative for state-like legitimacy and the imperative to extract as much profit as possible in order to scale up and ensure the continued inflow of capital. These imperatives play themselves out in ways that reinforce women's subordination within MFIS and coalesce class norms, giving women, and especially mothers, little chance of experiencing significant mobility within MFIS. Men and women on the front lines of MFI work perform benevolent protectionism. They act as a liaison to state services when appropriate and emphasize how they are serving the women whenever possible. Since most of these men and women come from modest or marginalized backgrounds themselves, they are able to forge personal connections with clients through class-specific, and at times, caste- and regionally specific performances of masculinity or femininity. Through these performances, women clients come to see that women *can* combine motherhood and work, that their children could be like their MFI workers if they provide them with a good education, and that MFIS are in their communities for the benefit of their communities.

But once we turn our gaze within the organization, we find that these performances do not reflect the internal structures of profit-oriented financial companies in an industry that actively upholds masculine norms at every level. At lower tiers, women encounter a sticky floor and rarely rise up, while at upper levels, class-privileged women find it difficult to carry out work that is actually valued by the firm and thus either quit or remain segregated in the social activities of the firm. Corporate masculinity, the organizing principle at the top of Indian MFIs, actively works against the very ethos of women's empowerment it outwardly aims to promote. The state-sanctioned special status of MFIS as providers of financial services translates into everyday interactions with clients that assist in the gendered extraction of value. Together with benevolent protectionism, corporate masculinity reinforces gendered extraction within the industry as a whole. I now turn to how MFI staff and clients together produce the condition that both the state *and* the profit-oriented corporate office want for their clients: creditworthiness.

3. MAKING WOMEN CREDITWORTHY

Interdependency

In the head office of Bhavishya, John explained the difficulty of getting clients to repay on time. Citing a Tamil proverb about loans, he laughed, "Before you give the loan, you are a *raja* [a king], but after you give the loan, you become a beggar!" The proverb helped John crisply convey the cross-purposes that clients and MFI employees experience from the moment a loan has been disbursed. The client must repay, which can be painful for her, and the MFI employee must collect the money on time, offering nothing more than the promise of future loans under similarly restrictive conditions and high interest rates. If a client is delinquent and her group fails to pay in her stead, the MFI must either report the default, which would undermine its impressive repayment record, or resort to coercion, which would undermine its legitimacy. Especially after the crisis, MFIs have been wary of political or regulatory blowback and so try to avoid coercive tactics. Yet, timely repayment is still required in order to ensure profit extraction *and* the impression that women are agents of development to a broader public. How, then, do MFIs promote timely repayment while maintaining their own legitimacy?

Microfinance initiatives have come to target women because microfinance providers worldwide regard women as better credit risks than men.[1] This assertion, however, is based on an assumption that women are a cohesive category, an idea that feminist scholarship has thoroughly debunked. When policy makers treat women as a unified group, more similar to one another than to men who may share some characteristics, they risk magnifying gender inequalities.[2] This critique need not deny the structural oppression that women around the world face. Rather, it asserts that women's structural oppression is always connected with other dimensions of privilege and marginalization that define women's social location. *mm's exp. vane)*

The existing feminist scholarship on repayment in microfinance illustrates how gendered vulnerabilities, especially tied to class, make women reliable borrowers in the eyes of lending institutions. In Bangladesh, Lamia Karim cites "economies of shame" as a reason women tend to be more reliable than men at repaying. Women borrowers, she explains, are squeezed in many ways—by pressure from their husbands to bring in loans, pressure from loan officers to pay for defaulting members of a group, and the risk of losing dignity within a community.[3] In India, Kalpana Karunakaran documents self-help group members closely monitoring one another for creditworthiness, expelling members who pose too great a risk and recruiting those deemed creditworthy according to the framework outlined by the National Agricultural Bank. Lending policies thus constitute self-help group members as neoliberal subjects who work with the microfinance system to survive poverty. Acting as agents on their own behalf in the absence of other options, women who are vulnerable to multiple kinds of pressure and surveillance keep loans flowing.[4] Here and elsewhere, state-led microcredit initiatives effectively transfer full responsibility for loans to groups of women, who must, through various forms of coercion, surveillance, exclusion, and recruitment, manage to repay. State-led programs ensure women's repayment through gendered systems of discipline imposed from above and enforced horizontally, between women. *social codes?*

As we have already seen, the for-profit microfinance system also depends on women's social ties to one another. In groups, women monitor each other to ensure accountability, for which each group member is individually liable. We might expect that commercial MFIS operate in the same way as state-run programs. An emergent literature, however, points to a slightly different dynamic, with the distinct institutional context of commercial microfinance producing perhaps more mutual interpersonal exchanges between clients and staff. Sohini Kar's analysis of loan officers and field-workers in West Bengal reveals two sides to loan-taking.[5] Women carry out what she calls credit-work, the meetings, planning, and financial discipline that constitute the everyday domestic responsibility of taking out loans and paying them back. This unpaid gendered labor, which I elaborate upon in chapter 5, provides MFIS with the foundation of their business model. Building *branding*

on state narratives, MFIS construct women borrowers as domestic and efficient as well as vulnerable and in need of empowerment. MFIS leverage
this characterization to attract investment capital. Women's credit-work not
only conforms to this characterization but also includes the surveillance and
discipline that Karunakaran observed in SHGS.

On the other side of the transaction, Kar reveals, loan officers carry out
intense emotional labor to ensure that loans are repaid.[6] They retain detailed
information about their clients' everyday lives, develop long-standing relationships of obligation and loyalty, and treat clients with deference and care.
When a default arises, therefore, a loan officer could draw effectively upon
strong ties of mutual obligation. Expressions of care allowed these loan officers to feel that they were better than the moneylenders, even as they sold
expensive financial products to vulnerable women clients. Their emotional
labor could also ensure a high repayment rate that would allow them to advance
in their careers.

This chapter builds on these studies to examine the processes through
which commercial MFIS leverage routines, procedures, and relationships of
familiarity to make women creditworthy. The construction of creditworthy
women lies at the heart of the broader state project of financial inclusion,
which has required transforming the historical status of Indian women as
inherently uncreditworthy. Yet after the 2010 crisis, the microfinance industry could no longer transfer all responsibility for repayment to women
because there was widespread recognition that MFIS also had responsibilities
around disbursal and loan recovery. Unlike self-help groups, therefore, MFIS
established a regulated system of relational work sustained through interaction between a client and a loan officer, usually a man.[7] Within this system,
women cannot make themselves creditworthy; rather, they must demonstrate
creditworthiness through loans mediated by loan officers. This ongoing process of lending and repayment involves various forms of discipline, as other
studies have shown, but it also involves institutional scripts and procedures
infused with expressions of care. Through gendered social ties supporting a
fundamentally economic relationship, MFIS balance their profit orientation
and their political legitimacy. Once accomplished, relational work between
clients and employees facilitates financial extraction, while also allowing
symbolic extraction, as MFIS record and publicize client stories that legitimate their work. By making all parties happy, MFIS appear to be serving
marginalized women who benefit from their services.

Viviana Zelizer's notion of relational work helps us conceptualize the intertwined forms of sociality and economy involved in making women creditworthy.[8] As Bandelj explains,

> people create connected lives by differentiating their multiple social ties from each other, marking boundaries between those different ties by means of everyday practices [distinctive names, symbols, practices, and media of exchange], sustaining those ties through joint activities (including economic activities), but constantly negotiating the exact content of important social ties. [Zelizer writes,] "It is the process of [r]elational work [that] includes the establishment of differentiated social ties, their maintenance, their reshaping, their distinction from other relations, and sometimes, their termination."[9]

As a frame for the interactions between client and MFI, relational work reveals the social character of financial inclusion in an economic transaction.[10] In a relationship simultaneously economic and social, MFIS and borrowers build and sustain lasting ties. MFIS can then make working-class women creditworthy, in cooperation with national policy. The process of building such ties, however, requires more than discipline or emotional labor; it requires a mutual understanding of interdependence. This interdependence is a prerequisite for the long-term gendered extraction through which the microfinance industry retains both its profit and its legitimacy. It is also the substance of what neither colonial nor postcolonial state banking efforts were ever able to accomplish. MFI success with relational work and their ability to carry it out in a reliable, scalable way is the precise skill that legitimized their operations to the state and the larger public. Thus, relational work is foundational to banking at the expanding outer edge of the financial system.

MFIS and their loan officers need clients to repay, while clients need to keep bringing loans into their households. Loan officers, trained in company procedures, create and mediate this interdependence through the accomplishment and sustenance of relational work. They leverage the honor and trust that clients afford to encourage repayment in lean times. They bend the official rules to lend to women who might not meet all the official criteria, leading to expressions of gratitude from clients who need the funds in the short term. They offer clients programs that sometimes benefit clients, which then allow frontline staff and the MFIS that employ them to extract the symbolic value of helping vulnerable women through stories of these

Shame

encounters. Through all these interactions, entwined forms of social and economic relationality between borrowers and frontline workers produce the high repayment rates and (often misleading) positive credit records. These conditions encourage vulnerable women to take loans as a livelihood strategy.

Relational work resolves the contradictions among three crucial tasks for MFIS: borrower recruitment, loan collection, and maintenance of legitimacy. The first two tasks are discrete, but efforts to maintain legitimacy pervade MFI activities at every level. Recruiting borrowers is tricky work. MFIS must find clients who are needy and not already targeted by mainstream banking institutions. At the same time, these potential borrowers cannot be *too* needy because their chances of repayment must be good. In the eyes of MFIS, mothers who are embedded in a particular neighborhood are a better bet, more likely to repay because of their ties to their neighbors. MFIS establish recruitment procedures strict enough to weed out those who cannot afford to repay but open enough to offer access to those without credit records. And because microfinance is a group loan, MFIS are not looking for individuals but groups of individuals with nonfamilial relationships to one another.[11]

Once an appropriate group has been recruited, vetted, and the loan has been disbursed, an MFI must undertake the second task, loan repayment. Clients must appear at the appointed time and place with the correct amount of money, adhering to a strict repayment schedule that is uniform throughout the year, despite the seasonality of income in most working families. At defined intervals—every week or two weeks or month, depending on the organization—clients meet collectively with their loan officers. Meetings forge solidarity between members and between the loan officers and clients, but the driving purpose behind meetings is simple: everyone must repay. Because income volatility is endemic in communities where microfinance thrives, one or more members are likely to be unable to repay. Nonetheless, the MFI requires repayment to financially sustain its own organization.

MFIS that care about repayment above all else then have two options: recruit only wealthier borrowers or engage in varying forms of coercion toward their more vulnerable clientele. Recruiting wealthier borrowers and offering larger loans have become commonplace in the industry, but the scope for this strategy is limited because MFIS cannot rely on borrowers who can get cheaper debt from other financial institutions. Coercive tactics are also, increasingly, a less viable option. Public discourse that linked the suicides of farmers in Andhra Pradesh in 2009 to microfinance caused a public outcry against such tactics, contributing to the industry's crisis in 2010.[12] By the time I began my fieldwork in 2012, new regulations for the behavior of loan officers precluded overt coercion, although my interviews suggested that loan officers did, at times, apply subtle coercion.[13]

This history of coercion and crisis informs MFIS' third all-consuming task: maintaining legitimacy. India's nonbanking financial institutions have historically drawn great suspicion across the class spectrum. India also has a long history of large-scale scams from the 1970s through the present day. In 2019, the Saradha chit fund scam, a massive banking operation with direct connections to members of the national parliament, defrauded millions of ordinary people in a Ponzi scheme.[14] MFIs have a better reputation than chit funds but still feel the heat of public scrutiny. As longtime MFI employee Velan explained, friends and relatives warned against his taking a job with Sowbagya, then a new financial company offering small loans to groups of women. Even though the job offered a fourfold salary increase, "in India, the general trend is that [finance companies] are all just cheaters," he noted. Still, despite hesitating, Velan needed a job and had the requisite skills. His story underscores the care MFIs must take with clients, ensuring that borrowers understand them to be scrupulous, helping rather than cheating their communities. To address this challenge, MFIs establish conditions for relational work, leveraging the social proximity of clients and staff and making them depend on each other.

When successful, relational work infuses the inherently conflictual, extractive work of microfinance with affective ties and establishes an ongoing relationship of helping and mutual obligation. Gendered performances of trainers and loan officers mediate the tone and terms of relational work. If both client and loan officer feel that the MFI is helping, the company can better protect its legitimacy, improve its chances of prompt repayment, and minimize coercion. The perception of mutual obligation is not merely performative. Frontline MFI workers are truly beholden to their clients for their own career advancement. Moreover, many come from similar backgrounds and neighborhoods and so understand the everyday conditions that clients face.

As they acknowledge, clients can aspire to microfinance work, if not for themselves then for a family member. MFI staff often extend job opportunities to clients. I observed Sowbagya's loan officers invite clients to bring their grown children to job fairs hosted by the company or inform clients about open positions for which their children or siblings might apply. I interviewed the CEO of a large rural MFI who proudly declared that more than half the staff had a mother who was a client. In these ways, the everyday lives of clients and workers are enmeshed, deepening their loan-related interactions and ensuring that they live what Zelizer terms connected lives. They rely upon one another to advance their economic chances, even as they carefully monitor the favors and information that flow between them.

The interpersonal ties forged between clients and frontline workers further our understanding of microfinance as gendered extraction by linking the institutional and macrolevel processes through which MFIs acquire profit with the everyday experiences of clients taking loans. When relational work between clients and frontline workers is successful, the state has successfully shored up its project of financial inclusion, and MFIs are able to smoothly extract both financial and symbolic value from their women clients. The production of creditworthiness, at once individual and structural, is the interpersonal lynchpin that makes all these processes possible. As I show in the next chapter, these interpersonal relationships work in concert with other relational processes between women clients living in the same neighborhood. The broader regulatory environment puts into context why the relational work I describe in this chapter unfolds in the particular ways that it does.

Regulating Relational Work

As chapter 1 outlines, the microfinance crisis of 2010 led to the creation of a slew of new regulations. Also significant was a change within company cultures. Where once few strong norms governed interactions between clients and MFI staff, MFI leaders started imposing more extensive training—with onboarding programs and longer periods of training in the field before workers were allowed to be on their own with clients—and careful auditing of interactions with clients. While much variation in these practices remains, Sowbagya and Bhavishya are widely viewed to be more rule bound and careful than some other organizations. Most companies, however, began regulating interactions at every stage of the loan process, thus routinizing this service work.[15] Although affective and relational practices had long been underway and enmeshed with repayment, the details of these practices came to be managed overtly.

My interviews with senior MFI staff who had cut their teeth in the industry in the early 2000s offered comparisons with an earlier period. Their accounts revealed the importance of rendering relationships between clients and workers nonsexual, and the corollary risk of too little intimacy. They *rapport*

also revealed the trial and error that led organizations to recognize that flexibility and understanding with clients would produce better results: higher likelihood of repayment, better rapport with customers, and ultimately greater legitimacy. During an earlier period of unscripted relationality, organizations were learning, ad hoc, that client-worker relationships had to be intimate, but not *too* intimate. → *resp. be mixed gender*

Ramanathan, founder-director of Grama Valachi in Tamil Nadu, explained that socializing staff to adhere to protocols with clients was a major challenge in the organization's early stage. While establishing operations in rural areas where women had never taken loans, Grama Valachi had found too much intimacy between clients and staff, even with what seemed like extensive training. Ramanathan called it the "problem of the sexes," wherein young men on motorcycles disbursing funds to women in rural areas fell in love or eloped, causing significant social disruption. Ramanathan was flummoxed. "How can you ever stop that which is a normal human tendency?" he declared.

> But society will not leave me so easily. I've had so many [instances] where people [villagers] have walked into my office in groups, saying, [angrily] "Where is that fellow?!" God! So we had to build in systems and processes to resist that. . . . Those are bad episodes, but good things happen also. Our fellows are so soft many a time, that if these ladies come and crib [complain] that I have a problem and can't repay, they'll put the money from their own pocket and say, "Okay, here's the money. Repay now." The reverse also happens! The fellows [young loan officers] go and crib [complain], and these ladies take him the money, and this fellow runs away [stealing it]!

balance

When the personal overtakes the economic, Ramanathan suggests, inappropriate sexuality or transactions can undermine the company's profits or credibility. As Ramanathan explained, the gradual establishment of systems, procedures, checks, and balances had made such incidents less common at Grama Valachi, although they could never be completely eliminated.

The opposite extreme—a lack of intimacy—also had to be avoided. Sarina, an employee at Jagruti, a leading MFI in Andhra Pradesh in 2008, recalled that strict adherence to procedures, without a mutual understanding between clients and workers, could cause a breakdown in trust between clients and the MFI and, possibly, the industry. Sarina recalled an instance from one of her many field visits that had shattered her image of the industry:

I had gone to a center meeting where somebody was not in a position to pay back their loan. . . . I think it had been going on for a while. And the group was like, "Well, we're not going to keep paying for her part. She's just not paying off her loan . . ." But the loan officer was like, "You guys are going to have to sort this out, while I'm just going to keep sitting here and not make any new disbursements or collect repayments from other groups until you sort this out." . . . Everyone was frustrated. They [the other women gathered] were supposed to give their portion or get a new loan, . . . and they were like, "Well, we're not going to keep sitting here because this one person is not paying off her loans." [But] No one [on Jagruti's side] was worried about the inconvenience caused to all of them.

Here, Sarina recalls, the relationship between the loan officer and client lacked warmth and understanding. If the company had ever been client centered, a frequent claim of early NGOs, that ethos had been lost. A cold employee response to one member's adversity had led customers to feel devalued and frustrated. The incident led Sarina, too, to begin losing faith in the company. She wondered whether the drive to expand and lend out as much money as possible was compromising its core mission to improve the lives of poor women. Months later, when the crisis of nonpayment hit Andhra Pradesh, Jagruti was indeed at its center, and Sarina felt her hunch validated. Many of the leaders I spoke with regarded Jagruti as a worst case for Indian commercial microfinance in India and had established practices explicitly to avoid Jagruti's fate.

Yet from their early days, organizations had to figure out, often in the moment, the best way to deal with default, which could set the tone for an organization's self-image and future practices. Ramanathan offered one example, a defaulting rural couple, whose story illustrated how the flexibility of his management team could make a client successful. In a village where Grama Valachi was working, a group included a loan to a couple, through the woman, though both husband and wife had been disabled by polio. They took the loan to begin a tailoring shop, but because about forty others in the village also took loans to open tailoring shops, their business failed, and they could not repay. At first, the other group members paid their share, but over time their help became unsustainable. Facing intense pressure from her peers, the woman reported planning to ask her mother for assistance and left with her husband, locking the store. When they did not return, another moneylender broke the lock and repossessed the sewing machine, leaving Grama Valachi with a default.

When group members then refused to repay, Ramanathan realized that any further pressure would lead the entire group into default. He sent a team to find the couple and discuss their problems, and he gave them another loan, to restart the business. Within two years, the couple had a successful tailoring shop with better processes for withstanding local competition and had repaid the balance on both loans. By returning a couple to a viable livelihood, the institution gained trust and standing within a community and the loyalty of a group that was on the verge of defaulting. The MFI also ensured that the woman who was the original borrower would become creditworthy.

Ramanathan used this example to explain the importance of flexibility with clients, learning the details of their problems, fighting against default by absconding, and, ultimately, preserving the firm's reputation and making this couple better off overall. The organization had prevented a group default by carving out a new solution and offering additional support that ensured repayment, albeit two years later. As Ramanathan's account also reveals, even before the crisis, some firms had linked their longevity and success to practices that would facilitate repayment and maintain lending relationships. This kind of flexibility informed how scripted and unscripted interactions would intertwine to define a new kind of relational work after the crisis.

When the industry began to recover from the crisis, companies understood the need to implement stricter procedures that would regulate workers' comportment with clients. Firms therefore instituted new practices meant to strike a balance between too much intimacy and not enough, to allow for negotiation with borrowers. If the conditions of a relationship became difficult, especially in cases of nonpayment, MFI workers might now be able to push boundaries by drawing on interpersonal connections established through relational work. I observed relational practices that broadly represented three types: prohibitions, auditing, and scripting.

PROHIBITIONS AND THE BOUNDARIES OF RELATIONALITY

Prohibitions related to bribes, sexuality, and food and drink (even water) were largely shared across the organizations I observed and the informants with whom I conducted interviews. Prohibitions constrained the development of social ties between clients and workers. Some prohibitions may have already been in force before the crisis, but I was unable to verify the timing. Under no circumstances were MFI workers permitted to be in any kind of romantic relationship with a client. To minimize the possibility, loan officers would refer to clients as "*ma*," a more informal form of *amma*, or mother.[16]

Bribes had long been prohibited, but new onboarding procedures emphasized loan officers' never accepting any kind of payment outside the amount designated to collect. Because clients might be accustomed to offering a bribe or even just a gift of appreciation to any official in a position of power, this prohibition had to be strong and clear cut.

The prohibition of gifts, which extended to food and drink, bucks the norms of Indian hospitality, even in the most modest homes, but MFI workers cannot accept even a glass of water from a client. I experienced this prohibition in person. A client would offer a drink that she had purchased, and the worker would decline, sometimes awkwardly. Yet workers seemed accustomed to the rule and expressed no resentment. As branch manager Vinay said, "If you have [food or drink] in one person's house, then you have to go to everyone's house, or they will feel bad. Or they may think you prefer one client or another. So we don't eat or drink with clients at all." In some training sessions I observed, trainers and loan officers would get food for clients, perhaps to thank them for attending a long training or to celebrate the end of a course (see figure 3.1). Even in those circumstances, when the company provided the food, employees ate not alongside clients but separately, eating leftovers after everyone else had gone. Industry prohibitions thus limit worker-client connections and define the boundaries of relational work.

AUDITS AND STANDARDIZATION

Whereas prohibitions restrict social ties that might jeopardize MFI legitimacy, auditing practices specify those ties that are imperative to MFI legitimacy. To protect against fraud as much as possible, microfinance companies specify procedures for handling cash. As a cash-based business, companies have needed to ensure that the money clients pay is correctly counted, posted to the correct account, and brought intact to the branch office. From there, it needs to be transferred to the main office, where it can be deposited. In the heyday of microfinance, when institutions were signing loans with almost no verification, wastage and fraud became serious concerns, and evidence led both companies and regulatory agencies to implement multilevel systems of auditing by both people and technology. Such processes are far trickier than they appear because of the difficult conditions in which loan officers work.

Companies met this challenge in diverse ways, depending on the head office, the location of their operations, and their approach to handling cash. Bhavishya applied a centralized model in which individual branches handle

FIGURE 3.1. A treat after training.

no money, relying instead on loan officers, who are directly accountable, and on material and technical systems that streamline operations and thus reduce the chance of fraud as cash changes hands. In contrast, at Sowbagya, branch staff must directly account for the money, serving as a check on loan officers. Each model has implications for the distribution of power and agency in the organization. At Sowbagya, rising to a branch position means handling cash and is a sign of advancement. At Bhavishya, advancing through the organization is unrelated to handling cash. There, the division of responsibility at the lower levels is less hierarchical, and frontline officers might have various tasks related to data collection. These divergent processes may not directly affect relational work between clients and MFI workers, but they do inform MFI employees' views of themselves, their power, and their positions.

Auditing extends to field-workers. Companies train officers to perform collection, and company leaders go to great lengths to ensure that the same information is delivered in each session in the same way. This combination of training and auditing ensures that the scripts for interacting with clients are followed in every interaction. When Chandran, the head of human resources at Bhavishya was hired to establish a strong culture, he advocated for more specific training related to interaction with clients. Predisbursal and postcollection audits, he believed, were insufficient, and company leadership had to ensure that employees were adhering to regulations *during* the loan transaction. Chandran explained his rationale:

> As a finance company, it is going to be very difficult for us to trust our employees. Because we are dealing with the most vulnerable section of the society [as clients]. [It's] easier for these guys to take some kind of money [a bribe from clients] for the loan. And people [clients] will give [the bribe] because they are used to giving bribes for different facilities they need to get.

Fueled by the conviction that employees were likely to take advantage of clients, Chandran forged an extensive, mandatory training program for new employees at Bhavishya. All the major MFIs I studied had similar programs.[17] In most cases, onboarding programs familiarized new employees with the company's mission and guiding principles and distinguished it from competitors. These programs presented company employment not as profit-seeking free agency but as an ethical service to the most vulnerable in society, even as employees help the company make a profit. Once deployed in the field, they are told, employees must manifest company loyalty through consistently fair, appropriate actions that develop reliable, enduring relationships with clients.

Once workers are fully trained, auditing practices ensure that the same information is delivered to each client reliably and comprehensively and that clients, who might be unaccustomed to formal financial transactions, know the expectations exactly. The combination of extensive training, followed by audits, produces a remarkable degree of uniformity and standardization in loaning operations, especially within companies.[18] Audits take place in person and so are expensive and time intensive for the company. Krishnan, head of MFI operations at Bhavishya, explained the process:

> We stand along with the customers in a meeting, and we sit and see what he [the employee] is explaining. If anything is not very clear, we pitch in, without interrupting [what he is already saying], as if we are giving some additional information [out of concern for the clients] that they should not miss anything. Then, when he [the employee] comes back to the branch, we will tell the employee, "This is what you missed out on. Why did you?"

Such audits ensure that the employees never experience disrespect by their superiors in front of customers but at the same time remind them never to forget that they are beholden to those in operations and human resources who decide what they should say and how they should say it. In other companies, I observed in-person audits were less exacting, but they remained an important means for controlling employee comportment.

Reinforced by intensive auditing, the training process not only regulates relational work but also produces a remarkable degree of uniformity and standardization. The affective labor of a more unregulated time remains necessary but now must be expressed as management directs. Both in my ethnographic observations and in my interviews, I was struck by the limited vocabulary and standardized tone of loan-related transactions, in contrast with training or other optional interactions. Especially in the larger, more established companies I studied, a high level of standardization was deemed necessary for fairness and good business practice. Krishnan explained a company leader's rationale for standardization:

> It should not be that each [loan officer] is telling something different in a different manner. The way he tells [customers] should be the same all over India. We started training people how to explain. Each and every point we say how it is to be done. [We explain] what is the [appropriate]

body language [to use with clients]. . . . Twenty-five people [MFI members] all should understand and focus on you [the loan officer], and they should be alert for that forty-five minutes. . . . So, they should understand what you are saying. [In] top management, we all sat together and discussed, point by point, how it has to be explained [to clients].

Krishnan's explanation reveals the extent to which top leadership extends control even to field-workers' body language. The communications must appear authentic, accurate, authoritative, and personally relevant for all women, from veteran clients to first-time borrowers. And through their conduct during meetings, employees must convey the company's ethos so that the clients will develop loyalty over time. Relationality thus develops in the space between a fixed script and its delivery. An employee who follows the script too closely or sounds overly rehearsed will not be successful. An employee who improvises too much, perhaps speaking from a personal understanding, may forge too individual a bond with the client and will not survive an in-person audit. Regulating interaction thus shapes and challenges relational work.

SCRIPTING AND ITS LIMITS

The practice of auditing illuminates a closely related relational practice, scripting, which is pervasive in the industry but far from uniform. MFI staff do differentiate among clients, creating both assurances of good faith and fear of reprisal. House visits are a vital, albeit routine, part of the loan approval process in most MFIS, and these, too, involve a performance. Interacting with potential clients, an employee establishes that taking a loan is a serious commitment by showcasing the MFI's attention to rules. As I observed during one round of loan verifications with Vinay, branch manager of Sowbagya, house visits are about more than verification. They also allow an authority figure even more commanding than the loan officer who collected the data to convey the rules of the loan to the client and her household. Yet house visits also reveal the limits of scripted interaction. However much companies standardize interactions through forms, specific questions, and calculated dialogues, staff members approving loans have significant discretion, which can promote relationships with clients.

On a temperate Bengaluru afternoon in June, branch manager Vinay of Sowbagya climbed to the second floor of a three-unit apartment building and asked the woman who answered the door for Sheila. Vinay was carrying out a house verification procedure. If all went well, he would allow Sheila to take out a loan for up to ten thousand rupees (about two hundred dollars at the time). I accompanied Vinay inside and found the apartment better appointed than most homes in the neighborhood. The floors were tiled, and I saw a television and settee, where Sheila's father was sleeping, surrounded by family members. Sheila emerged from a bedroom deeper in the home, wearing a stylish *salwar kameez,* a long, fitted tunic with pants.

Sheila carried herself with confidence. As she stood in front of her parents and siblings, Vinay asked—and she answered—a barrage of financial questions. She worked a customer service job, earning eight thousand rupees a month. She was also starting a small business, selling salwar materials and saris to neighborhood women. She had requested a combo loan, which can be used for both home and business. Vinay asked to see her stock. Sheila went back into the room from which she had emerged and brought out a large plastic bag full of fabric. As she started to open it, Vinay held up a hand, satisfied, and jotted something on the paperwork attached to his clipboard. He then asked to see receipts for the material, and without missing a beat, Sheila pulled them from the bag. He next asked her a few questions about her business plans.

By then, Sheila's father was awake, and to him Vinay posed a direct question: "Do you know your daughter is taking a loan?" Sheila's father nodded. In an authoritative, rapid-fire style, Vinay asked whether all family members understood the group guarantee that the loan required. Something about this interaction felt intrusive to me, yet the behavior of everyone in the room told me that it was expected, even routine.

> VINAY: If one person doesn't pay in your group of five, who has to pay?
> SHEILA: Four of them must pay.
> VINAY: And if two people in your group don't pay, who has to pay?
> SHEILA: Three people.
> VINAY: And if three people don't pay?
> SHEILA: Two people.
> VINAY: And if all four members of your group don't pay?
> SHEILA: I alone must pay.
> VINAY: So if four people [in Sheila's group] do not pay, then you [all] have to pay.

Vinay addressed her whole family in his last statement, making sure everyone understood. All family members agreed immediately, without hesitation or apparent unease. They appeared to be accustomed to the unsettling proposition that they would have to come up with money to settle the loans of up to four others if group members defaulted.

The call-and-response dialogue that Vinay initiated at Sheila's home unfolded in every home the branch manager visited. A visit to Mary's house was perhaps the most straightforward and typical. In her one-room, asbestos-sheet home near other members of the new group she had proposed joining, lunch was cooking on the stove, and two children played together. In a soft-spoken voice, Mary declared that this loan will be her first, ever. She answered Vinay's questions about terms and conditions, and he reminded her about the responsibilities that come with a loan, as he did with other clients. Because no other family members were at home, this exchange felt less intrusive than in situations involving a whole family. "Do you know what it means to take this group loan?" Vinay asked. Mary nodded. Vinay and Mary repeated the same arithmetic dialogue of obligation. Mary remained calm throughout the exchange. She knew what to say. She had her other documents ready. She produced her husband's original identity card, a wedding album, and a gas bill. She explained that she will use her loan for her children's school fees and for other household expenses. Her husband was a painter and she a domestic worker in two homes, she reported. Vinay quickly closed his sheaf of papers, thanked Mary, and moved on.

We moved on to Ishwari's house. When she opened the door, we saw a tiny, bare square room, devoid of any furnishings. When Vinay asked her where she lives, Ishwari insisted repeatedly that this was her "own house" (*sontha manne*). "But where do you stay?" asked Vinay. "Where is your gas bill? Where are your photos? Where are all those things kept?" Puzzled, Ishwari responded, "But do you need all those things to give a loan?" "Well," Vinay insisted, "we need to see where you are living." Finally, she relented, "Oh, I stay in Neelasandra [an adjacent neighborhood] because this house is too small." "Then," declared Vinay, "we need to see that house, not this one." While Ishwari might own the small room that was little more than a storage space, she clearly did not live there and probably never did. Her neighborhood was quite a distance from this place and certainly exceeded the five-hundred-meter limit that was to limit this residential group. We never got to the part of the conversation where Vinay asked whether she understood the expectations of a group loan. Unlike the others, Ishwari seemed not to know what to expect. If she had taken similar loans, the experience was not apparent. I assumed Ishwari's loan would be rejected and the group reformed. Nonetheless, we continued on to the home of the next group member.

Next, we met Nalini, who was napping when we knocked at her door. There was bedding on the floor that could easily sleep two people but little else in the windowless room, illuminated by a single light bulb. When Vinay began his questioning, Nalini explained that she cooked at her mother's house down the street but slept here. She said she was resting because she was unwell. She produced her husband's identity card, needed to guarantee the loan, but it was a color photocopy, not the original. "Look," Vinay stated stoically. "You can't provide this as documentation. We need the original to match with the photocopy you have already provided us." "Oh," she responded, "that's not here right now." Vinay moved on, asking about her livelihood and pointing out that her answers did not add up. "If you work in two houses and earn 1,000 rupees in each house, how is it that you have 3,000 rupees of income each month?" he asked. According to guidelines set by the Reserve Bank of India, 3,000 rupees is the minimum threshold to qualify for an MFI loan. "I make 1,500 in each house," Nalini backpedaled. "Then why did you say 1,000?" Vinay demanded. He was tough on her, more so than with the others. As in Ishwari's case, this exchange made clear that Nalini may only barely meet the official criteria for a loan. Here, too, Vinay avoided a confrontation about its terms.

Finally, we arrived at the most well-appointed home we had seen that day. Although located in the same slum just a short distance from the other women, Kalyani's home was a spacious second-floor apartment with a large balcony, an ample, well-furnished family room, and one or two bedrooms hidden from our view. Her mother and sister were present, and the walls were adorned with numerous photos of her children, including a soccer award for one of her sons. Kalyani explained that the house was rented. They had moved there because the house they owned in another neighborhood was too small. Kalyani was a loan veteran and the group leader. She reported a current loan from a competing MFI, slated to conclude within three months. She needed this loan for her son's business.

Vinay came to Kalyani with concerns, clear from the intensity of his paper flipping. In the corner of the room, barely noticeable to my eyes, he saw a carrom board, used for a game of finger pool associated with gambling. Vinay wanted to know more about her husband. Did he run a carrom board business? Was it a gambling business? Involvement with gambling is considered a negative occupation, and Sowbagya cannot loan to someone with a negative occupation. Kalyani replied that her husband was not involved in gambling and that he had given up the carrom board business and now worked only as a painter. Vinay seemed satisfied, asking no further proof of her husband's occupation, and we departed. Perhaps because she had already taken an MFI loan, Vinay avoided the dialogue about the group guarantee.

Contrary to my expectations, loans for all of these women were quickly approved, and the women commenced their three-day training the very next morning. Despite concerns about this group, especially with Ishwari's residence in Neelasandra, Vinay told me, no one would be rejected. Indeed, clients are rejected at the point of the house visit only in extenuating circumstances. The concern with Ishwari's residence was that she might be late for meetings and, perhaps, less likely to repay promptly without living near other group members. But Vinay was comfortable. He had interpreted Sowbagya's notion of flexible requirements compassionately toward these women.

In these accounts of house visits, we see how scripting and standardization appear to control the conditions for loan approval. In practice, however, MFI personnel only apply these rules in a limited way. Here, the branch officer, embodying a more authoritative interpretation of benevolent protectionism,[19] carried out his required tasks. At least some of these tasks—shuffling papers and consulting an official clipboard—appear performative. Sowbagya was more concerned with disbursing the loan and gleaning clues about clients who might pose issues than using the loan verification procedures to reject a client. This practice reflects the company's expectation that the women will work out repayment among themselves, with the help of their dedicated loan officer. Scripts around house visits help establish the seriousness of the loan commitment for clients, while also laying the foundation for the more intimate relational work of the loan officer who would work directly with clients for the duration of the loan. But the significant latitude Vinay offered clients shows that the priority for Sowbagya is loan disbursal, thus devolving responsibility for collection to the frontline workers and ensuring maximum financial extraction while still abiding by regulations.

The company's formal rules may be even more relaxed for longtime clients, encouraging decision makers like Vinay to overlook them in order to retain trusted customers. In one instance, we visited a customer taking a tenth loan. She was not in the house she had listed on her application but was found in another group member's house, where she appeared to be living. She then challenged Vinay about the importance of revealing her residence and dismissed his insistence that they needed her true address. When I later asked him about the importance of having addresses match, he told me that, in this case, the woman's address really did not matter because she was a longtime customer who now qualified for a large loan. Large loans from longtime customers are a significant source of profit for MFIS, as they are able to collect more interest while offering fewer services. The profit motive thus incentivizes MFIS to continue giving loans to these customers, whether or not it benefits the customer.

Microlevel interactions set up and sustain the relational work of microfinance. More established clients challenge standardized rules and procedures, relying on their economic stability and their relationships with MFI staff. Women who are newer to the company receive uneven socialization into the give-and-take of loan repayment. That give-and-take transforms women like Mary, Ishwari, and Nalini from uncreditworthy women, with no credit histories, into creditworthy women who will eventually learn the discipline and relationality associated with financial inclusion. The generosity of staff like Vinay, however, ultimately serves the interests of the company, facilitating gendered financial extraction.

Relational Regulations in Practice

Apart from optional trainings in entrepreneurship and financial literacy that many MFIS offer their clients, an orientation training is mandatory for all groups, including members who are previous customers, before funds are disbursed. Each organization has its own norms about the length of these trainings and the materials covered. Sowbagya's training was relatively extensive, with three two-hour sessions on consecutive days. The first session was usually the first time that group members met their loan officer, whom they would work with for the full year and perhaps for future loans as well. The training content was modified slightly from year to year, as interest rates and arrangements changed, but the basic terms and communication style remained the same.

The trainings I observed were largely didactic exercises in which the trainer delivered specified information in a highly standardized way. Yet the loan officer's softer, kinder approach, at least compared to the branch manager, suggested to clients that this relationship across lines of class and gender will involve mutual trust.

TRAINING INTERACTIONS

After the loan with Kalyani's group was approved, group members convened the next day for the first training with their new loan officer, Ajit. Mamatha, my research assistant, and I met Ajit at the branch office and returned to the neighborhood we had visited the day before. But rather than any of the houses we had visited, the training was held at Nalini's mother's house, where Nalini claimed she cooked but did not live. Compared to Vinay's direct and assertive style, Ajit was mild and self-effacing, retaining a calm, even stoic demeanor in his interactions with group members. Ajit had to verify that all group members were present and understood what he was charged with telling them. Emulating self-help groups, Ajit exuded a respectful manner, held the training in a group member's home, and seated everyone on the floor, creating a feeling of inclusion meant to invite participation.

On the first day, Ishwari was late, coming all the way from her house in Neelasandra, about a fifteen-minute bus ride away. She had told the group that she had to work in the morning but would arrive as soon as she could. We waited at Nalini's mother's house. Sparsely furnished, with only a cot sans mattress in the front room, the interior was airy and pleasant on a beautifully temperate day. I noticed a large fish floated in a tank far too small for its surprising girth. At last, Ishwari arrived, and we began. Ajit asked the group to repeat the Sowbagya pledge after him. He called out each line, and group members repeated slowly:

I will repay my loan on time.
I will educate my children.
I will go through good times and bad times with my group.
And for everything I do, God is my witness.

As Ajit called out each line in Kannada, the clients repeated it, whether or not they spoke Kannada well. These clients were Tamil speakers.

I was struck by the quasi-religious feeling of the pledge ritual. The group members were solemn as they formally agreed to take this loan together. This ritual, a streamlined, simplified adaptation of the Grameen Bank's "sixteen decisions" pledge, also invokes the feeling of a community-based cooperative or a self-help group.[20] But unlike these institutions, the MFI is a profit-seeking financial corporation establishing commitment, the interdependence that will eventually provide credit histories for the women gathered and facilitate the efficient extraction of financial value. Participating in this quasi-religious ritual promotes a group identity in relation to the loan officer and a sense of interconnection and mutual trust between members. These feelings would need to be leveraged in the year ahead if any member has trouble repaying her loan.

After this opening, the training began. The first day was all about the company—its rules (i.e., what they are, why they are in place, the importance of respecting them), its services (i.e., other loans and nonfinancial services available), and the terms and fees associated with the loan, including life insurance, administrative fees, and the interest rate. The first session was also an opportunity for the loan officer to learn about his clients. The women offered information about themselves and the loan they were taking. At Ajit's request, each woman explained her reasons for taking the loan. These opening exchanges established the ground for the relational work that must continue over the entire year and created a pool of information about the group that only group members and Ajit would know.

Departing slightly from the loan's stated purpose on her application, Kalyani reported plans to use it for household expenses. She never mentioned her son's business. Ajit asked again about her husband's occupation, gently inquiring about the carrom board business. "Only if it's seasonal, it's okay," he explained, softening Vinay's earlier stance that any negative occupation would disqualify her from the loan. "No," Kalyani insisted. "There is no carrom business. He only does painting now. And I do housemaid work, so those together are the main income." "You are sure?" Ajit pressed gently. "Because there could be a problem later. The loan could be cancelled." Kalyani maintained her position. Sheila also departed slightly from the stated purpose for her loan. Rather than using it to expand her home-based clothing business, she said, she would be releasing jewels from a pledge to a local pawn dealer. "Will ten thousand rupees be enough for that?" Ajit asked. Sheila did not answer. Both Ajit and Sheila knew that releasing even the most modest jewels from a pledge would require thirty or forty thousand rupees. Mary was consistent about plans to pay school fees.

Here, clients and their loan officer established a conduit of personal financial information, framed by the standardized MFI procedures that would cushion and advance their exchanges over the course of the year ahead. This basis for trust and intimacy, which would be leveraged in the future, set relational work into motion. This first day of training, then, offered Ajit an initial chance to assess the ease or difficulty of servicing this group's loan. He knew that meeting his own targets for the month depended on it. All personal details were crucially important. Ajit concluded the meeting by returning to the group guarantee and its meaning. The back-and-forth was identical to Vinay's dialogue, the arithmetic scenario laid out carefully, explaining that if four members abandon the loan, whoever is left is responsible. Each member had to understand that if the rest of the group defaults, she alone must repay the loan.

The next two days of training began similarly. On day two, Ishwari was late again. Ajit then explained that a penalty would be assessed for tardiness going forward, and that punctuality was critical. He asked Kalyani to sit at the head of the group and asked each member to sit in a line to her left, in the order they would assume at every meeting henceforth. No longer a circle signifying equality and unity, the loan was now experienced as a line, with the group leader at the head and every member in her designated place. As the training commenced, the women recited the pledge, and Ajit began reviewing concepts from the day before, starting with the company rules.

Ishwari could not remember the previous day's information. Kalyani prompted her, but Ajit implored Kalyani to let Ishwari answer "because someone from the head office could come and ask you," he warned. "If you learn quickly, we will finish this in three days, but if it takes longer, we will sit for five or six days, as long as it takes." Step by step, each piece of information from the day before was reviewed, with members asked to demonstrate their full understanding. Ishwari struggled with recall and recitation throughout. The process was painstaking, with members apparently learning slowly, but Ajit was patient, even in the most trying moments.

After reviewing all the terms of the loan, Ajit returned once again to the group guarantee. "This is like a job," he stated. "It is a big responsibility. You should have a fear (*bhayam*) about not being able to pay, and you should regard it as something important that you must take care of." Ajit reiterated this solemn responsibility in several different ways. Next, he covered the nuts and bolts of meeting procedures, including the precise conduct for meetings and what would happen each time. He concluded the session with reminders emphasizing the women's responsibilities to one another, adding that compliance could eventually reap much larger individual rewards. "If you follow all these rules," he offered, "you can graduate to a larger loan and, someday, to an individual loan or business loan for a larger amount."

Day three was delayed by a day because of scheduling constraints, but two days later, the group gathered at Sheila's house. She was the only one with a DVD player, which Ajit needed to play his training video. He had arranged this plan in advance with all the members, and when Ajit, Mamatha, and I arrived, everyone was lined up in the correct order. This time, Mary was late. While we waited, I noticed that Ishwari and Nalini had made notes on their hands and were looking at them as they tried to remember the company rules. Ishwari burst out, "You know, this is really hard for me! I never studied. No one ever taught me how to do all this. I cannot hold all these things in my mind. I don't know! I do not know what [any of this] is!" (see figure 3.2). Minutes later, Mary arrived; no penalty was imposed, and the meeting began.

The video, dubbed in Tamil, lasted thirty minutes and narrated three cautionary tales in the style of an Indian soap opera set in working-class homes like those of many MFI clients. In the first, a woman borrows from multiple sources at a moment when all seems to be going well for her. Unexpected circumstances, however, cause her sources of income to dry up, and she defaults on her loans, losing everything. The second episode narrates the dangers of ghost lending, in which a woman, at the behest of a senior relative who promises to repay her, takes a loan for him in her name. When the relative disappears after a few months, she defaults and loses the little she has. The last tale explains the newly established credit bureau and urges clients to be truthful about the number of loans they have when filling out paperwork. If the credit bureau finds that a borrower has more than two loans, a new application will be declined. Here, the MFI made clear that clients' loaning practices are rule bound and will be surveilled by a computer system they cannot influence.

After the film, Ajit asked group members to sit in a circle and prompted them to explain its lessons and identify what they had learned. Each member spoke about one episode, but Kalyani's comprehension of the last episode was inaccurate. "Well, that episode was actually about the credit bureau," Ajit gently corrected her, without actually saying that she was wrong. After the discussion, group members reviewed the lessons of the last two days, with Ajit's prompting, and then turned to material for the last session, detailing what Sowbagya offered them. Services complimentary for members, they

FIGURE 3.2. Customers experience stress while reviewing materials before training.

learn, include job fairs, health camps, training opportunities, and sports camps for kids. Ishwari interrupted with a non sequitor, meant to signal her understanding. "Don't worry, sir. We will repay promptly on time every month," she gushed. The comment was jarring but went uncorrected. With the lesson completed, Ajit reminded the women to bring proof of ID, along with the amount of insurance and processing fees to the branch the next day. They would then receive their loan. The group dispersed, with all members eager to get to work by 10 a.m.

These three days of training comprised a gendered, time-consuming activity at the core of clients' livelihoods. During trainings, group members internalized their financial responsibility and pledged to one another that they would repay their loans on time. Through time-consuming credit-work, they were both disciplined and introduced to the benefits of group membership with the MFI. While the branch manager verified their information, treating them with authoritative professionalism, he also emphasized that he was willing to overlook issues of qualification (e.g., Ishwari's residence, Kalyani's husband's possible negative occupation, and Nalini's inadequate documentation). This relational work then opened the door for a long-term mutual understanding between clients and Ajit, who would learn more detailed information about his clients while servicing the loan.

The discrepancies between a loan officer's knowledge of his clients and the official information collected in the company's records constitute the first building block of the relational work that will continue for at least a whole year. Ajit let his clients know what they could expect from him if they cooperate and trust him. He signaled his understanding of group members' lives and showed his commitment to their growth. He was never patronizing, never impatient with their slow uptake of detailed information, never openly skeptical of their fitness for the loan or its benefits. Through kindness and forbearance, rooted in benevolent protectionism, Ajit carried out the emotional labor of a loan officer, in an effort to build relationships that will sustain over time.

Group training constitutes a site at which financialized subjectivities are shaped and standardized. Through specific social and economic exchanges across lines of class, gender, and institutional position, a loan officer like Ajit must do two things at once: he must represent the lender, and he must be himself, with his own linguistic background, class location, and gender identity. The borrowers at once must be both social and economic actors, though in a transactional relationship with the lender they remained women with particular struggles and vulnerabilities who nonetheless symbolized all women in poverty, a group that the MFI could appear to serve. Ajit was required to manage their struggles to produce creditworthiness for them, efficient financial extraction for his company, and career advancement for himself. Ajit told them that they must consider repayment a job. But he knew this could not be a job they could complete on their own. From the very first moment, Ajit collected information about them that could allow him to help them resolve an unpaid debt in the future.

LEVERAGING RELATIONAL WORK

Nonetheless, some clients are unable to repay on time. How, then, do lenders' representatives leverage their intimate knowledge of their clients and their own social locations to create creditworthiness? As they strategize about clients' options in default, loan officers consider both the information they have acquired and their own jobs. Sundari offered me an example of a typical extra-procedural exchange. At age twenty-seven, she managed over 650 Sowbagya clients who had repaid almost perfectly. At her branch office, her name and photo appeared multiple times under the celebratory label "top performer of the month." As a woman who, for various reasons, had remained a loan officer (see chapter 2), she had established warm, friendly relationships with most of her clients, many of whom she had known for several years.

Clients and loan officers both can benefit from long-term relationships between them. For example, at one meeting, Sundari avoided imposing the ten-rupee late fine on members who arrived late. During that session, Sundari announced an opportunity for a computer class, as she had with all centers that day, but with the long-term clients at this meeting, she followed with a fifteen-minute discussion of who could qualify, what would be offered, and when and how to enroll. As Sundari attested to me, such longstanding relationships allow her to encourage collaboration in case of default. In one case she narrated, a customer owed 350 rupees and had not been attending meetings. "I know all the customers in that group because I had been going there from the beginning [of that group]. I told the members that I would lose my promotion because of this. All the group members discussed it and mobilized 350 rupees by paying 50 rupees per person. They told me to repay the money if she repays." Here, Sundari could leverage trust to call upon her clients' sense of obligation to her. Having invoked mutual dependence, she maintained her impeccable record, and the loan did not default.

In other instances, however, calling upon clients' loyalty to the loan officer is inadequate because the clients simply cannot pay on behalf of their absconding group member. Nadia, a twenty-two-year-old loan officer, had been employed by Sowbagya for three years and was frank about her experiences with nonpayment. She told me of multiple instances, some that she had experienced directly, others she knew only from colleagues. She expressed great regret at these circumstances, which were sometimes quite extreme. In one incident, a group in a poor neighborhood she serviced had trouble repaying because one member had abandoned the neighborhood, leaving her house locked and her possessions behind. Week after week, group members had to pony up money for her. Payments became excessively burdensome, as Nadia elaborated,

> They were very sad at that time and used to ask me, "Please do something, madam." I thought it should not go out [and be reported officially]. It should be cleared here itself [between myself and the clients]. It's simply not good telling others of their condition. And if the manager gets to know this, then we all [staff members, including managers] would have to go to their house. Their neighbors will think badly of them. We didn't want to hurt the families.
>
> So, I talked to those people and told them to pay the amount. I explained that if you pay, you can take more loans next time, so please try to pay the amount. They thought that if they pay the amount, we won't give them a loan again (because it was already so late). But I entrusted it to them and made them pay the amount. It was very difficult to convince them. They were paying the amount very late every month. I used to tell [my manager] that it was the absconding amount [that was late], but I didn't report a problem [to my branch]. Every month, I used to collect.
>
> At last the group members couldn't pay the amount at all. I told them to go to the home [of the absconding client], break the lock, and bring whatever they have left in their house. The other members did what I suggested. They sold the water purifier and all the other things and paid the money. . . . At last, when I gave them a new loan, and they were happy. Even now they come and tell me, "We trusted you and gave the money, and you respected our trust and gave us new loan. We are happy [grateful] for that."

Actively engaged in the production of a default-free record for herself and the company, Nadia expressed deep sympathy for her clients and wished to help them. But her own employment record was on the line with every vulnerable group she serviced. Her emotional and material entanglements with clients, together with her dependence on them for her own career advancement, thus remained at the heart of her success as an MFI employee. Here, however, her actions also made the non-absconding group members creditworthy. Protected by their loan officers' desire not to report a default, clients gain creditworthiness in the official records of the national financial system, despite their vulnerability. Their status then reinforces their subordinate positions and allows extractive financial processes to continue, even when clients can ill afford the terms and interest rates on offer.

Nadia's ongoing relationship with this group, which developed over months or years, facilitated clients' continued access to loans, making them happy. Expressing concern with their honor in the neighborhood, she strategically articulated benevolent protectionism. She wished both to help these vulnerable clients and be viewed as a resource, so she sought their trust for the future. As her actions exceeded typical expectations, clients viewed her as generously serving their community. Yet her solution to this problem—encouraging burglary—defied the norms of loan recovery for an absconding client. Nadia's emotional labor supported an economic exchange in which, beyond her wage, her reward was durable client relationships, even though those relationships could render her clients vulnerable in the future.

Analyzing these exchanges as relational work helps us understand why, at least on the surface, small loans appear to make everyone happy. Clients are grateful for the money, and loan officers are pleased with the work, as are office staff and other backend MFI workers. Ultimately, MFI leaders maintain their status as benevolent visionaries working for the upliftment of the country as a whole, even as the profit-oriented logic of corporate masculinity is strengthened and gendered financial value is efficiently extracted. Nadia's narrative, however, reveals the systematic concealment of vulnerability required to make working-class women creditworthy. These dynamics become visible only when viewed in the context of an industry, its institutions, and the diverse neighborhoods Nadia and others like her serve.

The gendered relationships between frontline workers and clients are always embedded in the larger structure of an MFI invested in building client creditworthiness, which then helps to advance the company's reputation and secure employees' good records and continued employment. These relationships must be navigated in a way that allows the company to conform to regulatory criteria that minimize fraud. Yet when MFIS routinely bend procedures to artificially depress default rates, the relevant actors construct this action not as fraud but rather as generosity and empathy toward clients who need worthy credit records. Relational work thus manages the contradictory processes through which MFIS transform vulnerable working-class clients into creditworthy women while continuing to facilitate gendered extraction.

Conclusion

In a loan transaction, institutions and individuals converge with contradictory imperatives rooted in MFIS' profit orientation on one hand and the vulnerable social locations of borrowers and frontline MFI workers on the other. Establishing relationships that are at once social and economic, clients and loan officers must engage in relational work to accomplish the lengthy, labor-intensive process of turning a working-class client from an urban slum or rural village into a creditworthy woman. Since the 2010 crisis, Indian MFIS have developed a range of policies and processes designed to streamline interactions, maximize efficiency, minimize fraud, and protect their companies' reputations. These changes became ever-more important with the increased regulations wrought by the crisis, and the narrowed range of exchanges allowed between clients and loan officers ensured mutually understood boundaries for these actors. Regulations, I have shown, certainly have reduced the chance of abuse and narrowed the scope of potential spontaneous relationships (such as romantic love). As I show in this chapter, the new regulations have set the boundaries for relational work by imposing the procedures of prohibitions, audits, and scripts. These procedures, however, still offer leeway for social and affective exchanges between clients and frontline staff. Loan officers and frontline staff acquire detailed information about clients' personal circumstances and thinking, mining financial data from sources that have previously remained outside the gambit of the financial system. Staff can then leverage these data when needed.

The accomplishment of relational work facilitates effective financial extraction from poor communities, while also preserving the image of MFIS as socially oriented organizations that empower and support vulnerable women as a group. The relational work of microfinance between MFIS and clients thus facilitates effective financial *and* symbolic extraction, as companies continue to be able to extract stories of women's success and upward mobility, however anecdotal, to legitimate their organizations. The regulatory changes since 2010 have only served to conceal the dynamic of extraction that links MFIS to client communities. Newly creditworthy women come to understand the process of taking loans and the gendered labor of repaying them and in the process become creditworthy in the eyes of the financial system. But they remain just as likely to default. Nonetheless, MFIS must continue making women creditworthy, in service of the state-led project of financial inclusion. Despite these significant issues with MFIS, this level of relationality and, consequently, compliance around credit and debt has not been accomplished by any state-led entity. Loan officers and the MFIS that employ them thus appear to be generous, always focusing on helping clients gain another chance for another loan.

As the bedrock of financial inclusion, creditworthiness requires not only scripts and procedures but also intimate knowledge of clients' financial lives and the willingness to act on that knowledge when, inevitably, default becomes likely for one or more members of a group. It further requires that particular loan officers' actions, such as accepting a bribe, be constructed as fraudulent, while other actions, such as avoiding a report of default or resolving it through burglary or favors, be constructed as generous. By enacting such policies and procedures, MFIS create what appears to be a virtuous circle of repayment when in fact most borrowers will experience little change in the conditions of marginality they experience.

Shankari, an accomplished carpenter, met Mamatha and me at the bus stop with her husband Kumaran and their six-year-old grandson, Venkatesh. Together, they led us through the narrow lanes of their dense urban slum neighborhood to their home. Along the way, it seemed as if everyone knew her. Around every turn, men and women alike gave her a nod or a smile or a greeting. She frequently introduced us. I had walked along lanes like this with many women like Shankari, but she seemed especially popular. Her neighborhood was close to the center of Bengaluru and was humming with activity on this warm day in May. We passed a pristine white mosque that stood in contrast with the humble residences, shop fronts, and narrow lanes that flanked it. This was an older neighborhood comprised primarily of Urdu- and Tamil-speaking migrant communities. We heard little of Karnataka's local language, Kannada, here, even though many of these residents have lived in Bengaluru for a generation or more. Though Shankari is herself a Tamilian, she is fluent in Kannada, and she switched between Kannada and Tamil to speak with Mamatha and me.

When we arrived at her modest two-room home, Shankari pointed out a photograph of herself hanging on the wall above the fish tank. In it, she is receiving an award from the Minister of Women's Rights for the state of Karnataka, for her work organizing women in her area. In recent years, Shankari explains, she formed and led twelve microfinance groups, each consisting of fifteen to thirty women, and she had helped form dozens of other groups in the neighborhood. She named five major MFIs and said she had organized groups for all of them. She saw herself as an advocate for her neighborhood. Her aim was to connect her neighborhood with loans and other private and government programs that could help them. In her narrative, the help provided by government schemes overlapped with the help of financial companies, and she was an important broker of all of these. "People with good family conditions are getting free laptops and schooling," she lamented, "but there is nothing to help the poor family. There are a lot of programs by the government for bright students from poor families, but we are not aware of them . . . So, I run around, travel, and learn about such things to help them."

She estimated that she spent about ten days of every month in this social work, which included microfinance group organizing. Shankari described the difficult work of organizing women:

> [The companies] find out who formed the groups and then they will select the leader . . . Leaders don't get any money and have more responsibility. Leaders have to visit every home . . . Sometimes, you need to go to their [members'] doorsteps and shout at them, "Why haven't you repaid your loan yet?" It's very difficult to be a leader, madam. If we are not strict, members in the group might take advantage of us, and ask us to fill in the money, saying they will repay later. Then, I [must] make the payment myself and then later collect the money from the members because it is not correct for us to make them [the loan officers] wait here, right?

According to Shankari, a group leader's helping work requires her to take certain financial and social risks. She, in short, insures the loan, cushioning the group she organizes from nonpayment as much as she can. Her narrative about the responsibility she absorbs to make sure that repayment is made on time flies in the face of the arithmetic dialogue that is baked into loan verification procedures, explored in chapter 3. For Shankari, all members in a group do not have equal liability to repay on time; she takes on more responsibility than others. But this responsibility also arises from her relative privilege, since both she and her husband earn stable incomes. This means that relationships between women in a micro-lending group, far from being democratic and equitable, are instead structured by inequalities of class and status.

Like the relational work of loan officers, who must carefully establish relationships with women that are at once rule bound and flexible, the women who constitute lending groups must establish relationships among one another that meet exacting MFI requirements, while allowing for divergent needs and divergent benefits among the group members. This understudied relational work within loan groups is, ultimately, the most important form of work required for financial inclusion. As with the relational work required for creditworthiness, the relational work among women in lending groups ends up benefiting MFI workers and higher-ups more than it does the borrowers themselves. This chapter examines two dimensions of relational work between women: the integrated financial management role that women borrowers take on when they become immersed in a gendered financial ecosystem composed of many kinds of debt, and the social work of powerful volunteers like Shankari, who organize women's labor around financial management within neighborhoods and communities.

Zelizer's notion of relational work[1] gets at the simultaneously social and economic character of the work that women undertake when they participate in unsecuritized group loans, but other feminist concepts help highlight the unpaid labor that women perform to meet MFI requirements. Caroline Moser famously coined the notion of women's *triple burden*, a term that recognizes that in most parts of the world, women have productive, reproductive, *and* what Moser calls "community management" roles.[2] Most women have long been expected to occupy productive roles; waged work can include agricultural work, domestic work for pay, or microenterprise. In addition, women's reproductive labor includes the bearing of children, primary responsibility for childcare, as well as all household work, including cooking, cleaning, and provisioning. Women's community managing roles includes the unmonetized work of keeping households connected to one another through social relationships, reciprocal borrowing and gifts, and work with others in the community for festivals, rallies, public health programming, or the like.

In the context of widespread group loans, reproductive, productive, and community management roles are merged into a unified *financial management* role. We might guess that women taking on the role of financial manager for the family would shore up her bargaining power at home and in her community, and indeed, there is some evidence for this in the context of self-help groups.[3] But because financial management integrates roles that were already devalued, without providing clear pathways toward new economic opportunities, the work of financial management supports the continued primacy of unpaid reproductive labor for women and the weak position women occupy in the labor market. This devalued financial management work thus makes women living in poor and working-class neighborhoods a vector through which interest can be extracted for MFI profit. Because financial management has been so thoroughly domesticated, I found that the women borrowers I studied often did not even view tasks related to their all-encompassing financial management role as work.[4] This work was completely integrated into their roles as mothers.

Women's financial management role includes Zelizerian relational work but extends beyond it to include decision-making and the management of relationships of power between and among neighbors, decisions about what kinds of debt to take on and for what purpose, as well as the consistent work of showing up for meetings and trainings, building relationships with MFI, NGO, or self-help group personnel, and coming up with creative strategies to repay in slim times. Women borrowers may also manage their own earnings and sometimes the earnings of their husbands, in situations where earnings are pooled. As I will explore further in the next chapter, MFIS promote the idea that husbands and wives should plan their finances together and that women should be the primary shapers of the family's financial habits. When the borrowers I studied took up financial management for their families, integrating productive, reproductive, and community managing work that was already devalued, responsibility for loans served to reinforce, rather than disrupt, their status as housewives with access only to the lowest end of the labor market.

While most women borrowers I studied had taken up a financial management role in their families, only some of these women were also powerful volunteers who played the role of organizing women and connecting them to MFIS, government programs, and other opportunities. Shankari not only managed her own loans and her income from her carpentry work, she also ensured that other borrowers would promptly repay, checking up on members prior to the weekly meetings, educating them on how to present themselves to MFIS when they come to collect information, and ensuring that members physically show up at meetings. Shankari and others I interviewed who did similar work named this work as helping or social work. Shankari did not distinguish between government and private sources for her services but instead sought out help for her community anywhere it might be on offer. From the perspective of the state, Shankari was doing invaluable work, as evidenced by the public recognition she received from the state government. Her work validated the state's programs and policies around women in development and ensured that such programs ran smoothly. When Shankari was successful, she also produced proof for the state that women-oriented lending programs furthered the goals of development. She offered the same kind of validation and success for commercial MFIS, who stood to profit far more than Shankari or any of her peers ever would. This unpaid volunteer labor, closely linked to the everyday gendered labor required for financial management, is a prerequisite for MFIS to function, yet it never figures into official accounts of how MFIS impact the communities that they lend to.[5]

Gendered Social Work in a Bengaluru Slum: Jayanthi and Satish

At the end of a busy day of fieldwork in a central Bengaluru slum, my last interviewee introduced me to her group leader, Jayanthi, who had just returned home. As she greeted Mamatha and me and led us into her second-story home, Jayanthi's tall and well-dressed figure struck me as imposing and influential. I found her home's tiled interior, large television, and desktop computer to be a striking contrast from the sparsely furnished single-room concrete and aluminum-roofed homes I had spent the morning in. Jayanthi's husband Satish was seated at the computer and immediately rose to welcome us when he heard I was a visitor from the US. Sharply dressed and well groomed, Satish plied Mamatha and me with cool drinks and began an impassioned speech about growing inequality in the city and the hardship his community had endured for the past twenty-five years.

"They have been calling Bengaluru the Garden City," Satish explained with a note of bitterness. "They say this is like a Singapore. Is this a Singapore? Where is the garden here? We don't even have basic facilities and we are just 4.5 kilometers from Vidhana Soudha [the grand state capitol building]. Just 4.5 kilometers." He was angry with both the Congress Party and the opposition because they cheated his community. "The politicians all come during elections, put a big *namaskaram* [a sign of respect], and then disappear. We have only ever gotten anything done by going and fighting with the Corporation [the city municipality] for a long time." He told us that his social work, which he carried out under the aegis of a trust that he and a few peers in the neighborhood had established, had been advocating for their community with some success. Due to the pressure of his group, pavement had been laid down in this area recently. Otherwise, Satish noted, I would not have even been able to arrive at his house because even a little rain used to turn everything to mud. And even now, he explained, I would not be able to come in the rainy season, when the narrow alleyways flood. Satish continued to explain the activities he conducted for his community through the trust. He and Jayanthi distributed books and school uniforms for the needy kids in their neighborhood and gave saris to older women without families during festivals. His brother, still seated at the computer, began pulling up photos from various events the trust has held and invited me to look at them.

When Mamatha and I interviewed Jayanthi a few days later, we came to understand Satish's narrative in a new light. Satish had worked in a number of jobs over the years, including painting, construction, and tile work, all typical jobs for men living in the neighborhood. But in a work-related accident eight years ago, most of Satish's hand was sliced off, left hanging from his wrist. After an expensive surgery that bankrupted them, the hand had been reattached but was immobile. A few years later, Jayanthi saved enough through her home-based sari business to pay for a subsequent surgery that recovered some mobility in Satish's hand, but his fingers curve in way that made it impossible to continue working as a tile mason. Satish refashioned himself into an unpaid community advocate, and Jayanthi stepped up to provide for her family. For years, she operated a profitable sari business and worked as a domestic. She quit working as a domestic for health reasons and left her sari business when her two older daughters got old enough to work. At the time of our interview, two of her daughters were employed at the global fast-food chain KFC and brought in small, vital incomes. Jayanthi pinned all her hopes on her third daughter, currently in ninth grade, Krithi. She told us that Krithi was smart at school, unlike her older sisters, and spoke good English. Krithi told her parents that that if they could just keep her in school, she would provide for all of them in the future.

Despite these economic realities, which emerged over the course of our interview, Jayanthi had introduced herself as a housewife who also does social work, using the English phrase as Shankari and other leaders I spoke to used it. She asserted that her husband, a tile mason, was the earner. This narrative emerged in interviews with many clients I spoke to, who considered themselves housewives and their husbands to be breadwinners, even when the story they told about their family's livelihoods did not match that set of constructions. Jayanthi had an understanding of social work that was distinct from her husband's as well. Where Satish's account of his social work was explicitly political, Jayanthi's emphasized education for children and organizing women for finance. She and her daughters offered free academic tuition for students in the neighborhood up to tenth grade, offering many poor students a chance to stay in school. Such tuitions were expected in most schools but were too expensive for poor families, so she offered them for free. Jayanthi also managed about thirty self-help groups in her area. With different price points for entry, the range of options made them available for women with different capacities for savings. She also organized and participated in various chit funds, rotating savings and credit associations, and of course microfinance groups. She convened these groups, set up the rules and norms, made sure everyone paid, and stepped in to solve problems when they arose. When the 2010 crisis hit, for example, Sowbagya and other MFIs pulled out of her neighborhood. Jayanthi sought out a Kanchan employee and brought the organization in to serve the unmet demands in her community, including her own demands.

As she explained each of the financial products she organized, she shared her detailed, mathematically precise knowledge of how the interest works in the rotating credit groups, who can afford to pay how much, and what members use the funds for:

> One group will save ten rupees. Another might save twenty-five rupees, depending on their capacity. Then they offer loans to members with five percent interest. The collected amount, along with the interest, is divided up between the members in the April/May/June time frame so that they can all pay school fees. If one member has put in one hundred rupees, they would get back five hundred rupees in a year. Suppose ten members each put in three hundred rupees. The total amount will be three thousand rupees. [But] once the amount is rotated as loans to members, after a year, each member would get back seven hundred or eight hundred rupees. That is how the interest amount helps in paying the [school] admission fees of children.

These savings and credit associations also contained the classic group guarantee mechanism of Grameen Bank, which MFIs have emulated. Just as in MFI-sanctioned groups, Jayanthi explained that in the community-based rotating savings groups, if someone has an emergency and cannot pay, the other nineteen members chip in to compensate and keep it going. She was trained to do this work by NGO field-workers who came to the neighborhood fifteen years ago. Their field staff stopped coming, but the women of the neighborhood, under Jayanthi's leadership, continued the arrangements that were set up. Jayanthi's account sheds light on the financial products that preceded commercial microfinance and continued to flourish alongside it. In this environment, MFIs simply provided these communities with another option for finance and the opportunity for slightly larger loans in the future. This was possible because MFIs leveraged familiar financial arrangements among women put in place by government and NGO programs that came before them.

The proliferation of diverse financial products requires slightly better off, entrepreneurially inclined women to be strategic organizers within their poor and working-class communities, particularly with regard to finance. For Jayanthi, financing from MFIS provides just one more avenue through which she can use her skills to help her community and shore up her own unstable financial condition. Like Shankari and other leaders I spoke to, she would hear about a particular MFI and learn through her networks how she could contact a loan officer. She would find that loan officer, learn the requirements, and then organize women around her to be able to meet those requirements. Due to medical expenses and her husband's exclusion from labor markets, Jayanthi had turned social work and loans into a livelihood for herself and her family, using her extensive knowledge of diverse financial products and the families in her own neighborhood to get by until a secure future came their way. In parallel, her husband had, through local politics and his own form of social work, reclaimed the masculinity he lost through his occupational injury. He, too, calls himself a social worker, but in contrast with Jayanthi's activities in tutoring and financial management for the family, Satish's agency lies in the masculine realm of politics, lobbying the state for community resources.

Among Group Members: The Politics of Complying with Social Work

In another slum neighborhood in Bengaluru, tucked away behind one of the city's most posh commercial districts, I interviewed four women in the same large group. Unusually, in this set of interviews, each client spoke about the group leader and about one another. Their individual narratives highlight both how the leader means different things to different people, depending on their financial situation. Because better-off women tend to exert greater power in lending groups, the transactions involved in microfinance can reinscribe class differences between women while reinforcing gendered reproductive work at the bottom of the labor market. In all these narratives, we see economic and social ties reinforcing one another as women's social relationships as neighbors are extended into economic relationships and incorporated into their feminized roles as financial managers for their families. This relational work places disproportionate burdens on those who are more marginalized to begin with.

SHANTHI: "HELPER" TO ALL

When we asked Kanchan's trainer to introduce us to someone in this neighborhood, we were first directed to Shanthi. While her home was located in a dense area of the slum, inside her doorway it was a different world, clean and new. Gleaming tiles in the entrance flanked shiny granite steps, opening into a modest foyer appointed with chairs and a cot. The walls, painted in maroon and dusty rose, were purposely subtle, in contrast with the bright colors preferred in most homes in the area. The traditional *gruhapravesham* ceremony, which celebrates the building of a new house, had just been completed, and partly dried marigold garlands hung from the inside of the door's frame.

Shanthi welcomed us in and introduced us to her adult son, who lounged on a nearby cot and watched the interview, interjecting when possible. From where I sat, I glimpsed a modern kitchen and a television just inside. Shanthi immediately asserted that she had no business at all, though she understood that you always must say you have a business to be able to get loans.

"My mother takes care of everything at home. That is a lot in itself," her son interjected. We voiced our agreement.

Shanthi explained that instead of having a business, she helped people in her neighborhood. She didn't need a 10,000-rupee loan herself, but the other women in her neighborhood were really needy. So, she helped them however she could. She had taken several loans from both MFIs and mainstream banks, including a Bank of India loan for over 700,000 rupees, repaid over eighteen years. That loan was used to pay for the home we were then sitting in, which cost much more money than that. Later in our interview, in direct contradiction to her previous statement, Shanthi explained that she had a phone business, charging people for local phone calls in her neighborhood. She told us she earned 150 to 200 rupees per day from that.

Upon exiting Shanthi's home, Mamatha wondered aloud whether Shanthi had told us the truth about everything. Or perhaps she told us the truth, but in a coded way. There were many inconsistencies and, seemingly, a huge emphasis on helping others. Was she taking loans and lending the money to other women at a profit? Mamatha wondered.

Over the next few days, we independently interviewed three other women in her group. While there was no way to either verify Shanthi's account or contradict it, her peers' accounts of her presence in the community suggested that at the very least, she was a powerful individual in the community and played a time-consuming, demanding leadership role. Shanthi's class position seemed to have protected her from the necessity of working in the low end of the labor market, and she may have had deep connections to local political parties. Whatever the case, Shanthi capitalized upon her residence in this prime neighborhood location near the center of town through an expansion of her role in her community, whereby she brokered financial services for those who were unable to acquire such services themselves. In so doing, Shanti cultivated webs of obligation and interconnectedness that she could then trade in for favors or support when she needed it.

VIJAYA: FORESTALLING DISTRESS

Vijaya, age forty-two, had just taken out her third loan at the time of our meeting. Previously, she had taken out two loans with Sowbagya. Her new loan was with Kanchan. Located along a by-lane off the main road, her concrete house was larger than some of the others we had seen—two separate rooms with some furnishings, rather than just one. But it was simple, a far cry from the style of her group leader, Shanthi. At the beginning of her interview, Vijaya identified herself as a housewife who managed her financial obligations with her husband's income as a baggage handler for Indian Airlines. Quickly, it became apparent that her husband did not contribute to household expenses due to his alcoholism. On the day of our interview, her husband ended up in the hospital with a stomachache and vomiting. She did not even express alarm about his condition to Mamatha or me.

Vijaya and her husband owned two other homes and collected rent from both of them, netting just under five thousand rupees per month (about eighty dollars). She had used her first MFI loan of ten thousand rupees to release gold ornaments that had been previously pledged to a local moneylender in order to pay for a much-needed hysterectomy. When asked about the purpose of her current loan with Kanchan, Vijaya hesitated. "I feel I should do something and have a business," she said, "and stand on my own feet." Sensing her reluctance, we requested further detail. She readily admitted that she needed the money for a routine medical checkup for herself and to pay the college fees for her twenty-nine-year-old son, who was still working on his Bachelor of Commerce degree. She had also purchased some materials for a small tailoring business, including sari falls, buttons, and thread. But she could not specify how much time she spent on the business or how much she earned from it. She said that she wanted to start a door-to-door sari business but that her husband did not like her going outside the house for work. She mentioned that she was quite worried about the expenses that would be involved in marrying off her twenty-six-year-old daughter, who was also living at home, not earning a wage.

Vijaya's narrative on its own provides a snapshot of a working-class woman's life, but her account of the financial interactions in her neighborhood suggest that these social relationships pervaded her livelihood and demanded constant labor and maintenance. We learned that Shanthi, apart from being the leader of the Kanchan group loan, also led another government-sponsored self-help group. As Vijaya puts it, Shanthi "guides us and motivates us to do some business." There was a woman in the neighborhood who ran an *idli*[6] stand, and another who had a good tailoring business. But most of the women in the groups did not have businesses, Vijaya explained. They used the savings association when they needed money. Shanthi provided assistance for everyone in securing loans, withdrawing money from their accounts, or any other financial task. Vijaya, like Shanthi and many others I spoke with, consistently used the English word *help* to describe Shanthi's role. When I asked Vijaya whether Shanthi needed the money, Vijaya replied, "She doesn't need it, but it's always useful for something, no?"

Vijaya struggled with many responsibilities, virtually no control over her husband's earnings, and limited opportunities to supplement her family's income with a wage. Loans provided income at crucial times, but the repayments were burdensome and expensive to keep up with. Under these difficult circumstances, Vijaya's livelihood depended greatly upon her relationship to Shanthi, who acted as a financial benefactor of sorts. Her financial life was also tied up with other women in the neighborhood, who all participated in diverse activities that comprised a complex, highly local gendered financial ecosystem. In the case of the Kanchan loan, a group had to consist of an ideal mix of entrepreneurial and non-entrepreneurial clients who could meet minimal income requirements and, as we shall see in the next example, a specific mix of clients who own and rent houses. These various requirements, designed to minimize risk for the MFI and maximize repayment odds, ultimately fell to the women in their communities to shoulder, and Vijaya was one of the more vulnerable ones in her group because of her poor health and her husband's alcoholism. But as a homeowner, she was still a good risk for a company, and her relatively stable economic standing made her an important member of the group.

Vijaya's narrative signals the significance of several aspects of the gendered financial ecosystem that are particularly significant for women borrowers: pawnbrokers and property ownership. The practice of pledging gold jewelry for cash to pawnbrokers at a high interest rate is a common practice in South Asia, and most of the women I spoke to leveraged this form of debt as a cushion throughout their lives.[7] Vijaya and many other women I spoke to also stabilized their incomes by having rights over property, usually with their husbands. Bina Agrawal's work has established the importance of property ownership for women's well-being in rural areas of

South Asia, but less is known about urban areas.[8] I found anecdotal evidence that women who owned their homes seemed to have slightly stronger entitlements within their communities and entered into group lending arrangements in a stronger position than their income or livelihoods would otherwise suggest.

DARSHANA: "SHE FORCED ME"

On the third floor of a bleak concrete apartment structure, twenty-three-year-old Darshana lived in a two-room flat with her husband and two young children. Unlike her peers, Darshana spoke excellent English and had completed two years of college in her home city of Coimbatore, Tamil Nadu. She married against the will of her family and came to live in Bengaluru. With two young children at home, a thriving tailoring business, and a gainfully employed husband working a manual printing job in the advertising industry, Darshana reported that she had sufficient funds coming in each month and had never considered taking a loan. Darshana was clear about her priorities: "My first child always gets first rank in the class. She's an outstanding student in school. Because I have given full effort to her. That is the main thing. First preference for my children, second preference to my husband, and third preference to myself." We learned, however, that this prioritization belied other interests. On weekends, she tutored twenty neighborhood children in her home, none of whom had any other opportunity for academic help. Darshana seemed indignant when we asked her whether this tutoring business was profitable for her—she did not charge anyone a penny. When we turned the recorder off and her husband, who arrived for lunch in the middle of the interview, left, she inquired earnestly about the possibility of continuing her higher studies. Did we know about correspondence or distance courses? She wanted to know. She knew her husband would not allow her to leave the house for work or education, but she wanted to do something from home. English literature, perhaps? As with so many women with requests for information that would come up at the tail end of our interaction, I had to admit my ignorance.

Darshana's tailoring skills, learned at a young age in Coimbatore, worked in tandem with her middle-class tastes and aspirations to protect her from the stresses of the low end of the labor market, but not from the social and economic pressures of living in that particular neighborhood. Though she and her husband owned a home in Coimbatore, they lived in a rented home in Bengaluru. According to the stipulations for Kanchan's group formation, for every five members in a Kanchan group, one must live in a rented home.

As a result, Darshana was pushed into participating in the group. "That [Shanthi] Aunty—she forced me to take the loan," she lamented.

> Really. Whatever is the truth, I have to tell you. I have sufficient money for my house. And now monthly, I have to pay [this loan as well]. Not even monthly, weekly! It's a big stress, no? Because I have the capacity to pay the loan [back], [I told her,] "Okay, Aunty, I'll pay it." The fact I'm telling you will not be a problem for me, right? This is the first time I have done anything like this.

When asked, Darshana said she had no idea what the interest rate on the Kanchan loan was. Although she had previously taken conventional bank loans, she knew nothing about the current terms. She just felt she had to participate when Shanthi Aunty, knowing fully well that Darshana had the financial wherewithal to repay, asked her to join. Darshana explained that many in the group—though she would not name anyone in particular—took loans from MFIs at low rates and lent that money to others in the neighborhood who could not qualify. This practice, known as ghost lending, is strictly prohibited by MFIs. There is an entire video devoted to explaining to clients about the dangers of ghost lending in Sowbyga's orientation training, although it may not have been so thoroughly covered in Kanchan's training. Darshana's statements seemed to verify what Mamatha had suspected—that Shanthi was herself an informal moneylender who used her power and networks to help other women in the neighborhood, while putting pressure on those in the neighborhood who could repay to take loans they might not need. In Darshana's case, she had used the money to prepay the school admissions fees for her kids for the next year, since she had already paid the current year's fees in full.

In the commercial lending groups that I observed, there was often at least one younger woman like Darshana (such as Sheila from previous chapters and in the next section of this chapter), with a potentially stronger position in the labor market, combined in a group with significantly more vulnerable peers. Like a health insurance pool that mixes high-risk and low-risk clients, MFI groups must include some clients who might not even need the loan. However, in the world of MFI lending, it is the women themselves who must forge those groups through social relationships that become laden with economic meaning, rather than institutional algorithms forming them into anonymous pools. Powerful women exercise social pressure to bring these groups together and funnel financial services into their neighborhoods. In these unofficial contexts, social relationships are reconfigured for economic reasons. While successful relational work might make these relationships durable over time, they can be laced with coercion. For clients like Darshana, involvement in the group loan did not necessarily provide help for her own family in the short run but nonetheless required a significant investment of labor and intensive relational work. By feeling beholden to Shanthi due to Shanthi's relatively higher social position, and consequently stretching herself to take a group loan, Darshana was now tied to her neighbors in a way she would not have chosen, with untold consequences in the future. Although we might expect that members of an MFI group each have similar needs and issues, Darshana's narrative shows that taking a loan does not always indicate an immediate need and may in some cases draw women into exploitative forms of debt that do not serve them in order to keep peace and uphold the social order within their neighborhoods.

GOURIAMMA: JUGGLING FINANCES

Gregarious and smiling, forty-two-year-old Gouriamma was the most talkative woman of all those we spoke to in the neighborhood. Income from her husband and son's occupations as drivers, and income from rental properties, gave her financial stability. Gouriamma was also very well versed in the neighborhood's gendered financial ecosystem. As she put it, she participated in these financial activities to the benefit of herself and her family. Apart from the neighborhood rotating savings association that Vijaya mentioned, and the Kanchan loan, Gouriamma mentioned a "calling chit fund" in which members paid premium monthly fees for access to a large loan of one lakh of rupees (about sixteen hundred dollars) or more to support a big expense, like a car purchase or a wedding. Gouriamma reported that at the time of our interview she was part of two calling chit funds, one with forty women, requiring a monthly payment of three thousand rupees for a 1.2 lakh loan, and another with a similar monthly fee for a 1.6 lakh loan. Finally, she had a loan of ten thousand rupees from Kanchan, which required weekly repayments. Later in the interview, she remembered that she had also taken an informal hand loan from her husband's friend to construct the new home we were sitting in. For a one lakh loan, Gouriamma had paid over fifty thousand rupees in interest. These informal loans from moneylenders have long been viewed as the most exploitative form of debt, and one of the many arguments that MFIS make about the importance of their services is that their rates are lower than that of the hand-loan lenders. But as Gouriamma's narrative suggests, even well-off borrowers use high-interest loans, and if anything, MFIS have shored up the need for informal moneylenders.[9]

Gouriamma shared with us that Shanthi had worked hard to form the Kanchan group. When she heard of Kanchan's presence in their area, Shanthi approached a Kanchan official with a group of ten women. But the group was rejected for having too few members. "Shanthi was so angry," Gouriamma shared, "because she had organized these ten members among all her hectic work." That was when Shanthi asked Gouriamma to join the group. Gouriamma agreed and produced all the documents needed. Her husband disagreed with her decision and felt the weekly payments would be too burdensome. Since she had already made the commitment to Shanthi, Gouriamma convinced her husband to agree to the extra loan and promised to revive her failed sari business. She then joined the existing group, which eventually grew to fifteen members to meet Kanchan's requirement.

Out of the all the members in the Kanchan group, Gouriamma estimated that five or six members are doing fine financially, while the others really needed the money. She understood that the need in her community was great and stated that she felt comfortable taking a loan from an MFI and lending it to another woman in the neighborhood who did not qualify herself but needed the loan. But she expressed hesitation alongside her willingness, since she could end up with a problem if they did not repay. This was the second clear statement from this set of interviews indicating that ghost lending was a common practice in neighborhoods such as these and that such practices were not just making some women creditworthy: it was also extracting interest from women who could least afford it and who would not even reap the benefits of creditworthiness. Women were forging groups strategically, across lines of class especially, to gain access to financial services for themselves and others in the neighborhood. This hidden relational work, linked to the relational work between clients and loan officers, made the state's financial inclusion policies successful.

Gouriamma's narrative might have foreshadowed a future in store for someone like Darshana, who was potentially poised to accumulate status and cultural capital in the community through inclusion in gendered financial arrangements. In contrast, Vijaya, the same age as Gouriamma, had not enjoyed similar financial security and thus found herself in a subordinate position within the neighborhood's financial ecosystem, as one of the women in the group who really needed the loan.

What was clear from my examination of these four interviews in relation to one another, however, was the central role of neighborhood women's groups for organizing access to various kinds of financial products, wherein MFIs are just one source in the mix. Every product in that financial ecosystem, however, required at least one person to be familiar with different interest rates and terms and, at the same time, to have an intimate understanding of the livelihoods of all the women in the surrounding areas. As women with secure finances absorbed the risk of those with fewer resources, they gained status in the community. Along the way, these powerful volunteer women may pick up financial brokering skills that would serve them in other informal, but potentially lucrative, arenas, such as community-level politics or real estate deals.

In the narratives of these four neighbors and group members, we learn that engaging in simultaneously social and economic relationships with other women neighbors is required, whether or not they choose it as individuals. In this Kanchan group, a powerful leader, potentially with political connections, rallied considerable time and energy to broker her community's access to an MFI loan that she did not necessarily need for her own subsistence or entrepreneurship. Shanthi seemed to have intimate knowledge of her neighbors' housing statuses and incomes and relied on this knowledge to strategically bring together this group. She also likely advised members about what they should say to MFI officials to secure an approval. For many, like Vijaya, the loan provided access for funds that would be immediately useful for medical and other necessary expenses. The loan also allowed them to abide by their husband's preference for them staying at home, keeping them at the outer margins of the labor market. As long as the women repay on time and at least some of the women can appear successful for the MFI, however, the state's financial inclusion mandate is accomplished and women are affirmed as worthy targets of development programming.

Loan-Taking as Reproductive Labor

Over several days in May of 2012, I observed how a group of Sowbagya customers were approved for loans and trained prior to loan disbursal, the topic of chapter 4. After observing these processes between the MFI and the customers, I interviewed four of the five group members independently. While these interviews revealed less about the in-group dynamics than in the previous example, they illustrated vividly how financial management as a gendered role fuses women's productive, reproductive and community managing roles without disrupting the subordinate position of working-class women in the labor market. Women engage in loan-taking within a broader landscape of limited prospects for work or class mobility. Furthermore, in support of Jayanthi's narrative from earlier in the chapter, the narratives of women in this group show how lenders—whether MFIs or moneylenders or employers—target women for particular kinds of loans by engaging them within their roles as housewives or domestic workers, reinforcing that role over time. Furthermore, in the following vignettes of the various group members' social and financial circumstances, we find that, like in the previous group profiled, the inequalities between group members are prominent.

KALYANI: THE LONG ROAD OUT OF DOMESTIC WORK

At thirty-nine years of age, group leader Kalyani had given up business ventures to engage in loan-taking as a primary source of income, in cooperation with her part-time work as a domestic in a single home. Kalyani was the least educated in the group, having dropped out of school in fifth grade. But she had taken loans for a decade from a competing MFI and felt her life had improved over time as a result. Through housing loans, she had managed to get her family of six into increasingly better homes. Other efforts to improve herself involving her own labor, however, had not proved to be profitable.

For three years, she took MFI loans to invest in what I had by then understood was a ubiquitous sari business. Like others, she bought saris in bulk and sold them on an installment basis to women in the neighborhood. Like others in her neighborhood, she failed to turn a profit in this business. Neighbors knew how much the saris cost and did not wish to pay Kalyani's markup. Likely due to MFIs' emphasis on microenterprise, soon there were far too many women selling saris at people's doorsteps, so Kalyani decided she could not compete. She concluded that she would much prefer going to a job daily than taking up a business at home.

At the time of our interview, Kalyani had been working for the same family in a nearby apartment complex for fifteen years and continued to work for them because they insisted on it. Kalyani did not enjoy domestic work, however. When her grown children were younger, she explained, "I used to work in seven houses every day. It always involved working with water, and I ended up having a bit of a [health] problem. I could not continue with it. When my children grew older, I had too many other responsibilities. Now, I just work in one house."

Kalyani's narrative suggests that loans from MFIs have helped her improve her housing situation and support the education of her children. She quickly learned that if you can repay smaller loans on time, you will gain access to larger loans. With another MFI, she first gained access to a loan of ten thousand rupees, but at the time of our interview, she had access to a loan of twenty-five thousand rupees (about $420). She had used the loans for school fees and for paying off more expensive debts. As a result of these loans, her two daughters completed tenth grade, and one of them planned to look for work in a year's time, once she turned eighteen. That daughter was unable to gain admission to college but did not wish to marry for the time being. Her son, whose photos I had observed on her wall, had been selected for the Indian Junior Football League, so he was training in Goa and did not contribute to the family's finances, though she expected that he would be able to within two years. Access to increasingly large loans had been helpful for Kalyani's family. These loans may even have prevented her family from falling into dire poverty. Notably, Kalyani did not disclose much about her husband's occupation or income, other than noting that he was a painter. Sowbagya officials had raised an issue with her husband's side carrom (finger pool) business, but Kalyani did not discuss this in our interview.

Despite her hard-won gains, Kalyani's scope for improved work had not improved as much as we might expect. A decade of loan-taking as a primary occupation has done little to develop her skills to expand opportunity for herself, despite her interest in working. Instead, she used her know-how of microfinance to organize a new group for Sowbagya. She implied that Sowbagya might have even bent the residential requirements slightly to allow her to organize this group, perhaps referring to Ishwari's distant residence. She appreciated the training but found it quite similar to others she had experienced with the competing company, though that was with a group of twenty. "From that film I learned that we should not take too many loans," she declared. "We should only take what we can repay."

Unlike some of the other group leaders I interviewed, such as Shankari and Shanthi, Kalyani's situation was vulnerable too; she was invested in being a group leader because it was one of the only skills she had. Unlike some MFI workers I had interviewed who were men, however, Kalyani was unable or unwilling to parlay that know-how into a salaried opportunity with an MFI or another similar organization. In the new Sowbagya group she had organized, composed of just five members, the varied levels of vulnerability suggested that this group may have trouble covering the amounts in the future.

NALINI: INDEBTED BUT OPTIMISTIC

Nalini, age twenty-seven, cooked at her mother's house but claimed to live at another. She had a ninth-grade education and had married a young man from the neighborhood with whom she fell in love. Their marriage created tension in the family, as her parents—especially her mother—did not approve of it, likely due to caste differences. Her parents eventually relented, but due to the rift between her husband and mother, her husband never visited her mother's house. This is why Nalini went to cook at her mother's house and then brought the food back to their sparse rented house each day. She told us that she had worked for years (she did not specify doing what) and did not wish to work again, other than as a part-time domestic worker. She had stopped that work when she married and was now focused on having a child and gaining enough financial stability to own a home.

An outsider might consider Nalini to be in dire financial straits. When I heard more about her circumstances, I certainly did. Apart from the loan she was about to take from Sowbagya, she also had another loan from a competing MFI that had been stuck in the approval process for several months. Together, these two group loans would cost approximately one-third to one-half of her total household income, which she estimated to total about nine thousand rupees per month (about $150). Apart from these group loans, Nalini and her husband had taken numerous hand loans for five hundred or one thousand rupees, which are offered at a 10 percent per day interest rate. Nalini stated confidently that they have no problem repaying. She did not connect the lesson in the film about the dangers of multiple lending to her own situation. In the situation in the film, the husband pushed the wife to take a third loan, whereas in her situation, no one pushed her to do anything. She took a loan because she wished to gather the funds to put a deposit down on a larger house for them to live in. For Nalini, this was a more viable strategy through which to move up in life than finding more steady work or beginning an entrepreneurial business, which she reported no interest in. She seemed to believe that loan money could be used to put down a deposit on a new home.

Nalini's narrative helps us understand how gendered processes of extraction can occur in a way that targets the most vulnerable groups, who have few options and thus feel happy that they have the opportunity to take a loan. Because of the circumstances she finds herself in after marriage, Nalini has few pathways toward stability and has been largely alienated from any property or income rights she had as a member of her family. Becoming a mother and owning a home is a top priority for her, and she optimistically believes that taking more loans will help her attain those goals. As she and her husband sink deeper into debt without a chance to improve their position in a stratified labor market, however, these odds appear to be long.

Relative to her peers, Sheila, the only single woman in my sample of fifty-five clients, entered into loan-taking with relatively more cultural capital and less liability. The youngest in her group at age twenty-four, she was also the most educated, having received a two-year diploma in office management after finishing twelfth grade. She was engaged to be married next year. When asked why she had never taken a loan before, she explained,

> All finance companies consider [the income of] husbands in their eligibility criteria. Only married couples will get the loan. But for the first time, Sowbagya said that I can borrow for a loan, even if I am not married. They [the companies] want surety. Most wives don't go to work. Therefore, they [the companies] assume that if they [the women] don't pay, their husbands will pay back the loan.

Sheila understood well that her loan-taking as a single woman was exceptional. While most MFIs lend to women and encourage them to either work or start small businesses, they also collect the IDs and information of husbands, making them guarantors who can be pressured for loan repayment if their wives fail to repay. As shown in the house visit vignettes in chapter 3, a client's husband's identification and income made up a critical piece of documentation in the loan application process, even though husbands are conspicuously absent from success stories.[10]

Sheila's education and strong position in the labor market, however, gave her access to a set of financial tools that were unattainable for other married group members. Sheila wished to eventually start her own data entry business, so she had already looked into an individual loan from a conventional private bank, for whom she works as a data entry provider through a subcontractor. "They said you need two lakhs (about $3,300) for that, so if I want that, I need to start contributing to a chit fund." While someone like Nalini was oriented toward using microfinance and hand loans to secure a house, Sheila could access more expensive, high-yield chit funds open to men and women alongside her loan from Sowbagya, which she was using to help release pledged jewelry that would be needed for her upcoming wedding. For someone like Sheila, her Sowbagya loan was a stepping-stone precisely because she had significant access to other resources and competencies. If Sheila were to open her business, however, Sowbagya could claim that their loan helped make her independent, an appropriation that reinforces the symbolic value of the company.

Ishwari, who also had issues with verifying her residence with Sowbagya staff, revealed in her interview a history of indebtedness and vulnerability as a single mother of four children. When I met her at age fifty, Ishwari was already a loan veteran, having labored for decades as a single mother at the bottom of the labor market to provide for her children. Thirty years prior to our meeting, she migrated from a Tamil Nadu town with her husband, a painter and an alcoholic. He experienced kidney failure when their son was a newborn and was unable to receive any treatment at the hospital. "My brother-in-law admitted my husband in the hospital," Ishwari recalled. "Then, I was totally ignorant. I did not know a thing. No knowledge of housework also. My brother-in-law asked the doctor about a kidney transplant. He was ready to spend for that. He pleaded with the doctor, but they said it wouldn't work . . . my son was just three months when my husband passed away. I was a nursing mother. I struggled and brought up my children [three daughters and one son]. All people here know." Despite the blow of losing her husband, Ishwari secured a proper cleaning job at an office while her children were still young.

Ishwari repeatedly commented on her ignorance as a new migrant and a young mother. She recollected the circumstances under which she was hired for the office cleaning job, a position she has held for decades: "When I got married and came here, I did not know one word of English. Ask my children. Even in the office, I didn't know how to sign [required papers]. Sir [my boss] would yell at me . . . He would say, 'You've been married for so long and mothered four kids but you do not know a thing, Ishwari.'" Despite the remarkable feat of bringing up four children under such adverse circumstances, Ishwari had clearly internalized at least some of the message that she had consistently received from her superiors for decades: that she was stupid and ignorant. Her lack of confidence about her intelligence came up repeatedly during the training, detailed in chapter 3.

By her own account, what she thought she lacked in book smarts, she more than made up for in her punctuality, reliability, and multitasking abilities. Unlike others in her group, her cleaning job at an office building was an official one, not an informal one, and she had held it for two decades. Although the salary was low, she drew some benefits. She also continued to work in another home as a domestic. And if there was one thing Ishwari understood well, it was loans and money management. She readily shared information about her most recent loans. Two loans from a competing MFI, and the new Sowbagya loan, all went toward providing upfront expenses for her son's business. She also detailed a past loan that she took from an employer, who ended up not collecting half of it. That employer had promised her continued employment in another neighborhood further away. But because it was too far a commute from her residence, her son decided that she should not continue there, a decision she did not overrule.

In an earlier time period, she had taken loans from moneylenders for her daughters' weddings, and the pressure was intense. Ishwari recalled with emotion, "I had to get my daughters married and it became so difficult. I have struggled. We took so many loans for the weddings. The moneylenders would come and keep knocking on our doors. I used to cry." Once she got through that rough patch, she ponied up jewelry she owned and loans from MFIS to help start her son's card printing business. After all these experiences, she decided that MFIS provided the most convenient option for her. "This is better than getting loans on interest elsewhere. If we pay interest on time, we are comfortable here. This is better. For other lenders, there's one hundred rupees interest for one thousand rupees. Here, if we pay the loan on time, there is no hassle. And I am very prompt." Ishwari's justification for why MFIS loans are convenient echoed the justifications provided by MFIS themselves about their usefulness in clients' lives.

Ishwari took pride in the fact that her son no longer wished for her to work outside the home. "He says, 'You have slogged for twenty years. Why not stop working [as a domestic worker] in the evening at least?' He wants me to rest. But I can work, so I can also help and earn money." Twenty years later, Ishwari labored in the same subordinate position in the economy but had more options for loans than she used to, thanks to MFIS.

KALYANI'S GROUP: MOTHERING THROUGH LOANS

Kalyani, Nalini, Sheila and Ishwari's narratives paint a gendered picture of urban India in which raising children with the assistance of loans is the only way forward. While some narrate the involvement of sons or husbands, the work of making ends meet through loans is largely borne by women. Whether through the pawning of jewelry, microfinance, loans from employers, or hand loans from moneylenders at interest rates of 10 percent per day, mothers juggle loans while surviving as domestics in a social context that fails to provide basic amenities and protections, from sanitation to health care to education. Furthermore, while this group of women did not narrate their interconnections with one another in their interviews, we find in this group different levels of vulnerability, different ages, different livelihoods, and ultimately different levels of risk coming together in a single group, managed by Kalyani, perhaps the savviest borrower in the group. In this environment, MFI loans are one kind of gendered loan among many, but through the group, MFIS are able to extract both financial and symbolic value from all the members. Should any of their enterprises be successful, Sowbagya could take credit for it with a selectively appropriated story that ignores the other contingent opportunities and forms of capital that each person brought to the group loan. But should Nalini or Ishwari grow more vulnerable in the years ahead, Sowbagya would bear no responsibility and, indeed, might even continue to appear generous if these group members continue to successfully repay even if their overall financial stability declines, reflecting poor conditions in the labor market.

These accounts also give us a clear sense of the variations that make this group a good risk pool for an MFI like Sowbagya. Nalini and Ishwari may be more likely to default, while Sheila and Kalyani have the connections and resources to pay. Mary, the fifth group member whom I could not interview one-on-one, was also young and employed part-time. As the group leader, Kalyani leveraged her intimate knowledge of neighbors to construct a group that would allow her to take out a loan for her family, but in so doing, Kalyani absorbed the financial and social responsibility of others in the group with less social, economic, and political capital than she. The relational work of loan-taking, then, involves borrowers themselves managing inequality to support the production of creditworthiness.

Conclusion

Examining the relational work within microfinance groups reveals new kinds of gendered labor within the context of class inequalities. As with relational work between MFI employees and clients, relational work among clients is embedded within deep structural inequalities but it is highly contingent and, thus, unpredictable in its trajectory. Social work by powerful volunteers has become an unpaid form of gendered labor through which better-off women leverage their intimate knowledge of other women in their communities to bring opportunities for lending to their communities. Emulating the benevolent protectionism of MFI employees, women like Shankari, Jayanthi, Kalyani, and even Shanthi aim to do well for themselves and their families by also doing well for others in their community. Regarding MFI loans as a form of help, relationships within urban slums familiarize especially mothers with the expectations of loan-taking and accustom them to the condition of indebtedness.

This chapter illuminates how gendered extraction requires relational work for all actors involved but disproportionately benefits MFIS, while allocating modest and often nonmonetary benefits of honor and status to relatively better-off women in a neighborhood. Relational work between women living in the same neighborhood is constantly underway, involving a constant interchange of help. Through relational work, people within neighborhoods form simultaneously social and financial alliances, not always entirely of their choosing, and through those alliances either improve their social standing, address immediate financial needs or desires, or perhaps even earn a profit in cases where better-off women might be taking loans for poorer women who do not qualify. Highlighting such relational work not only in between the MFI and borrowers but also among borrowers themselves highlights the extent to which fraught, intimate relationships lie at the heart of financial inclusion projects. It is the private financial companies who benefit most from these intimate negotiations.

Second, this chapter highlights the unpaid labor of group finance that is folded into women's integrated financial management roles. This work may protect a family from starvation at times but also reinforces the status quo for women borrowers. MFI loans and other sources of financing tie their loans to their husbands in most cases and provide little or no incentive for any kind of work outside the lowest end of the job market. The labor of group finance is class- and gender-specific and draws together the burden of low-wage work and the labor involved in managing relationships of reciprocity and support in one's own neighborhood. The processes and criteria that are in place keep leaders like Shankari on the hook for repayment, while protecting the MFI from excessive financial risk. It is left up to borrowers to manage their own economic and social risks, as well as their affective ties to one another, a situation that involves cooperation but also coercion. Class and residential differences between clients in the same group draw them together more closely in their indebtedness without reducing the vulnerabilities of the least well off. When MFIS extract symbolic value in the form of success stories, they also selectively appropriate individualistic stories, leaving out the social and economic fabric of relationality that makes vulnerable women borrowers repay on time. Finally, when these complex relationships result in repeated loan-taking and occasional success stories, those outcomes validate the state's financial inclusion project, appearing to empower women as champions of their own financial destinies through their MFI partners.

5. EMPOWERMENT, DECLINED

MFIS present a variety of optional offerings to clients, meant to supplement their loan products with additional opportunities. Training programs geared toward entrepreneurship, financial literacy, or skills development are common program offerings for borrowers, and they serve to enhance the reputation and legitimacy of MFIS. I have long viewed these trainings as critical sites for understanding the ideological and political dimensions of MFI work. Through trainings oriented at empowerment, microfinance companies communicate to their clients what kind of woman they want them to be.

While the preceding chapters focused on the lending side of the microfinance industry in India, in this chapter I explore empowerment training, which has been long conjoined with lending in India and in many other parts of the world. I investigate the materials that microfinance companies offer their borrowers, how facilitators manage these materials in real interactions with clients, and how microfinance clients respond to the experience of training. This area of focus helps uncover the gendered ideologies at the core of microfinance and how they resonate (or not) with women borrowers. I found that the two training programs I studied—Shaktisri from Kanchan and Vriddhi from Sowbagya—while different in many respects, both promoted the ideology of *working motherhood*, a construction of femininity meant to resonate with working-class clients. Trainings encouraged women to embrace many roles, all of which should ideally support their roles as mothers and primary caregivers at all times. With proper planning and time management, facilitators suggested, women borrowers could earn a wage and manage their household responsibilities to reduce their vulnerabilities, provide for their children, and live a prosperous life. As I show in this chapter, however, this message resonated unevenly with clients and was often rejected. I focus on what I witnessed frequently during my research: women's (polite) refusals to internalize what was on offer, particularly in the context of entrepreneurial training. These refusals suggest that the power of MFIS is limited. Nonetheless, empowerment trainings allow MFIS to effectively extract symbolic value; trainers selectively appropriate success stories from clients whose stories reflect the kind of femininity MFIS idealize. Because of both the symbolic value MFIS extract through training and the positive company image that empowerment trainings help build, many commercial MFIS continue to invest in programs that neither yield a profit nor meet customers' real needs.

In the middle of a baking afternoon, I sat alongside twenty-eight working-class women on a concrete-floored veranda in a small outlying town of Coimbatore, Tamil Nadu. We had been sitting together for almost four hours, participating in the "Self-Management" module of Shaktisri, a free training program promoting entrepreneurship among Kanchan's clients. After a series of participatory games, discussions, and activities led by Nandini, an experienced trainer, we began watching a film on a laptop screen. The asbestos sheet above our heads created a shade over the film that allowed us to see the images despite the blinding sun. I found the dubbed Tamil dialogue a bit hard to follow. Others seemed to be following along, albeit without much apparent enthusiasm.

In the film's first segment, a dancer in classical Bharatnatyam[1] regalia acted out on stage the daily tasks of an Indian housewife, including cooking, cleaning, and taking care of children. The dancer used the mimetic language of the highly stylized traditional dance form, with instrumental music in the background. She swept invisible floors, made unseen beds, cared for imaginary children, and ran an illusory store. Then the film transitioned to a narrative style, in which a "real" woman—presented to us as a light-skinned, upper-class woman living in a modern Indian flat—woke up in the morning from a clean and comfortable bed, cleaned the house, prepared breakfast *dosas* for her family, sent her husband and kids off to school and work, and then managed her own tailor shop. In the last segment of the film, four different women, who looked more like the women seated beside me, described their businesses—tailoring, beauty salon, doll sales, and candle-making—and how they succeeded or failed in them. Few women remained in rapt attention over the course of the thirty-minute film. But they were quiet, and most of the women stayed until the film concluded. Food was served afterward.

Although the women gathered for the training were the explicit audience for this Shaktisri film, we had an audience of our own for the entire afternoon. Along the fringe of the veranda stood half a dozen men, arms folded across their chests, watching us watching the video. Standing in the harsh sun, their white handkerchiefs mopped sweaty foreheads, as their button-down shirts and polyester slacks exacerbated the effects of the heat. These men, from Kanchan's local office, had come to observe how the company's corporate social responsibility (CSR) initiative was going. They were evaluating Nandini, the trainer, also a Kanchan employee, but they were curious about my and Bagya's presence as well. They were looking for evidence that the program was working so that they could give a positive report to their superiors at the head office later that day. Over the course of the afternoon, men rotated in and out of the periphery of that veranda, all the time careful not to disturb the proceedings. They could not really see the film, but they were impressed by its existence nonetheless.

At the conclusion of the film, Nandini asked the clients what they understood from each part of the film. "What did you understand from the dance in the beginning?" she inquired. The question hung in the long, humid silence that followed her question. Some women shifted their positions uneasily. Others stared blankly at one another and at Nandini, wondering whether they were supposed to know the answer. Finally, one woman admitted, "I couldn't understand anything from that. Madam, you must tell us." Nandini had a response at the ready. The dance and the film, featuring the woman with the tailoring business, she explained, show us that "ladies" are responsible for so many things, but they are also capable of taking care of their home and their business simultaneously. The last segment of the film, she continued, introduced different ideas for businesses, but also showed what they as clients ought to be thinking about when they began their businesses. It was not just about deciding on a product to sell, you see, but also about market demand, price point, and quality.

I had been sitting next to the same woman for a few hours now, and we had exchanged a few polite smiles. During the earlier round of introductions, she identified herself as Kamala, a construction worker. Kamala participated enthusiastically in a few parts of the training, and I had the impression she was enjoying herself. But she had made impatient comments about how long it was taking as the afternoon wore on. When the film was over, and Nandini concluded her explanation, I asked her if she had found this training useful. "All this is not for me," she said dismissively. "I should bring my daughter next time. Maybe she would be interested."

This Shaktisri training aimed to convince the women gathered that they could earn a living through a small home business while also fulfilling their family duties. They encouraged women to embrace the idea that they were entrepreneurs while also being mothers, and to take pride in the convergence of these identities. These discourses did not just target women borrowers; they also targeted another audience just outside the training session. In this instance, the group of men from the local office eagerly observed the training in order to document and report on it to superiors. But even when there was no physical audience present for a training session, there was always another invisible audience: the corporate office and its donors. That audience was hungry for stories that would portray MFI clients as hardworking women who had leveraged microfinance to make their lives prosperous. In particular, corporate actors wished to document the cases in which clients became success stories. Such success stories abound in popular and business-oriented accounts of microfinance.[2] I show in this chapter that training programs, rather than being beholden to the interests of the borrowers enrolling in them, are instead accountable to these more powerful actors and serve as a channel through which decontextualized success stories can be directed from clients to higher-ups.

The Conflicted Rationale for Training

Given the extent to which India's microfinance industry has become embedded in the broader financial industry, it is surprising that most companies continue to offer expensive training programs to their clientele that seldom pencil out financially. The growing dominance of commercial microfinance should have, in theory, obviated empowerment-oriented training programs. But in India loans for women remain entwined with social programs intended to improve their lives, whether through entrepreneurial training, financial literacy programs, health-care provision, health education, or job training.[3] Increasingly, this focus on women has become peculiar to India; MFIs in Latin America and Southeast Asia now lend almost equally to men and women and have largely eschewed women's empowerment as a justification.

The persistence of such programs stems from the microfinance industry's central place in national financial inclusion policies, in tandem with self-help groups, which aim to reach underserved groups, including Dalits and women. Government programs in all states offer various kinds of trainings to self-help group members, ranging from health and hygiene, training on agricultural techniques and inputs, and women's empowerment. MFI programming imitates these state offerings, while also trying to produce and maintain distinction from the state. Some MFIS offer trainings as optional value-added components of loan programs, while others sponsor them as CSR initiatives. Trainings allow MFIS to improve their public image, strengthen their relationships with local communities, and procure success stories for company websites and glossy brochures. All these activities, which occur in tandem with training, allow for the extraction of symbolic value that would not be possible through lending alone.

While women borrowers could be trained to engage in a wide variety of collective projects, the empowerment trainings I observed were primarily focused on borrowers as individual actors, a reflection of the global consensus among dominant development institutions around neoliberal feminism. Katherine Moeller argues that when the World Bank's policy regime shifted away from redistribution with growth to positioning individual productivity as the key solution for ending poverty, women became a key priority. This transformation led to greater emphasis on investments in women's productivity and a peculiar emphasis on women's education. This emphasis became so commonplace in development discourse that, by the 2000s, educating girls and women for the purposes of ending poverty had become "common sense," thus fueling corporate CSR programs, particularly at US corporations.[4] In the programs I studied, this common sense influenced the content of programming in Indian financial corporations, providing a core logic about individual responsibility that effectively deflected attention from structural constraints while enticing individual clients to increase their productivity and thus become more reliable clients. As in programming sponsored by US corporations like Nike, Kanchan and Sowbagya training programs defined empowerment as the individual management of multiple productive and reproductive roles by women clients. This approach not only departed from the collective training approaches of self-help groups and feminist movements in India but also denied the importance of caste, occupation, and residential location in producing significant obstacles to clients' success.

In India, the notion of offering women training that will aid in their own empowerment has a long, ambivalent history that runs in parallel to global discourses around gender and development. Aradhana Sharma's study of women's empowerment NGOs in north India finds that the work of empowering women is dangerous because, often, the type of empowerment that organizations seek from the women they train does not emerge. Instead, women targeted by such programs may flaunt their superiors, deepen social divisions among themselves, or subvert official projects to serve their own interests. In Sharma's study, women embraced empowerment as a paradigm but internalized it in unpredictable ways.[5] Similarly, Richa Nagar and the Sangtin Collective found that the empowerment of Sangtin members through work in their community could be transformative, but such changes were unwelcome for the NGO that fostered their group formation, and the women faced punishment for interpreting the lessons of empowerment and using those lessons to advance their own critique of the organization and circulate it widely.[6] In both these examples, targeted women participated in the diverse forms of engagement, employment, and training that NGOs offered poor and working-class women in rural communities and often internalized its core ideas, even though the result of this process separated them from NGO aims.

Despite the lack of evidence that training programs achieve observable results that benefit marginalized women, organizations are driven by an imperative to do something concrete for clients that will be perceived as helpful, regardless of its eventual effects. Such programs serve different purposes in different firms. At Kanchan, the Shaktisri program was part of the company's CSR initiative, which came from the top and evolved in its implementation over the course of a few years. Kanchan leadership wished to provide this added feature to prove its distinction from other organizations and demonstrate its care for clients. Thus, Shaktisri programs were meant to impress clients and enhance the reputation of the firm, hoping to deepen customer loyalty. At Sowbagya, Vriddhi programs originated from a sister NGO that managed all of Sowbagya's social impact programs. From the outside, at least, the NGO's leadership appeared more committed than Kanchan CSR to making sure that their programming was directly relevant to Sowbagya clients. Nonetheless, Vriddhi was aimed at improving customer loyalty and, in the long run, making women borrowers more reliable clients. The aims of both empowerment programs, at least on paper, served the MFI. If clients were more financially literate, the reasoning went, they would be able to take on greater loans and ultimately leverage a wider range of Sowbagya's financial services.

Other firms I studied did not visualize client education as a viable part of their CSR offerings. Grama Valachi, for example, saw no value in training clients and instead committed its CSR activities to building schools in the communities they worked in, not necessarily just for client families. Bhavishya, in contrast, conducted an ongoing minimalist training model that involved a standardized letter for all clients containing key information about topics such as hygiene, schooling, or women's health. A new letter, penned as if from a woman pen pal, has been read at every weekly meeting for women clients by their loan officers across the region for years. The company had more than 230 such letters on file when I visited them in 2016, and the leaders felt strongly that these letters have made an important impact on client knowledge. These diverse approaches demonstrate that MFIS lack a unified approach to empowering women and regard such programs as subordinate to their central business strategies. Notably, none of these programs are influenced by a drive toward the transformation of gender relations long called for by feminist scholars in India and beyond.

Despite a lack of cohesive strategy among MFIS, and often within firms themselves, during my research, I observed that such programs occupied an outsize amount of time and resources relative to their financial importance, indicating how important they were to the overall morale and legitimacy of many MFIS. In my study of the Shaktisri program, for example, I saw that Kanchan workers were required to invest considerable time in training to become effective trainers for clients and in keeping their skills and knowledge updated. The Indian branch office of Prosperity worked hard to oversee the program, albeit with ambivalent results.

Making Trainers Who Will Empower

Twice a year, Kanchan workers attended extensive trainings for trainers that stretched into several days, requiring them to live at a hotel in Bengaluru, attend sessions all day, and do homework at night to prepare for the next day's session. During one such training I attended, which participants informed me was typical of these trainings, a supertrainer with decades of experience training trainers emphasized the core values of the Shaktisri program: that each person is a valuable individual, trying her best, and that all she needed was to be empowered by the world-class entrepreneurial trainings that would be offered. The supertrainer aimed to motivate and inspire trainers to constantly improve to meet the needs of clients. During the six days of training that I observed, trainers responded to this laudable philosophy with skepticism. In many sessions, they complained that it was difficult to recruit clients for trainings and let the supertrainer and Kanchan leadership know that they lacked adequate space and resources with which to conduct the trainings. They also suggested that the clients they were supposed to target, Kanchan's microfinance clients, were inherently unsuited for these trainings. But the supertrainer, Kanchan managers, and office staff tried repeatedly to convince mostly young trainers that it was their job to make the training attractive and appealing to clients. These leaders assured trainers that the materials were of the best possible quality and that, as one leader put it, "it is *you* who must take it up. It is *you* who must motivate them."

Despite Shaktisri's participatory ethos in relation to clients, the process of training trainers relied upon organizational and status hierarchies. Trainers complained privately, and sometimes publicly, that Prosperity leaders did not take their concerns seriously, a suspicion that was further amplified by obvious class divisions between the two groups, especially in the training for trainers' session. Kanchan leaders expected trainers to operate as productive individuals who overcome constraints, rather than taking seriously the limited space, resources, and reception that trainers received with the client base. These internal dynamics are in themselves important, and I have written about them in more detail elsewhere.[7]

The extensive training-for-trainers program and the many contests within and around it, however, highlight the sustained investment in auxiliary training programs that MFIs like Kanchan continued to make, even when demonstrated results were dubious. The elaborate arrangements, investment of time, and constant working and reworking of the program, even in the few months I was there full-time, revealed that Kanchan leadership, trainers, and loan staff all wanted the program to be successful, or at least to appear to be successful. To serve this end, they searched for and validated success if and when they found it. They were convinced that the program was both helpful for their clients and for the legitimacy of their organizations, and this conviction sustained enthusiasm for the program as a whole.

But the fraught internal organizational dynamics I witnessed around the Shaktisri training also revealed the presumptions that both organizations—Prosperity and Kanchan—had about their clients' own subjectivities. I expected that client responses to empowerment programming would help me understand whether MFI assumptions about what was best for clients panned out in the real world. Prosperity claimed, both through staff in interviews and in pamphlets that were circulated in hard copies, that impact evaluations had been conducted by independent research organizations previously, and 75 percent of the clients trained experienced a benefit from their training experience.[8] But I was looking for something more than a polite statement from well-meaning clients that they enjoyed the training. I was interested in how clients engaged with trainers and the materials. How did training materials connect with clients around constructions of empowered womanhood, if at all they did? Quickly, I came to understand that clients and organizations came together around constructions of motherhood, which both sides of the divide viewed as crucial for borrowers' identities.

Financialization at Work: Working Motherhood and Self-Making

The vast feminist literature on globalization suggests that the material and ideological dimensions of motherhood are constructed, adopted, and contested in the context of the imperative for gendered subjects to work for a wage.[9] Such negotiations are critical for the continued expansion of global capitalism.[10] Building on our understanding that the financialization of poverty means the poor, especially women, are "enfolded"[11] by finance, what kinds of gendered subjectivities are needed for financial inclusion to be successful? Are they similar or distinct from neoliberal or entrepreneurial subjectivities[12] that have characterized the spread of neoliberal global capital?

Existing studies of subjectivity in the context of microfinance suggest that women's interactions with financial services relate to the contexts of both local and global ideologies of womanhood. A few studies suggest that microfinance specifically collateralizes women's status as married women who are mothers. Jude Fernando's study of NGO-led microfinance programs in rural Bangladesh found an NGO leader who explained, "Who but our mothers can run the family. [sic] She is the one, not father or the children who forgo their meals in order to meet the needs of the family."[13] Echoing these findings in rural Andhra Pradesh, Stephen Young found that field officers lend only to married women because they viewed unmarried women as too likely to move and thus give up membership in the group.[14]

But for the microfinance borrowers I studied, motherhood alone was not enough, especially for trainers who were interested in inspiring women to do more than "sit at home," a condition associated with being a stay-at-home mother. Being a mother with a certain level of income and need could be enough to gain access to a loan, but MFIS also wanted women to either work for a wage outside the home or be entrepreneurial. The Shaktisri training described above aimed to inspire women to become entrepreneurial, an ideology that has been observed with microfinance clients in other contexts. In Turkey, for example, Özlem Altan-Olcay's research with entrepreneurial training programs found that borrowers were interpolated as entrepreneurial mothers, and this positioning served to keep them at the lowest end of the labor market.[15] The Vriddhi training I observed, in contrast, interpolated clients as mothers who worked outside the home and managed the family finances. The program managers I spoke to did not expect their clients to be entrepreneurial but rather to be "working." They expected that their clients were domestic workers or engaged in other forms of low-wage, likely informal employment and that their husbands were similarly employed in semi-skilled or low-skilled professions. Still, like the teachers and designers of the Shaktisri program, Vriddhi managers wished to inspire women to manage their many roles in a way that would allow for greater financial security and, eventually, upward mobility. Both trainings emphasized how their clients' agency around work and finance could transform them as women and as mothers.

The program I call Vriddhi sought to empower Sowbagya borrowers through the promotion of financial literacy, a popular initiative in funding circles in recent years. Such trainings socialize clients into the responsible consumption of loans and other financial products and teach basic accounting skills. Each of Vriddhi's five modules consisted of an animated video featuring two sisters, one of whom is financially responsible and another who is not. In the first module, an animated video of two sisters sets up the ideal of the working mother:

> Khushi and Vishadi are two sisters who worked as daily laborers in the city. Six years back, both of them moved to the city with their husbands to earn a living. Khushi was married to Sandeep and had a son named Rupesh. Vishadi was married to Ramesh and had a son called Manohar. Khushi was older than Vishadi. Both Khushi and her husband were hardworking construction laborers who worked extra hours and saved money for their son's future. Sandeep had given up drinking two years back, and now, along with Khushi, saves money for their future. Each evening after dinner, Khushi and her husband count the money they have earned and their expenses for the day. Vishadi loves shopping and spends a lot of money on expensive toys for Manohar or cosmetics or jewelry for herself. Vishadi's husband Ramesh is a drunkard and spends his entire earnings on expensive liquor and gambling with his friends.

During this first film, Vishadi explains to her sister that she has taken out many loans from moneylenders and must now plan her sister-in-law's wedding, which will cost 1.3 lakhs (about $2,200), and put them in debt for years.

Khushi tells Vishadi that she has saved forty thousand rupees in the past two years due to financial planning and suggests that Vishadi start saving too, starting with the wedding. She advises that Vishadi distinguish between a want and a need, and scale back the wedding to something more modest. Vishadi protests and wonders what the neighbors will think if they put on a simple wedding. Khushi admonishes, "Vishadi, you should be worrying about your future and the future of your family, rather than thinking about what the neighbors will say if you serve three dishes instead of ten." Vishadi relents and agrees to speak with her husband.

In this module, as in the entire Vriddhi program, Khushi models responsible financial behavior for her irresponsible sister. Khushi works hard, keeps accounts, saves a bit of money for the future every day, and works with her husband to send her son to school. Khushi is always prepared, even for unexpected familial obligations or medical needs. Vishadi, in contrast, is sad because she is irresponsible. She does not seem to work for a wage, and she is constantly flirting with financial disaster, whether it is a big wedding or an unexpected accident. While oversimplified for pedagogic purposes, a clear ideal is being set out in this narrative: a working-class woman who is a good mother, a good worker, a responsible individual, and a savvy financial subject. This ideal, while not explicitly entrepreneurial, resonates with the ideals of heteronormative working motherhood expressed in the Shaktisri film.

The Shaktisri film I described earlier came at the end of a day-long module that aimed to introduce learners to a host of concepts that would support it. Beginning with the simple question, "Who am I?" ("Naan yaar?" in Tamil or "Naanu yaaru?" in Kannada), this module emphasized the idea of realizing oneself as someone with many strengths, rather than as "just" a woman or a mother. Once realized, the module suggested, these strengths could create new livelihood possibilities. Training activities in this module teach clients about money management by prioritizing wants and needs and always putting needs first. Time management activities ask women participants to list the tasks they have to do each day and identify areas where time is wasted. This will allow for the time needed to start a small business. Ultimately, every woman should think of herself as an entrepreneur (*thozhilmunaivor* in Tamil or *udhyemi* in Kannada). The film described at the opening of the chapter usually followed the various lessons and activities of the Self-Management module. The culturally specific illustrations underscore the idea that a borrower could be a tailor (see figure 5.1).

Both the Vriddhi and Shaktisri programs reveal the extent to which MFIS rely on women borrowers to be mothers first, while also modeling ideal

FIGURE 5.1. Shaktisri suggests that clients should empower themselves by becoming tailors in these culturally specific drawings from training materials.

women who do more than mothering; they work for a wage and manage family finances. Both modules presume that the audience members identify first and foremost as mothers and build upon the presumption that their clients' primary ambitions would be geared toward their children's care and education. For Vriddhi's audience, this ambition can be fulfilled through careful management of one's finances. Money and credit, the films emphasize, are resources that women clients can and must control in order to be, literally, "Khushi"—happy. These can be maximized by managing expenditures and saving. For Shaktisri's audience, the ambition to have one's children advance through good mothering can be fulfilled through careful management of one's time, which will in turn make space for entrepreneurial activities. These entrepreneurial activities (which implicitly require a loan to start) will allow you to be your own boss, a strong woman who builds on her own strengths. Together, the Vriddhi and Shaktisri films, and the training activities that accompany them, offered women clients a framework for a new set of gendered ideals around organization and productivity that MFIs have been promoting in the name of women's empowerment.

The *working mother* ideal set forth in these programs merges the imperative of work or microenterprise with the ideals of motherhood and in so doing encourages small-scale, low-wage work for women at the bottom of the labor market, while collateralizing their status as mothers. Drawing from a relatively standardized complement of global themes and images that merge women's productive and reproductive roles, trainings offer new ways to integrate those roles—entrepreneurialism, financial literacy, and management—without challenging the subordination that clients face both in their families and in the labor market.

Model Entrepreneurs Make Success Stories

Selvi sat on the doorstep of her modest, free-standing home to speak with me, my research assistant, and her local Prosperity trainer, Nandini. Selvi had taken four Shaktisri modules and ran a business making and selling plates made out of the leaves of areca nut trees, harvested from a type of hearty indigenous tree common to the area. A year after my interview with Selvi, she appeared in a publicity video about Prosperity's client education programs. In the video, Selvi's areca leaf plate-making machines run in the background, as she praises the Shaktisri program for sparking her ambition to be an entrepreneur (see figure 5.2). The narrative she shared with me in her interview was equally admiring of the Shaktisri program, especially with

From these modules I learned about time management and how to efficiently manage my own business while tending to my family life.

FIGURE 5.2. Selvi's areca plate-making machine in a Prosperity publicity video.

regard to its time management training but considerably more complex in its account of her entrepreneurial journey.

Selvi finished twelfth grade and was married by the age of eighteen. She then lived in a joint family with in-laws who did not wish for her to work outside the home. Once she had two children, however, it became clear that her husband alone could not manage the household expenses, and the family relented. Selvi and her husband opened a petty shop together—a joint entrepreneurial venture. Soon, they opened a cab agency, accessing financing from local banks. The cab agency was running fine, but business was erratic due to the seasonal nature of temple tourism in her area. She decided she wanted to do something on her own. She began a paper plate manufacturing business, taking a small business loan of 1.5 lakhs of rupees (about $2,800) from a bank. Due to dishonest clients, poor knowledge of marketing strategies, and depreciation of the machine she purchased, she only recouped eighty thousand rupees (about $1,300) of the original loan. She put in forty thousand (about $650) of her own funds, from a gold loan,[16] to pay off the bank loan and began afresh.

For the next five years, along with fourteen other women in her self-help group, Selvi tried out a number of microbusinesses requiring hand-powered machines (such as mat weaving) or no machines at all (such as jewelry making). Then Selvi and her group encountered the Shaktisri training program for entrepreneurs. For her, it was transformative, especially the section on time management, which is part of the Self-Management module described above:

> I used to work to suit my comfort level. I used to get up a 6 a.m., have my milk, and sit and laze until 7 or so . . . After they gave me a time-table and asked me how much time is getting wasted, then whenever I started the day's cooking, I would cook for my daughter as well. If I save that time, I can weave ten extra mats . . . We have now started working for eight hours a day. Now, I save the time and use it to earn money.

Over the next three years, the members of Selvi's self-help group learned how to work together. They learned how to market their products and how to repay on time in order to procure larger loans in the future. A year before our interview, and after much research and thought, Selvi's group secured a loan of two lakhs of rupees ($3300) for the areca nut leaf plate-making machine from a government-sponsored program for promoting small businesses in rural areas. When we visited, the machine was stalled due to state-imposed power cuts in her area, but Selvi felt confident that once they had power again they would have a successful business. Selvi's narrative reads like a textbook for women's empowerment, as she explains:

> I am not dependent on my husband now for all my needs . . . He will occasionally say, "After you started earning, you are not respecting me," . . . but that is not so. When I go out and tell him that I will be spending this much money, he will say, "It is your money. Spend it as you wish." To that extent, I am happy.

By Selvi's own account, she has reaped tremendous benefits from the Shaktisri program, making her a credit to the program as a whole.

When we put her story into the context of her group and my broader sample, however, we come to see just how exceptional Selvi was. In her self-help group of fifteen women, thirteen were construction workers, and Selvi was the only one in her group who wished to run an entrepreneurial venture rather than work in the formal economy for a fixed wage. Her twelfth-grade education made her the most educated of her peers, and more educated than the majority of my client sample. Her husband, already an entrepreneur with a successful cab agency business, provided a stable livelihood for her family, even while they were waiting for the power to come back on so they could start making the plates. This means that Selvi was similar to the most well-off women in my sample, though none of the women I met through chance encounters at training sessions were as entrepreneurially inclined as she. While the Shaktisri program surely had a catalyzing effect on Selvi, she was already privileged compared to her peers and thus in a prime position to take advantage of the training. Through the Shaktisri program, she not only learned the skills needed for business, such as marketing, but learned how to restructure her time such that it complied with the recommendations of the module and resolved any tensions between childcare, productive work, and loan repayment. And yet, despite her embrace of a working mother identity, Selvi continued to wait for real entrepreneurial success. At the time of our meeting, her success had been in securing the loan and the machinery, but she had not yet earned a profit from any of her businesses. This extremely delayed reward for her efforts raises the question: was Selvi's success really a success?

Selvi's experience is critical for understanding an ideal situation in which MFI trainings help to transform the subjectivity of a talented woman, turning her into a mother who is also an entrepreneur. At first gloss, her success story showcases the benefits of MFI loans and trainings, and the promise of financial inclusion. But closer examination reveals that Selvi was already well integrated into India's banking system and had access to many forms of formal and informal financing, including a loan from the government and from conventional banks. Indeed, the training that Selvi's group had received for the businesses they had started had been aimed at their collective success, rather than Selvi's individual time management, and the business itself was a result of state funding for small businesses. Yet, Kanchan was able to selectively appropriate her story in order symbolize women's empowerment, even though Selvi is yet to experience any financial benefit from her long journey with entrepreneurialism.

Kanchan's narrative about Selvi's success purposely overlooks the reality that Selvi continues to be firmly situated within her self-help group, which is benefiting from a government program. Although Julia Elyachar showed that microfinance in Cairo promoted an individual instrumentality that undermined social relations,[17] in Tamil Nadu it was possible for Selvi to embrace both the entrepreneurial subjectivity on offer from Kanchan and the collective business model promoted by state programming. Selvi's empowerment, then, while consistent with dominant global narratives of neoliberal subjectivity, articulated in a distinct, collectively oriented regional context, resonant with state priorities. Selvi's vision for her community draws on strategies for surviving poverty within her community and fuses them with available opportunities. Such efforts to make microfinance fit within local frames of sociality have been found across various regions in India.[18] While Selvi makes these accommodations, Kanchan is able to dub her story a success and take credit for Selvi's sheer grit and persistence in the face of steep odds and multiple failures. They must make it appear as if it was the loans and training made the crucial difference and brought Selvi empowerment and her family financial stability, even if this interpretation misrepresents the fuller reality of Selvi's situation. The extraction of Selvi's story furthers corporate aims, promoting Kanchan's legitimacy and standing among local and international audiences.

Empowerment, Declined

In a small room situated in a Bengaluru slum, fifteen women were gathered expectantly as Prashanth, an experienced trainer, began the Self-Management module of the Shaktisri training. Most of the women seemed interested and enthusiastic, and broke into groups to discuss the "Who am I" question. But by the time the group came together again for discussion, Padmavathi, one of the group leaders, loudly questioned how long they were expected to be there. She had a lot of work to do. Without waiting for an answer from Prashanth, she got up and stated for a second time that she had a lot of work, and so did the other group members. Prashanth said he could come back tomorrow, quietly acquiescing to her request on behalf of the group to end the session, even though it had only just begun. Within minutes, the group dispersed with Padmavathi leading the way. In my field notes, I observed that the expressions and body language of the women gathered suggested that many would have stayed if Prashanth had requested it, but he did not.[19] Several of the women who had gathered returned to their homes and stood or sat in their doorways, which lined the narrow urban lane, appearing to be less busy than their neighbor claimed. But Padmavathi and the three other women supporting her disappeared from the area, signaling their lack of interest (and busyness) strongly. As I saw it, Padmavathi had single-handedly sabotaged the training session.

A few weeks later, I managed to track down Padmavathi with the help of my research assistant Mamatha. Padmavathi, age twenty-five, a wife and mother with a tenth-grade education, was a longtime Sowbagya customer who took a loan from Kanchan for the first time that year. She spoke approvingly of Sowbagya, appreciating that they offered her many types of loans with different interest rates (i.e., education loan, water filter loan, building loan), shared useful information, and otherwise let her be. But she had grown impatient with Kanchan's Self-Management training session. She ran a flower business but considered herself a housewife. When I asked her what she thought of the training, she laughed. "They [Kanchan] should know that lecture was of no benefit," she opined. "They asked us, 'Who am I?' Generally, a women's reply would be 'I am a housewife,' or 'I am a woman,' or at least they might say, 'I am a girl,' to that question. Will they say, 'I am a working woman'? Nobody would say that, right? Women laughed when they asked that question. When they came outside, they were joking about that. What kind of a question is 'Who am I?'" Padmavathi's rejection of the discourses being presented in the Shaktisri training suggests that the very idea of being a working woman was not just distant to her but distasteful: why would anyone say they identified with that? By her account, her friends were joking about it, even though I had observed smiles and affirmative body language from them, suggesting appreciation. My surprise at her dismissal of the entire training was reminiscent of the earlier training described above, where I had mistakenly interpreted Kamala to be enthusiastic about the materials.

Although trainers and Kanchan staff interpreted such instances as evidence of women's lack of confidence or inherent unfitness for the training, Padmavathi's narrative suggests that MFI borrowers may self-consciously decide they are not interested in programs that encourage them to adopt a working mother identity. Most clients do not identify with a working mother identity on a personal level, nor do they see how this identity relates to the improvement of their lives or the enhancement of their status in their communities. For Padmavathi, walking away from the training represented an affirmation of her existing identity and a push against further efforts to increase her productivity or change how she viewed herself. Compared to Selvi, Padmavathi's educational profile and livelihood are more similar to those of most MFI customers I met. Thus, while Padmavathi was more outspoken than most, her views may reflect those of many members.

Still, there were cases in which women from modest working-class backgrounds expressed outward appreciation and enjoyment of Shaktisri's materials. I attended four screenings of the Shaktisri film promoting entrepreneurship, and they evoked varied responses. While the women I described at the beginning of the chapter responded indifferently or with confusion to the film, just the day before, in a similar setting with the same trainer, an audience of forty women had a long, animated discussion of how important it is for women to have confidence in their own abilities, grasping the importance of women's empowerment (see figure 5.3). An older woman, Parvathy,

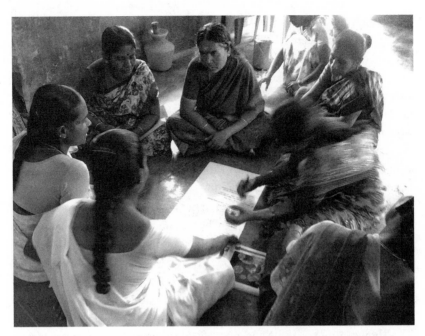

FIGURE 5.3. In some circumstances, clients participated in the training with apparent enjoyment, as in this session in Coimbatore.

who had been selling a special type of bhaji made of chilies, a delectable fried treat, for over twenty years, felt that the training had spoken directly to her. During the discussion, she raised her hand to say how much she liked it. Wasn't she an entrepreneur like the women in the film, she asked proudly? Everyone smiled and applauded for Parvathy. Still, the group did not follow up with Nandini for a second training.

In two other instances, with charismatic trainer Rajiv, women focused on the end of the film, in which women who looked like them discussed why their businesses succeeded or failed. Rather than inquiring about the abstract concepts presented in that segment (i.e., Was the product a good fit for the market? How can you innovate on your product?), the participants wanted to know whether they could receive training to make candles or soap or dolls, much to Rajiv's dismay. When he was unable to provide concrete leads on trainings for these products, this group also politely refused Rajiv's offer to return for the second module.

Leaders and trainers alike thus found themselves frustrated by what they viewed as the inability of their women clients to learn world-class lessons, adapted specifically for these working-class Indian clients.[20] Maya, the director of Client Education at Shaktisri, narrated such an instance in her interview. Maya recalled that a group of twenty-two members had gathered for a training session in Bengaluru, and one of the group members had received a large order from Saudi Arabia to embroider four thousand burkhas. This member was complaining that she could not find anyone to help her with such a large order. The facilitator had tried to recruit embroiderers and had failed. On the day Maya attended the training, she examined the registration cards of the women gathered and found that five women had written on their forms that they were tailors who did embroidery. Maya continued to recollect:

> So, I just stood up and I said, "Look, Hussaina is asking for five tailors who can do the embroidery for her. Why were you sitting quiet? You know, instantaneously, your empowerment and motivation should be to just stand up and get that order. What made you keep quiet? . . . You come to Self-Management. What does Self-Management teach you? What was the welcome letter all about? It was to empower you as an entrepreneur. And what was the question on your worksheet? Who am I? What did you write?" She said, "I wrote I am a housewife." And I asked the second one and she said, "Yeah, I wrote I am a mother." I said, "Why didn't you write you're an entrepreneur or you're a tailor?" She said, "Nothing great I am doing. So, I thought, you know, should I put that on paper?" Then I realized they are shy to disclose their identity as an entrepreneur.

Maya's tone in recounting the story was admonishing toward the women gathered, while also casting doubt on whether the facilitator had done a good job. From Maya's perspective, women with skills who consider themselves mothers first must also be proud of their skills and conceive of themselves as entrepreneurs. Maya expressed frustration that she and her team had offered them an incredible opportunity for empowerment, and they were just not taking it.

Some of the women who frustrated Maya so much might have genuinely suffered from a lack of confidence, but many others might have self-consciously chosen not to participate. Contrary to Maya's assumptions, there are many reasons why they would not wish to do that work. The clients I interviewed understood embroidery as difficult, devalued work that was usually not worth the time they put into it. One MFI member I interviewed, Halima, used to embroider dresses but decided that the paltry wages were unsatisfactory. "You spend the whole day doing a dress and try to sell it for 170 (under $3), and people want it for 150 (about $2.50), which would barely cover the costs." Halima chose to stay home while her daughter was young. She continues to take loans and repay them, knowing that consistent repayment would qualify her for larger loans in the future. Eventually, Halima thought she might be able to obtain a loan large enough to put a deposit down on a commercial rental space, out of which she could run her husband's mobile phone repair business.

As I observed in the trainings, women I interviewed expressed the wish to learn a worthwhile business that would help them earn money for their families. And some were still willing to give Shaktisri a chance to do that. Shortly after a Shaktisri training I attended in Bengaluru, I went to a client's house for an interview at an appointed time. Lakshmi was a twenty-four-year-old mother of three with a seventh-grade education. Youthful and bright-eyed, she welcomed us with a smile into her tiny one-room, asbestos roof home, situated in a narrow lane. When Mamatha and I arrived, a tanker drove precariously into the narrow lane, inches from the homes that lined the street, to drain the sewage from the area, leaving little space for us to chat. Unlike many other clients I visited, Lakshmi had no television, almost no furniture, and no refrigerator. Her husband Chandra had directed us to their home on a motorbike, which was likely their most valuable possession. Chandra ran a small tailor shop with inconsistent income. As she put it, "Sometimes one thousand rupees a day (twenty dollars), sometimes one hundred (two dollars)."

Lakshmi had attended a Shaktisri training recently and had really enjoyed it. She liked that they were encouraging her to do a business, and she was very interested in "doing something," rather than "sitting at home." "What is the use in that?" she asked rhetorically. After further conversation, we learned that she had been exposed to many trainings encouraging her to start a business, but none had quite panned out as she had hoped. Her mother, a woman in her fifties who was there in the same room while we were interviewing Lakshmi, interjected at one point in the interview that they had both learned to make candles in a training recently. But the high-quality wax was ninety-five rupees a kilo, and it took much time and practice to make the candles and set the string straight inside. And local churches were only willing to pay one hundred rupees a kilo for candles. So, business did not turn out to be worthwhile.

Through Mamatha, I told Lakshmi that Shaktisri was different from these other trainings because it aimed to show her how to actually run a business well, not just how to make a particular product. Shaktisri was aiming to train women to figure out how to decide what to make, how to market it, get customers, and keep the business going, I explained. Lakshmi did not seem to understand what I meant by this. As if to respond to my explanation, she grabbed the glossy booklet that Prosperity had handed out in the recent training and turned to the back cover, which showcased women from all over the world making various indigenous crafts for sale. The image was meant to portray a global view of women's empowerment through entrepreneurship. "This," she pointed out to me, indicating a photo of a South American woman who had woven a large shawl with an indigenous print. "Of all the options they show here, I pick this one. When will the training for this one be?"

Like many of the women I spoke with, Lakshmi was more interested in an outside party coming to tell her, in very specific terms, exactly what she should do. Like others, she was looking for a real income stream. Not a set of concepts, not a framework, not inspiration, not personal transformation. She wanted directions. Even though the last attempt—candle-making—had not penciled out, Lakshmi expected that Shaktisri would provide her another chance. She was likely to be let down once she realized that the trainings provided no concrete directions. When she looked at the training materials, which were meant to inspire her to self-reflection in order to make her into a savvy entrepreneur, she saw something else entirely: a menu of options for unique handmade products that she too could learn to make. Trainers who worked in her area, including Prashanth and Rajan, simply could not offer Lakshmi such a training. This discrepancy made her not suitable for the trainings in Kanchan's eyes and would eventually make the Shaktisri trainings disappointing for her. But the profound disjuncture between her wishes and the offerings of the program would not threaten the existence of Kanchan's programming. The company was uninterested in the aspirations and hopes of a client like Lakshmi. Excluding the stories of women like Lakshmi is as essential for effective symbolic extraction as selectively appropriating Selvi's story for a vast corporate and foreign audience.

Conclusion

MFI trainings meant to empower women clients, as well as client responses to such offerings, help us understand both the ambitions and limits of financial inclusion as a set of policies that have created a gendered financial ecosystem in India. They also illuminate a site at which the extraction of symbolic value occurs, primarily through selective appropriation of relatively prosperous women's biographies. MFI trainings reveal that financial inclusion is not merely about providing financial services to those who do not have them, nor is it about diverse forms of financial capital having new social groups that offer a new opportunity for profit. It also involves a distinct cultural project that promotes a specific kind working-class womanhood that is compatible with the financial capitalism prevalent in her given context. This understanding amplifies the discussion of the governance of gender introduced in chapter 2 to show that these training programs emulate state programs and aim to cultivate specific kinds of women, albeit not often successfully. Running in parallel with global gender and development discourses aimed at producing women's productivity through education, training programs aim to convince women that their individual decisions around time management, financial management, and savings can improve the situation for themselves and their families.

When a borrower applies for credit, her request might be declined, perhaps because she has a poor credit record or because the lender does not believe she has the resources to repay. In the case of empowerment trainings, which many MFIs bundle with loans, it is the borrower who "declines" the promise for self-transformation on offer because they do not believe it can improve their lives. Clients wished instead for a concrete pathway to a more reliable livelihood given their marginalized circumstances, something which none of the organizations I studied were willing or able to provide. There might be many other reasons women declined the transformed sense of self on offer in these training sessions; the women I saw rejecting the promise of empowerment trainings did not belong to any single group. But whatever their varied backgrounds, clients sought to preserve their own existing assumptions for what worked in their lives and what they aspired to in the future. These clients remained willing loan takers but politely refused the opportunity to be subject to symbolic extraction.

In contrast, those who truly embraced the notion of self-improvement through a working mother identity, such as Selvi, were more highly educated and financially stable than most of their peers. In rural Bangladesh, Karim also found that better-off women made the most successful borrowers.[21] While better-off borrowers may be more successful, ironically, they may also be more vulnerable to global finance's soft power. Their superior education and status may predispose them to find the ideal of working motherhood more appealing than their peers. Still, they are unlikely to materially benefit from the internalization of that ideal. As shown in Selvi's case, MFI ideals, oriented toward individual success, may even work at cross-purposes with the state's vision of women's empowerment, which are often collective.

While Selvi appeared to benefit from empowerment training, she was still stymied by structural factors outside her control (i.e., power cuts), waiting for her day in the sun of self-sufficiency.

In urban India, MFIS are beholden to clients in unexpected ways. They must compete with other MFIS for the opportunity to lend small amounts of money to women who are difficult to train or discipline. Field staff must deal with myriad forms of rejection from clients, especially when they bring in new ideas about empowerment, entrepreneurialism, or financial literacy. These ground realities provide a snapshot of the fraught negotiations that constitute financial inclusion processes on the ground. Women clients contest the material and symbolic extraction of gendered value. Nonetheless, MFIS manage to extract that value from a small group. The legitimacy they gain from these interactions allows MFIS to pass as state-like in relation to clients, offering similar combinations of loans and training and thus validating financial inclusion as a state project. Through training, MFIS produce and circulate discourses that encourage women clients to combine their productive and reproductive roles through entrepreneurship or financial management, activities that further expand and extend credit-work discussed in earlier chapters. When women clients develop identities as entrepreneurs or financial managers for their families, they reduce risk for financial companies by ensuring that new recruits to the system can repay, no matter what. But when clients decided they wished to be just mothers who took the loans and went on their way, they pushed back against the expectations of financial companies. In so doing, they defied any presumption that financial inclusion would entail intimate transformation.

6. DISTORTIONS OF DISTANCE

When I started writing this book, I expected that MFIS located in the US, especially those who had previously provided funding to Indian MFIS, would have significant influence in shaping the worlds of loaning and training in India. But as I have shown in chapter 1, for Indian MFIS at least, state and institutional environments, as well as domestic banking capital, together determine the shape and trajectory of the industry. All-India regulations limit the influence of foreign capital, and Indian MFIS were unable to scale up until the Reserve Bank made a rule change that allowed Indian banks to funnel money toward commercial MFIS to fulfill their obligations to lend to marginalized groups. But it is undeniable that influential microfinancial actors in the global North continue to shape funding, ideology, and knowledge. To explore these influences, this chapter pivots away from the specific context of Indian microfinance to explore the perspectives and actions of microfinancial actors located in the global North, often an invisible audience for Indian firms seeking global visibility and legitimacy. Microfinancial actors in the global North—and here, I identify these actors as everyday citizens lending online in the peer-to-peer platform Kiva.org as well as professionals employed in US based MFI firms—feel personally responsible for taking action against the devastation of poverty. Yet, as I will show here, the specific interests, knowledge base, and social and political environments of these social actors keep them at a distance from the real policies that shape borrowers' lives. Adopting an actor-oriented perspective on these agents of development,[1] I show that they produce an artificial relationality that obscures the real relational work of microfinance, which unfolds among clients and between clients and MFIS (see chapters 3 and 4).

The existing literature leads us to believe that Northern publics play a significant role in MFI operations. Ananya Roy's work on poverty experts shows that policy makers at global financial institutions set the rules and standards by which MFIS around the world must play.[2] Lamia Karim's ethnographic work also suggests that corporations based in Europe and the US have a significant presence in Bangladeshi MFIS.[3] Philip Mader's work on the political economy of microfinance emphasizes both international and intensely local influences in India but still suggests that the disciplining effects of microfinance operate from the top down; much of the venture capital for microfinance comes from companies in the global North who have increasingly turned to financial products in order to earn profits. These investment companies view microfinance as a smart investment when new opportunities through which to lucratively invest capital in developed markets seem to be saturating.[4]

Furthermore, we know that microfinancial actors located in the US and other global North countries exert an indirect influence on the Indian microfinance industry. The World Bank's Consultative Group to Assist the Poor (CGAP) has long served as a validating stamp for the industry worldwide. Even Mohammad Yunus has admitted that MFIS need CGAP's validation for legitimacy.[5] Other stakeholders include philanthropic investors, financial companies that specialize in social impact investing, venture capitalists, and microfinance institutions such as ACCION, Kiva, Excelsior Growth Fund, and Grameen America. These companies provide microloans within the United States and also partner with organizations in other countries. In addition, as mentioned in chapter 2, US college graduates seek work in MFIS at home and abroad regularly and thus provide a pipeline of young talent to companies around the world. Others take up work for CGAP, the largest consultant on financial inclusion matters worldwide. When Northern microfinancial actors enter into the space of microfinance, they enter from a position of strength due to their wealth, education, or employment and can be highly influential.

Northern actors also matter to microfinance because of the imagined connections between these actors and actual microfinance borrowers. In the previous chapter, I showed that empowerment trainings in Indian microfinance reproduce the neoliberal logics of prevailing gender and development paradigms that focus on the individual. The audiences for these trainings are often funders or investors abroad who are eager to see such programs put into effect. Building on this, this chapter reveals a relational sleight of hand that Northern development actors carry out through their engagements with a purposely decontextualized, gendered, and racialized understanding of microfinance: they can fabricate socially meaningful relationships between themselves and end-borrowers based on false or limited information that can then fuel a misplaced sense of satisfaction about making a difference. These relationships help to create a halo for MFIS around the world that acts as a powerful cover for the gendered extraction that drives the industry. Rather than lobbying for new policies that would address the global structural conditions that make life for women in the global South precarious, these agents of millennial development justify and promote commercial microfinance operations in India and around the world while at the same time erasing the real work of lending and training that allows MFIS to run profitably.

Professional and nonprofessional agents of microfinance in the global North make women in different parts of the world appear similar to one another, while sometimes forging an intimate, emotional connection to specific borrowers or groups of borrowers. Yet, when these groups encounter critical information about those operations that conflicts with existing understandings, they ignore or discredit such information, particularly if they are already deeply invested in the ideology of microfinance. These affective, professional, or charitable activities can provide cover for MFIS around the world, allowing MFIS to escape sustained scrutiny for their practices. These actions also allow the racialized, feminine face of financial inclusion policies to continue to be a false symbol for women's empowerment.

How Similar Are Kiva.org Lenders and MFI Workers in the US?

Does it make sense to draw a comparison between everyday humanitarians like Kiva.org lenders and MFI professionals employed in the US and other Western countries? Kiva.org lenders feel compelled to address global poverty but do not necessarily have any specific specialization related to poverty or development. In contrast, MFI professionals located in the US have made a decision to work in the global microfinance industry and often have qualifications in Economics, Education, Development, or other related fields. MFI professionals located in the US view microfinance as a viable career that can also be virtuous. I suggest here that despite their divergent positions and levels of knowledge, their geopolitical location and perspective makes them similar kinds of actors in the global field of development discourse and practice. Both US-based MFI professionals and Kiva lenders carry out their development work with (at best) an arm's length understanding of the women who are served by their partners in other countries.

Kiva.org lenders and MFI professionals share a largely visual imagination of a generic Third world woman, forged through well-composed photographs that make poverty into a spectacle. Conventional images of microfinance also perpetuate an idealized understanding of entrepreneurialism and femininity.[6] Because of these influences, a relatively simplistic understanding of financial inclusion, gender, and poverty exists in both groups. When considered together, the actions of both Kiva.org lenders and microfinance professionals sustain what Chandra Mohanty has called an "ahistorical, universal unity among [Third World] women based on their subordination"[7] that then appears to be easily addressed through small loans and microentrepreneurialism. Microfinance clients are similar to one another because they are understood as existing outside social relations, not constituted by them.[8] Northern microfinancial actors dismiss the real relationships of power and affect that women clients around the world live in, such as class and political dynamics, even among women in the same lending group, as explored in chapter 4. These actors regard the limitations that women face, often a result of complex inequalities, as a factor of "culture," which can (perhaps) be surmounted through entrepreneurial activity and economic self-sufficiency. Such constructions are typical of neoliberal feminism and current prevailing regimes of corporatized development.[9]

Because both groups possess decidedly different levels of investment in the very idea of microfinance, their commitment to microfinance as a cause or solution differs as well, making microfinance professionals sometimes more resistant to new information than Kiva lenders, who can simply find another way to be charitable. For most Kiva lenders, the financial investment in their charitable act is small (as little as twenty-five dollars), and thus the emotional investment can also be quite small. A compelling critique of Kiva, a decline in interest, or just a lack of motivation can lead all but the most committed lenders to drop off the platform.

For MFI professionals, however, the investment is much greater. They have dedicated their careers, or at least some part of their careers, to the enterprise of microfinance and training. When conflicting information arises, then, I found that there is a deliberate effort to avoid or discredit the information in order to get on with their work and feel secure in their altruistic motivation. They are able to do this because, unlike Indian MFIs, they are not accountable to either state governments or a particular polity. Instead, they work to provide equity investments to partner institutions and sell training products to partner organizations. Their only audience, then, are other financial companies, including their own investors and their financial partners abroad.

This lack of political accountability allows MFI professionals and Kiva lenders alike to sustain a conviction that they are helping, even when presented with evidence to the contrary. Both groups often feel doubtful about the impact of their activism or virtuous work, but many continue to engage and support microfinance, sometimes with surprising tenacity. Doubts about microfinance can easily dissuade most Kiva lenders. But even microfinance professionals are not entirely convinced that microfinance improves women's lives. Still, they aim to expand the business in service of trying to "do something" in an ethical way, without ever considering that a deeper understanding of client lives could go a long way toward making their work ethical.

Kiva and Prosperity in Relation to Indian MFIs

But how are Kiva and Prosperity connected to the commercial companies that I studied in India and to India's commercial microfinance sector more broadly? Kiva is a San Francisco-based nonprofit that has maintained its four-star rating on the highly regarded charity ratings website, Charity Navigator. Since their founding in 2005, however, the company has faced criticism. When journalists and economists showed that funds lent on the platform often went to for-profit financial companies without explicit social aims, Kiva started including more information on its website about its partner organizations. The vetting process for partners became more stringent, requiring companies to articulate explicit social aims and programs. The company soon introduced a social badge on the website, allowing lenders to seek loans provided by organizations with an explicit social mission. In India, Kiva loans started going to small NGOs and cooperatives reaching out to women in remote areas, rather than funding large MFIs such as those I studied. I discovered, then, that there was little direct funding from Kiva's platform to the most successful and widespread Indian MFIs. On the whole, Kiva has made fewer loans to South Asia as the commercialization of microfinance in the region has accelerated. This was a surprising finding for me as I delved into the virtual world of microfinance and realized that the visually engaging, convenient, and popular website had few direct links to the specific companies I was studying or their competitors.

Prosperity, on the other hand, was directly connected to commercial MFIS in India. In the early 2000s, Prosperity had provided equity capital and technical assistance, consulting to improve the efficiency of business processes, to several major MFIS in India, fueling their rapid expansion. Leaders like Vikram Akula, Samit Ghosh, and others actively sought out US-based venture capital to scale up their businesses and succeeded. Once those operations were successful, however, US investors exited the company, taking their share of profits with them and (in most cases) left behind a larger, sturdier company than before they put their money in. Thus, infusions of equity capital from Prosperity and other companies bolstered the business operations of Indian MFIS and made them larger and more efficient companies. Prosperity continued to maintain some contact with those organizations while continuing with technical assistance. Prosperity also continued to participate in the Indian microfinance industry through the provision of client education offerings. Client education comprised a small but important part of Prosperity's operations. Those involved with client education felt passionately about it and were eager for the programs to be successfully implemented in India. Thus, even though Prosperity was not necessarily directly funding Indian MFIS, its indirect and continued influence was evident, and operations in India always remained visible in corporate discussions.

Given these disparate material orientations to Indian microfinance, what shared discourses have informed the views of both Kiva lenders and professionals at Prosperity? And how might these groups carry out important political and ideological work for the industry?

Histories of Helping Women, and the Neoliberal Twist

Ananya Roy argues that millennial development "relies greatly on the modern, Western self who is not only aware of poverty's devastation but is also empowered to act upon it in responsible ways."[10] This action can take multiple forms, from active humanitarian intervention to the pursuit of careers in the development sector to passive consumerist action through Kiva.org loans or donations to Heifer International.[11] All of these actions have embedded within them an emotional sense of connection, which Anke Schwittay terms affective investments Roy similarly identifies this emotional element, arguing that millennial development is composed of "intimate transactions"[12] that are anchored in a singular view of the Third World woman. This Third World woman seems accessible in these interactions, especially on platforms like Kiva.org. "It is the Third World woman, Millennial Woman, who . . . transforms the distance of gender and race into a liberal intimacy with the world's poor."[13]

As Mohanty and others have pointed out, this universalizing Western gaze emerges directly from the "old" justification for colonialism—that "white men are saving brown women from brown men."[14] The oppression of women in so-called traditional cultures has long provided a justification for both colonialist rule and subsequent nationalist reform. The literature on these dynamics is particularly developed in the Indian context. Subaltern studies historians have shown that the "women's question" provided a compelling impetus for colonial, and later nationalist, intervention.[15] But as Edward Said's (1978) classic work on Orientalism shows, these discourses, far from being particular to India, undergird resonant notions of cultural power between East and West that extend beyond the colonial encounter or nationalist movements. These discourses continue to structure current scholarship, debate, and political discussion.[16]

But in millennial development, neoliberal ideology transforms that justification. Rather than the white man saving the woman, the woman seems to be saving herself, with the assistance of a loan. Thus, empowerment tropes underpin microfinance in the West and are seldom critical of the relationships—material or otherwise—in which women borrowers are embedded while engaging in loan-taking. This trope does not openly rationalize Western cultural or economic intervention but rather relies on a "flattened" understanding of microfinance to hold up poor women as saviors of themselves and the world. Lacking the perspective of social and material relations on the ground, then, Northern publics are unfailingly supportive of microfinance, in whatever form it happens to appear. The loan allows the new Third World woman of millennial development to be empowered by shedding the weight of her patriarchal culture and becoming an efficient allocator of scarce resources.

But this claim is not as obvious or liberatory as it appears. As I have shown in this book, the reliance on women to save themselves emerges from a neoliberal regulatory regime and an abdication of the state's responsibility to provide fair financial services to all its citizens. The notion that women can save themselves emerges not as a radical inversion of colonial discourse but rather as an extension of prevailing global dynamics that continue to locate previously colonized countries in a subordinate economic and cultural position within the global economy.

Despite the empirical reality that funding from Kiva plays a miniscule role in the expansion of India's microfinance industry, the website gives borrowers an exaggerated belief in the impact of their lending for the world's poor. Lenders on Kiva.org believe that the website gives them familiarity with India and other countries they may have no understanding of and encourages lenders to shop for a loan to fund and feel good about. At Kiva, lenders believe that microfinance is fundamentally about promoting microenterprise among poor women, an image that most companies in the industry have left behind long ago. The stubborn innocence of Kiva lenders, which I explore in the next section, gives cover for the industry's extractive practices and allows these financial companies to largely escape scrutiny in the US. This most public face preserves a halo that the industry has itself dispensed with and continues to promote the ideology of microfinance as a path toward women's self-sufficiency.[17]

A nonprofit founded in 2005, Kiva.org has become arguably the most visible advocate for microfinance in the US. The compelling idea of lending to a businessperson in the global South, getting the money back, and then lending it to someone else finds an easy audience among especially liberal, well-traveled citizens in the US. Kiva.org's superior online experience of choosing a borrower and conveniently sending her money sweetens the appeal, making the process as enjoyable and flawless as an Amazon.com purchase. Kiva.org presents a vision of microfinance focused on the compelling stories of mostly individual women pursuing a small enterprise. Through this highly appealing storyline, laden with moral imperatives that promote self-sufficiency, women's causes, and global solidarity, Kiva.org continues to present a simplified portrait of global microfinance, supported by lenders who rely on Kiva to address their sense of responsibility for poverty worldwide. Publicized widely by the *New York Times*[18] in its initial days, Kiva.org's scope and influence has continued to grow.

Today, the organization boasts over 1.6 million lenders, has programs in every region of the world, and has expanded its loan offerings to include loans for education, green building, green technology, and home improvement. Increasingly, Kiva.org appeals to anyone who feels that they must personally do something about global poverty and creates the urge to do something for those who may not yet feel so compelled. The website finds its way into gifts between family members and friends, social studies courses in high school, and economics courses in colleges. Here, I draw from interviews, survey data, and a data scrape of the open-access website conducted in 2015 to show how Kiva.org helps to keep alive a misleading fantasy about how microfinance works for the women who take out loans. At the same time, I find that lenders themselves connect the small amounts of money loaned and re-loaned on the website with their own sense of personhood.

Lenders on Kiva.org, usually in the US, can choose from thousands of predominantly women borrowers from nearly every region of the world. Each borrower is represented online with a photo and a biographical story, detailing their marital status and children and their aspirations to establish or expand a microenterprise. Lenders are invited to get acquainted with these borrowers, pick one or more whose stories resonate with them, and lend as little as $25 before a loan campaign for a particular borrower runs out. When the borrower pays back, the lender gets the money back as well and can lend to another worthy borrower of their choosing.

TRYING TO DO THE RIGHT THING

Christina was a librarian with a new baby and plans for another in the future when I interviewed her in 2015. For her wedding, she and her husband invited their guests to contribute, in lieu of a wedding gift, to a joint loan portfolio on Kiva.org. Christina and her husband gathered over $500 from their wedding guests and immediately selected deserving borrowers to lend to. They had been recycling those loans for many years now, and the experience gave her the illusion that they were giving back. In her interview, she acknowledged the illusion, realizing that recycling the same loans hardly qualifies as giving $500 year after year. Christina articulated exactly how and why Kiva.org provided a perfect salve for a responsibility that she feels for poverty but otherwise feels quite helpless to address:

> Doing this charity stuff is hard. I want to do the right thing. I have a little, well, I have more money than lots of people in this world, but from my perspective, I have one baby. We may try to have a second. We are looking at buying a house. And we are so privileged and it feels so horrible for me to feel like I'm looking at my budget and I don't have the money to give to charity. That's awful because we make an absurd amount of money compared to other people, [. . .] But in my area [of the country], and the price of daycare, and looking at the price of homes in the places we're looking. [. . .] So because of all that, it's like I don't have the mental energy to be doing all the research . . . And I like the idea of micro-lending.

Christina feels guilty, not only for living in the global North and making much more money than many others in the world but also for prioritizing her own family's immediate plans over the effort to find a way to give back. The uniquely American conviction that charity to unknown others is required of any household with disposable income contributes to the discomfort that Christina feels, but there is something more to it. Christina does not *just* want to give to a charity. She wants her contribution to do good in the world by building up the capacities of another person. Along with other interviewees and survey respondents, Christina was eager to give to good charities. Kiva .org is indeed such a charity, consistently receiving a four-star rating from the independent Charity Navigator website.[19]

Kiva inspires a high level of trust and loyalty among those who had previously loaned on the website. Of the sixty-five snowball-sampled respondents who took my online survey, 75 percent were confident that they would lend again. Most shared similar explanations for what inspired them to begin lending, including a positive outlook on microfinance as a model for poverty alleviation and women's empowerment, the feeling that even one person's limited funds could make a difference for someone else, and that it was easy. These explanations rely upon a set of convictions about individual impact, self-sufficiency without the use of continuous donations, and the belief that these features can alleviate poverty. As one survey respondent put it, "I like the idea that Kiva allows users to make the most of a donation when they don't have a lot to give. Fifty dollars, for example, can be invested over and over. Additionally, I like that it is meant to help users get a small business off the ground rather than require them to look for sustained donations." Another wrote, "I liked the fact that I could lend a relatively small amount and still feel like I was making a difference—when you give $25 to a giant charity, it just seems insignificant and pointless." Several other respondents mentioned popular books, such as Nicholas Kristof and Sheryl Wu Dunn's *Half the Sky*, which encouraged readers to make loans on Kiva.org to contribute to the global cause of women's empowerment. Both the book and the TV documentary based on it prominently featured stories of women developing businesses as a result of small loans.

Interviewees frequently contrasted Kiva.org with "bad charities" that raise huge amounts of money but may not spend that money responsibly. During the time of my interviews, a story had just broken about the Red Cross's relief efforts in Haiti, which had raised over four million dollars and had not managed to build a single structure with that money three years after the disaster. Several interviewees mentioned the story and felt good about contributing to a charity that was not the "big bad" Red Cross. The contrast between Kiva.org and more traditional charities, which was important and obvious to most of the Kiva faithful, underscores the particularity of Kiva and microfinance more generally to the sense of self required for millennial development.

The loans on the website themselves reflect a marketplace of small loans, based both on the supply of loans available for funding and the demand for particular kinds of loans on the part of lenders like Christina and others. In my study of the Kiva's website, I collected data for nine months on the top fifty most-viewed loans each day, a snapshot of the loans that were most appealing to borrowers. These 4,700 loans were almost evenly divided among major regions of the world and were composed of 74.5 percent women, a reflection both of Kiva's commitment to promote women entrepreneurs and lenders' preferences to lend primarily to women. The popular loans supported a wide variety of activities, including food or service provision (34.4 percent), livestock (16.1 percent), and retail (14.2 percent), and went primarily to individuals (63.7 percent) rather than to groups (34.1 percent) or couples (2.1 percent). These popular loans represent a pool of typical loans on Kiva.org and both reflect and go beyond the expectations of lenders living in the US. The various micro-entrepreneurial activities showcased on the website have limited capacity to scale and aim primarily to provide a subsistence level income to a typically individual, woman entrepreneur.

The characteristics of this loan pool on Kiva provide a snapshot of how everyday humanitarians in the global North view microfinance in the global South. Lenders aim to lend specifically to microfinance recipients who align with their own ideas of gendered empowerment. Lenders have their own ideas of what the person they lend to ought to be doing and how consistently they should pay back. These ideas are influenced by racialized understandings of poor women's capacities in the global South as well as by a profound ignorance of the structural conditions of marginalization that impoverish women and men around the world.

FINDING A BORROWER, MAKING A CONNECTION

When a lender visits the Kiva website, she encounters both individual stories and the sense that there are endless worthy loans that need fulfilling. Prominently displayed features include the ease of choosing a borrower, lending the money, getting repaid, and repeating the process, which can be done from your phone. The website displays innumerable capable, enterprising brown or black woman in need of a loan for a business, usually highlighting a single photo prominently for emotional gravitas. The dilemma for the lender quickly becomes: how to choose?

When I began studying Kiva.org, I went on the website to invest fifty dollars of my own in order to experience being a lender. I was simply overwhelmed by the sense of wonder and responsibility of encountering thousands of photos and stories representing real people the world over and having to decide to choose one or two (see figure 6.1). How could I decide who was deserving of my insignificant amount of money? Quickly, without thinking too much, I picked loans from remote countries with loans that were unpopular. I paid and left the website. As months rolled by, I received periodic updates, such as "Margery in Sierra Leone has repaid $0.36!" I felt embarrassed to be involved with receiving such an update. I wished I could discontinue them. I also received periodic appeals for loans from Kiva teams I joined and from the company itself during various campaigns. Over time, the strong emotions I felt during my first encounter on the website dissipated, and I grew less interested in the details of what was happening with my loans. When my fifty dollars was repaid, I picked two other borrowers with even less thought than the first time. But I did not pull my money out.

Interviews with borrowers suggest that my experience was not far from normative but that there is something about the process of choosing a borrower that lenders felt reflected upon them as people. Francesca, a forty-eight-year-old professor of medicine in the midwestern United States with extensive travel experience in Southeast Asia filtered choices based on region to funnel her loans to where she had traveled. Because she came from a farming family, she lent to women requesting agricultural loans. In this way, she forged a personal connection between the loan and herself. Francesca had been lending on Kiva.org for five years and continued to enjoy the experience. She initially bought Kiva gift cards for various members of the family to see if the younger members in the family would get excited about the idea of helping folks in other parts of the world, but it really didn't "take." For her part, however, Francesca continued to make loans regularly. She loaned on Kiva because she was interested not just in helping, but in making sure borrowers could fulfill their full human potential:

> For me it's not about accountability . . . what's important to me is building
> a sense of mastery and self-efficacy. So, knowing that if I give something
> to somebody who's motivated, and all they're lacking is the resources,
> which to me is a huge injustice. And I'm sitting over here, and I have a

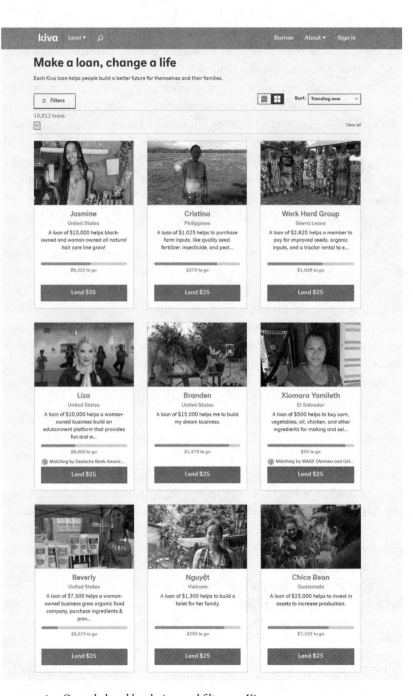

FIGURE 6.1. Overwhelmed by choices and filters on Kiva.org.

ton of resources, and you're over there, and you and I could be no different except for our circumstances. So being able to provide resources to somebody who is going to be able to do something with it is, I guess, compelling to me.

Through small peer-to-peer loans, citizens all over the world can establish an affective and personal connection to a needy borrower, usually a woman from a developing country, and seemingly make a small but significant contribution to her future. For lenders like Francesca to actually believe in this story, they have to also believe that the poverty that women are experiencing is due to a lack of access to funds and not due to conditions of social, political, and economic marginalization. By offering a backstory for a charitable donation, Kiva.org also offers a kind of salvation for lenders who wish to think of themselves as socially responsible. The selective biographies of borrowers, which are relatively free of social or political context, invite the donor to get to know a person and make a difference in their lives. Through the stories showcased on their website, lenders believe they are getting acquainted with individuals and the conditions in which they live. For Francesca, her own familiarity and connection to a region and a livelihood made her feel committed to the women she funded on the website. Through Kiva, Francesca also set up a normative benchmark for thinking about what small loans in the global South should do for their recipients, helping to generate a model for what kind of person a microfinance borrower should be: self-actualized, ambitious, and resourceful, just like Francesca.

A combination of knowledge, interests, and values inform lender strategies on Kiva.org, but over time those strategies become routinized, and borrowers have less and less specific things to say about how they lend. The most active borrower in my sample, Craig, who had been lending for over ten years and had given out dozens of loans on Kiva.org, said in his interview, "Here's what I do. I go on the site [. . .] I tend to look for women doing agricultural kinds of work. And that's it . . . No, I don't read the stories." Craig mentioned that there were many other things that caught his eye in the process. One loan may only need fifty dollars until it's funded, which he found tempting. He strenuously avoided lending to men, who tended to want to set up car shops. But he avoided details too. The hope was to get on the site, find, as quickly as possible, a borrower who would allow him to feel that the money was going to a good cause, and then leave the site.

For some lenders, the idea of connecting with a person through a loan and a biographical story provides an opening to understanding a wider world that would otherwise remain buried in depersonalized news headlines. Anne, a longtime Kiva lender I interviewed, explained one such experience:

ANNE: In Kenya, I sponsored someone and the loan fell through and at the time there had been rioting in Kenya. I think after an election, maybe. Some months later, I got a notice from Kiva saying, "We're really sorry, but," I think she was a fish vendor, "her stand was destroyed." And that was one of those [instances in which] you think, oh, right. This is why you read the news. You hear about these stories . . . When you see it in the abstract, it's like "oh, another disaster." But—

SR: If you were loaning to someone who had a business who could now no longer do it—

ANNE: Right! I mean, I really felt for them [the fish vendor's family]. I forget her name. I felt much worse for her and for her neighborhood than I had when it was just, you know, here's something going on in Kenya. Now I have a little story in Kenya.

For Anne, this newfound, seemingly personal connection with a fish vendor in Kenya established a personal, affective connection to a part of the world where she did not previously have such a connection. That sense of interconnectedness lies at the heart of Kiva's effectiveness in addressing the imperative to "do good" that Anne and others feel. The affective attention to Western donors' own sense of self and subjectivity fulfills a drive toward social responsibility that simply donating to a charity does not. Once this drive is fulfilled, most lenders do not feel the need to interrogate the action further.

OBLIGATION AND GIFTING

Like the microfinance industry at large, Kiva loans are also embedded in gift-giving relationships. A large literature on international aid has shown that development aid possesses many gift-like qualities, creating an expectation of reciprocation in the form of performance on the part of the aid giver.[20] Kiva makes that relationship even more personal, and therefore more compelling, because of the peer-to-peer character of the transactions on the website. For those that actually give Kiva gift certificates, the relationship goes further and interlinks two friends or family members to a Kiva loan, such that a set of values and preferences on how to be a good humanitarian come to bind together family members or friends. Several Kiva borrowers I interviewed shared that they had either given or received Kiva gift cards.

Sometimes, these cards sparked long-term interactions with the website and the giver, and other times these gift cards were something of a burden, not easily used and not easily disposed of.

Kiva lenders often found themselves tied down by the money on Kiva .org, unable to take the step of withdrawing it or releasing it to the company and consequently finding themselves re-lending out of habit or guilt. These relationships often came from gifting relationships, which came with their own strings attached. Almost all Kiva lenders I interviewed mentioned either giving or receiving Kiva gift cards in lieu of traditional holiday gifts. These gifts were almost all exchanged within immediate families. Anne and Craig both noted that their families have turned completely to donations at holidays and birthdays as a conscientious social decision. Francesca had also noted that she tried giving Kiva gift cards at one holiday, but her kids were not interested in taking it up.

In the most dramatic instance of large-scale Kiva gifting I encountered in my research, technology giant Hewlett-Packard (HP) signed a seven-million-dollar agreement with Kiva in 2013 to distribute a twenty-five-dollar gift card to each of HP's 275,000+ employees, who were then free to go online to find someone to allot that money to.[21] The campaign, Matter to a Million, used a gendered and racialized image of impoverishment to motivate HP employees to lend money being earmarked for them by the company (see figure 6.2). I tracked down two HP employees involved with the program, each of whom had divergent perceptions of the program. One employee, Richard, found the whole project to be an annoying, unwanted divergence from his work and mildly resented the repeated email reminders from management to use up the gift cards. His sat unused for nearly a year before he logged in, made the loan to the first person he found, and logged out. Richard never returned. As a global North resident who had not experienced an urge to "give back" that was not fulfilled by his family's routine donations to Charity Navigator-vetted charities every year (he did not seem to know how highly Charity Navigator consistently regards Kiva), Richard was exactly the kind of employee HP's corporate social responsibility team hoped to transform into a global citizen who "does good" for global poverty. But in his case, it failed.

In contrast, William, another HP employee, embraced the program and promoted it within his own team, beyond what was pushed by upper management. While William also routinely donated to traditional charities, both local and national, he especially enjoyed the opportunity to give loans to striving black women entrepreneurs, whom he identified with as a Black

FIGURE 6.2. Kiva's partnership with Hewlett-Packard aimed to motivate HP employees to lend money to poor women in other countries.

American. Since his employer provided him with the initial $25 gift card, William had added his own funds and regularly loaned out $150 at the time of our interview, nearly three years after the start of the program. William praised the program and was glad to have the opportunity to carry out this type of charity at his workplace.

In rare instances, the Kiva gift card forges a relationship across political differences within families in a way that exposes the concept's appeal across the political spectrum. Keira purchased a Kiva gift card for her politically conservative father in order to foster some kind of substantive conversation and exchange between them. It worked. Keira says her father strongly agreed with the idea of people wanting to help themselves. "He's told me in as many words," Keira explained, "that 'honey, I love that there's all these people I didn't know. All these people, these Africans who want to go and do things for themselves and get their own jobs. I think that's great.'" Since Keira gave him a fifty-dollar gift card for Christmas in 2010, he had consulted with her on every loan he gave out and updated her when he received a repayment.

"He views it as a bonding experience," Keira explained. "Honestly, my main motivation at this point, the number one motivation that slightly beats out microloaning, is that it's a bonding experience with my dad. It's something we can do together and something that gets him interested in my thoughts. I mean, he is interested [otherwise], but we don't talk about my professional life. So, this [the Kiva account] continues that dialogue with him." For Keira, microfinance provides an ideologically unifying activity to bring her closer to her family and the country of her Senegalese fiancé. Recently engaged to a Senegalese man, Keira started filtering her own loans to lend mainly to Senegalese women, a culture and place she now felt personally, intimately connected to.

For lenders, activity on Kiva.org is a way to participate in the type of millennial development that requires an enlightened Western self who is aware of the evils of poverty in the world and is particularly aware of the poor Third World woman and her struggles. Engagements on Kiva.org, whether through direct lending or gifting relationships, demonstrate and develop that enlightened self. When challenges to Kiva's representations emerge, however, there is rarely a parallel challenge to the self that relies on Kiva to demonstrate its enlightenment.

Deception and Controversy on Kiva.org

Toward the end of 2009, after several years of positive publicity and rapid growth, Kiva encountered a public relations nightmare. David Roodman, an economist working at the Center for Global Development who had been running a collaborative online blog devoted to microfinance, brought to light that certain information displayed on its website—namely, the ticking clock—was misleading.[22] Each loan on Kiva.org displays a ticking clock, a feature that has existed since the website's founding. The ticking clock makes up a key feature of a loan because it creates a sense of urgency for viewers, indicating how much time is left for the loan to be funded. The website offers an option to search for expiring loans so that lenders can chip in during that final crucial amount to bring a loan to fulfillment. Some interviewees I spoke to indeed sought out expiring loans to lend to when the time came to re-lend their funds.

But in a widely circulated blog post by Roodman, he revealed that the ticking clock was nothing more than a marketing gimmick, due to the structure of MFI funding. When a borrower comes to her local MFI, a Kiva partner, and presents all the necessary documentation, the MFI does not then wait for her loan to be fulfilled on a website before giving her the money. Rather, the company (rightly) disburses the money as soon as the requirements for the loan are met. As a result of this on-the-ground reality for MFIs, the vast majority of loans featured on Kiva.org had already been disbursed, though the borrower stories were real. When a lender picked a worthy borrower, then, they were really picking a particular MFI partner to direct funds to. Kiva directs a lender's funds to an interest-accumulating floating fund that the MFI can then tap into for its next loan. What appeared on the website to be a democratic, peer-to-peer interaction, then, really was not. And it was not peer-to-peer because of the pressing ground realities in which MFIS operate. Kiva.org's genius, however, is that through various marketing techniques, it flattened the complexity of those ground realities to create the perception among lenders in the US that they were contributing to a particular person's individual business or worthy cause.

While lenders like Francesca were thinking about building self-actualization among the borrowers she chose, her interest-free loan was instead contributing to a capital flow at an MFI in the country she chose. This capital flow contributed to the chosen borrower's empowerment only insofar as it was financially sustaining the organization that gave her loans so that it could provide loans to the next borrower who applied.

The backlash resulting from Roodman's revelations was swift and remarkably widespread. Many lenders perceived Kiva's (mis)representations as deliberate deception on the part of Kiva and stopped lending on the platform. But I also found that some lenders who knew about this controversy and were upset by it still did not pull their money out of Kiva. As one anonymous survey respondent explained, "While it doesn't make me rethink my lending, discovering a couple years ago that with Kiva, when I loan to Rita for her banana business, and I get updates from Rita about her business, that my money didn't go to her, that she *already* had a loan when I contributed my money, that took a lot of the joy out of Kiva. I still make loans because I think micro-lending may be an effective strategy, but I just pick the first one on the list and don't pay attention to the individual borrower details."

Another interviewee, who had been given a Kiva gift card, mused, "I mean, that would definitely to me constitute misrepresentation. Because their website clearly has individual profiles. And it's like, 'Give $20 to this woman,' and it has a name and a story. So, if it weren't going directly to her and if it was going through someone else and there's no way of knowing she's getting the amount I gave, yeah. I mean, I think in my case, once it was there, it wasn't really something I felt I could ignore [. . .] [If I were to have made the initial decision to put money into Kiva] I probably would assess that that twenty-five dollars might be better used just in a direct service sort of way."

Roodman's exposé on Kiva's inner workings did nothing more than reveal the complex workings of microfinance as it is embedded in social and economic contexts where it is accountable to real borrowers. This fact conflicted with the feel-good, shopper's paradise that Kiva lenders encounter online. As an organization, Kiva has been fully aware that the website needed to create the feeling of an affective person-to-person linkage between borrower and lender and, further, had to create a sense of urgency in the relationship. The ticking clock may be fictional, but it served as a bridge, translating the time-sensitive, relational, highly embedded process of identifying and verifying borrowers and disbursing their loans, in a timely way, into something that remote lenders in the global North could understand from their limited perspectives. Like a "one day only" sale, expiring loans spur action and commitment in a way that other presentations of the same "products" do not. Kiva's choice to display a ticking clock in the manner of a retail sale further highlights the highly commodified character of the loans on offer on the website. Through powerful marketing techniques and a compelling user interface experience, Kiva.org flattens the uneven, contradictory contours of the business of global microfinance into a sea of virtuous, gendered choices, one as good as the next, with no opportunities to do wrong.

Kiva necessarily responded to the heavy criticism it received by implementing symbols to indicate to lenders the true status of any loan (i.e., pre-disbursal, post-disbursal), and lenders can even search according to those characteristics on the website. But this controversy quickly died down. When I conducted interviews with lenders in 2015 and 2016, many had not even heard about it, and even if they had, they had chosen not to concern themselves too much with it. As Francesca put it, she had to trust some party, and she felt fine with trusting Kiva as an organization to make sound decisions that she does not have the expertise to make. As Kelly, a recent college graduate and Kiva.org lender, put it after a lengthy discussion of Kiva.org's controversies and the potential problems with microfinance, "Well, other kinds of charity have similar issues too, right? It doesn't make it acceptable that those practices occur, but at the same time, what can you do? And then the response is, well, then don't give money to anyone. Just keep it all. But that doesn't sit right with me either. Because I feel so fortunate and I want to be able to give." Kelly's will to do good, as well as her belief in the basic good of microfinance, overpowers her doubts or concerns about the everyday workings of the organization. And Kiva.org continues to earn her trust, whatever problems may have come up in the past.

Lenders on Kiva.org are compelled by the guilt they feel to take action against global poverty by doing something—namely, giving money to an organization that is doing something to counter global poverty. This type of poverty action ends up being more about the lender's feelings, convictions, relationships, and justifications than about what that money actually does in the world. Whether or not people pulled money out of Kiva once they discovered that their connection to a borrower was fabricated, the premise of lending to women abroad for microenterprise was so compelling and satisfying that there was never any reason to question that premise. Neither the social relations of microfinance nor the women who take loans were ever of interest to lenders. It did not occur to anyone to think about how US policies might be contributing to poor conditions for women in the global South. By continuing to contribute to the organization, their beliefs and attitudes unwittingly upheld the notion that circulating money to microfinance companies promotes women's empowerment and fights global poverty, while providing powerful ideological cover for the gendered extraction that MFIS actually carry out.

Profit-Oriented Microfinance and Its Discontents: MFI Professionals in the US

MFI professionals, we might expect, are quite different from Kiva lenders. As a part of the industry, they are engaged to a larger extent with its everyday complicated realities. While I found this to be true, I also found that MFI professionals, particularly in the client education department of Prosperity, were eager to "do good" in another way, albeit equally disconnected from social relations on the ground: by providing a counterbalance to profit-oriented operations and serving a social mission, but only in theory.

At the global New York headquarters of Prosperity, Clara, the director of client education programs, acquainted me with the organization's offerings in the areas of financial literacy and entrepreneurial training. Prosperity's entrepreneurial training program, BizTalk, supported microfinance clients who have small businesses of their own, teaching them skills such as marketing, accounting, and financial management of their businesses. BizTalk had been running in Latin America for fifteen years. Financial literacy training, in contrast, was meant for any microfinance client and teaches basic financial literacy skills such as budgeting, calculating income and expenditures, and saving for an emergency. Prosperity has developed several of these financial literacy programs in Latin America and India. Both these programs were developed in-house at times when prominent donors funded such endeavors or, sometimes, when a partnership with a local organization at one of their offices around the world required it. Clara was passionate about client education but found it difficult to convince her superiors at Prosperity:

> I mean, this is very personal and this is my position. We *should* be doing this because we're so commercial. This is what Prosperity *should* contribute . . . I think that we need to be contributing to our clientele by educating them in this way. [We don't have to] make it mandatory, but at least tell them, "Here it is. I will encourage you to absorb this information, but if you don't want to know, then that's fine." But at least we should do that. But . . . some people, especially the people who make the decisions [at Prosperity], do not think in that way.

This personal conviction she had about the importance of client education was more of a gut feeling, and she was unable to convince upper management to expand the budget for her programs because there was no proof that it improved Prosperity's bottom line. Indeed, experience with the existing entrepreneurial education program, BizTalk, had yielded no return on investment and, after many years of trying, was all but defunct in Latin America.

Despite the decline of the program, Clara saw herself as someone on the inside of a large commercial finance organization who was fighting for the individual client's benefit. She felt strongly that her job was to "do something," something that was (presumably, hopefully) good for clients. For her, that meant waving the flag of client education within the organization. She narrated anecdotes from her travels in Latin America and South Asia that led her to believe strongly that loans, in combination with these education programs, would lead women to become empowered. As in the managerial cultures of financial firms that regard the business of the firm to be in the best interest of society as a whole, Clara believed her work was something she could do for the clients.

Yet, Clara, like other US MFI professionals I met, was uninterested in the details of client lives. Clara felt she knew the clients because she had "seen" them. She regarded each of them as structurally similar to one another—similarly disadvantaged, similarly poor, and similarly oppressed. Despite this gap in her knowledge, her understanding of doing good was linked to doing something positive for women clients, a big contrast from most microfinance professionals I spoke to. Most commonly, MFI professionals in the US viewed their social responsibility as something that could only be addressed through financial sustainability, words that simply mean long-term profitability (for the company, not the client) in the microfinance industry.[23]

Clara's worries about the importance of these education programs within Prosperity were justified. Indeed, the program did not fit neatly into any of the key business areas within the organization. Janine, who served as the director of Prosperity's Asia programming in 2016, explained to me in an interview that client education played a relatively small role in Prosperity's business. The company had developed a lucrative strategy of funding and expanding the capacities and business operations of local MFIS in regions around the world. But this strategy, it turned out, assigned a minimal role to client education. It sounded important to do but could not quite be relied upon for funding:

> You know we love, really, we consistently promote financial literacy as one of the technical areas [in which we provide expertise]. We do bring financial literacy training to the institutions. It's an easy sell in India given what they have gone through [the 2010 crisis]. It is a harder sell in other places where they have not seen how important it is for clients to understand the risk of taking a loan, to understand the difference between taking out flat or declining balance interest rates, etcetera. And [clients should ask] just, "Should I use a credit product or a savings product? What is insurance?" All that stuff. It is so important to what we do. [But] that is still a piece we need to clarify within the organization . . . When we went through this whole strategic planning exercise two years ago, there were a lot of questions about that, I'll be honest.

Janine explained that at last the organization had come to view financial literacy education of clients as a core "driver" toward a "financially inclusive society," but they could not agree on what exactly Prosperity would focus on within that space, given that it was one business that was never going to be profitable in the way that microcredit or other financial services were. They wanted to focus on low-income households, but then that would move them away from their traditional area of strength in promoting microenterprise, since so much of the low-income microfinance market does not involve a small business.[24] There were a few programs working in India, including the Shaktisri program I was studying, but even that, which appeared to be a success, was gaining limited traction within the wider organization.

Janine's careful comments about the future of their client education initiatives reflected crucial divisions within Prosperity, and within the US-based microfinance industry more generally. As client education has become increasingly decoupled from loans and the drive toward profitability and scale became ever more important, large global companies like Prosperity have had to cut back on value-added programs, even as organizations like Sowbagya were rushing to provide trainings that might help them retain customers. For all these reasons, Clara found herself in an awkward position in the organization.

A Chance at Relevance: BizTalk Adaptations in India

Still, Clara was on a mission to advocate for client education programs. She was convinced that financial literacy programs, which encouraged personal thrift, detailed accounting, and regular savings, would be helpful to clients accessing financial products, perhaps for the first time. But she was still responsible for BizTalk, which had been developed by dedicated educators in Latin America and had fizzled out in recent years. This program was composed of more than fifty modules and contained detailed lesson plans, games, readings, and conversations planned for a year of weekly trainings, ranging from an opening self-reflection on "Who am I?" all the way to the details about learning how to market the specific product the client decides to produce. Clara's real job was to manage these two portfolios of educational offerings and try to make a go of them with half-hearted support from the organization.

Prosperity's operations in India had given her hope and had given BizTalk a new lease on life. Maya, the director of client education at Prosperity in India, had successfully set up a contract with Kanchan as a partner MFI. Kanchan and Prosperity were offering BizTalk trainings to Kanchan clients, encouraging them to become entrepreneurs. Clara was eager to find out whether or not the Indian version of BizTalk, Shaktisri, was successful in India and whether that success might help her advocate more strongly for client education as a more central part of Prosperity's business. Over the course of many meetings with Clara and other Prosperity staff, however, I saw that Clara was fighting a losing battle, and to a large extent, Clara knew it.

Maya visited Prosperity's headquarters in New York in November of 2011. Maya and Clara both hoped to convince Prosperity's leadership to commit more institutional and financial resources to client education by emphasizing the successes that Maya's team had in India and by charting a vision for what future work in the country could look like. Over a series of three meetings, Maya made her pitch about the programs she was in charge of in India.

These offerings included Shaktisri, as well as Prosperity's financial literacy trainings, which were partnered with another financial institution outside my study.

The opening meeting was conducted in Prosperity's large conference room with local employees, and videoconference participants from Prosperity's other branch offices around the world. Maya detailed the process, in cooperation with 650 Indian entrepreneurs in focus groups, through which the original fifty-plus modules were whittled down into nine modules that would be most suited for the Indian context. These materials were paired with relevant case studies, stories of real customers, and then translated into multiple regional languages. Maya claimed that an independent group of impact assessment evaluators had verified that this program was "well received" by clients, without going into further details about that evaluation. No one in the meeting questioned it, although I later learned that this was not a formal evaluation but rather a small-scale study carried out by undergraduate student volunteers. The results of that study showed that 75 percent of clients reported that they benefited from the trainings. As discussed in the previous chapter, I found instead that clients were ambivalent about the training and often did not find its main point relevant for their lives.

Maya then started charting out her vision for the future. She put a slide up with a multicolumn table displaying the program's projected growth over the next three years. Her chart indicated that she wished to hire staff to conduct the training, a data entry coordinator to record and organize client data, and managers to keep the program running smoothly. She outlined an expensive, but also far-reaching, vision of how existing programing could expand with the right infrastructural and staff investments from Prosperity.

Before asking further details about whether these programs had been shown to be effective, Prosperity employees asked a few related questions about the proposed program's potential for income generation. How could this program make any money when similar programs in Latin America had failed? Maya did not offer a fulsome answer and responded only to say that they were working on it.

Clara soon stood up. She explained that client education was not a money-making venture and never would be but that the benefit would come in terms of reputation, brand value enhancement, and of course attracting better clients. "It's not possible," she explained, "to make a spinoff [of previous materials] and make money." But that was not the point, she explained. It needed to be a csr initiative that Prosperity would invest in, just as many

MFIs around the world were investing in education initiatives for their clients.

The case that Clara and Maya together were making was on shaky ground. On one hand, they were trying to validate and recycle an existing program that they both believed had considerable merit. Their reasoning, which I had learned from my individual interviews with them and their colleagues, was that their existing materials, made for Latin America by dedicated educators, were essentially good materials containing generalizable insights on entrepreneurship that would be beneficial to working-class women around the world. That these trainings had not been successful in Latin America was not a deterrent because, in that case, the rollout had been inefficient and expensive. If these existing materials could be culturally adapted to fit the Indian context, then it would save the trouble of creating altogether new materials and could provide an opportunity for Prosperity to advance its social goals.

But this approach was unconvincing to multiple audiences. At the top, leaders such as Janine were not on board simply because there was no way that these programs could make enough money to be meaningful to a US-based MFI. Those gathered for Maya's presentation had the same concern and didn't question the underlying assumptions of what was being proposed, its effectiveness, or its suitability for clients. The only thing that mattered—as with most MFI practices I analyzed—was the bottom line.

Maya and Clara's idea did not resonate with donor priorities at Prosperity either, albeit for entirely different reasons. The next day, Prosperity leaders and donor relations representatives met with Maya and Clara. I was invited to attend as well. The donor relations director, Samantha, was interested in Maya's ideas, since donors were very interested in client-centered offerings. But donors wanted to partner with schools and community centers to deliver those offerings, and not necessarily with MFI partners who were linking these products with loans. Maya explained that she supported de-linking loans and training and reaching out to new organizations, but to do that, new infrastructure to reach out to diverse institutions in India would be needed. Prosperity leadership informed Maya, in the politest way possible, that she would have to make do with the institutional infrastructure already in place. Maya tried to explain why what they were asking her to do would not be possible in India without additional investments, but additional details did not seem to advance her case.

By the time Maya left for India a few days later, she received much praise for all the great work she was doing but few promises about additional investments from the company. Thus, although Prosperity leadership had invited Maya to present her ideas about expanding client education in India, they were not interested in advancing those ideas without significant financial return or, alternately, a close alignment with donor priorities. Being unable to deliver either, Maya returned home rather frustrated.

Maya's visit also left Clara frustrated, even though she had her own doubts about the effectiveness of, particularly, the entrepreneurial training materials. Based on her experience in Latin America, where she had met very sophisticated, cosmopolitan entrepreneurs, Clara suspected that some of the stories in the BizTalk materials were condescending, and she was not sure the lessons resonated with women clients. Clara, like the donors Samantha represented, saw more promise in financial literacy programs. But even Clara had little patience for analyses of client responses or materials that might suggest that Prosperity's financial literacy materials, a completely separate suite of client education materials from BizTalk, were ineffective. Like Prosperity staff in India, she believed that the training materials were of high quality and just needed to find the right audience. Because they were successful in finding that audience in India previously, she felt that Prosperity should be obligated, as a commercial MFI, to find it again and make it work, even if the math did not pencil out. Clara believed she was standing up for clients, but she had little interest in or understanding of what clients in India would find useful. Because she was doing devalued work within Prosperity, she had limited bandwidth to imagine or push for a completely new perspective.

A year later, I assembled a report of my findings for Prosperity about my observations on the trainings in India. My report provided clear and specific recommendations on how the program could be improved to be more attractive to clients. I explained that clients had access to many kinds of trainings but were interested in concrete plans that would help them generate income. I explained that it was difficult for most clients to relate to the lessons about the self and the attractiveness of an entrepreneurial identity. I heard back soon from Maya, who told me that my findings were inaccurate because I had not visited all their sites, with no further questions or engagement. There was no response at all from the head office. Although they had initially asked me to come to present at the head office about the findings of the study, as soon as they learned that my findings were not universally glowing, they were not interested in my participation. Even Clara, who had been hoping that my findings would ultimately shore up her case about client education, did not invite me back to the office to discuss my research.

The discomfort within Prosperity about any remotely critical findings about client education programs exposes that client education efforts, like lending on Kiva.org, provides legitimacy and cover for MFI practices that are almost exclusively concerned with commercial impact accomplished through gendered extraction. Prosperity's client education programming, while seemingly robust from the outside, turned out to be flimsy on the inside, staffed by well-meaning MFI professionals committed to countering, in a general way, the commercial impulses of the organization but without the tools or resources to make a client-centered approach viable. They were uninterested in learning more in order to shore up their arguments for serving clients in their real contexts. Clara and her colleagues had a vague idea of what Indian clients were like and how complicated microfinance was in India, but they were not interested in improving their perspective or creating new forms of activism within their organizations to connect effectively with the women they were supposed to be serving. Any time that Maya or I presented information that suggested detail beyond the broadest generalization, the information was met with disengagement, denial, and resignation. These forms of intentional ignorance further the injustice of structural inequalities that separate well-meaning actors in the US and the financial worlds of women borrowers in India.

Conclusion

In a powerful opinion piece for the *New York Times*, Serene Khader explained how and why "empowering women" is a "solution" that powerful actors in the global North use to "deflect attention from what the problems really are."[25] Khader pointed out that liberating women from their cultures, the implicit subtext of most efforts to bring empowerment to women, does not address what oppresses them: a subordinate position in global hierarchies wherein neither they nor their families have access to good jobs. Conscientious actors in the global North, Khader argues, should be lobbying lawmakers to change the policies that continue to perpetuate global disparities, including unfair trade policies that restrict access to goods from global South countries to markets in rich countries and patent laws that restrict the access to lifesaving drugs for patients in poor countries. These policies do not seem to be about women, but the conditions they produce indeed perpetuate gender inequality. These policies require disadvantaged women to provide extra care to the sick and vulnerable, to work three low-wage jobs to get by, or to take even more subprime loans.

Lenders on Kiva.org and microfinance professionals located in the global North are both Northern development actors committed to women's empowerment and development in parts of the world with which they have little familiarity or, as I have shown, interest. An imperative to do good in the world motivates them, but they are typically looking to carry out development action in a way that would be least disruptive to their schedules, worldviews, or organizations. An actor-oriented perspective on development helps us situate how well-intentioned microfinancial actors in the global North end up reinforcing, rather than disrupting, patterns of economic marginalization for women borrowers due to the preoccupations that structure their everyday lives. But there is more to it: microfinancial actors presume they understand why women all over the global South are poor, a conviction that permits a lack of interest in on-the-ground details of women's experiences. A racialized, decontextualized understanding of women's lives, as well as of microfinance, allows microfinancial actors to "do something," even though their actions do not directly affect the financial flows or institutional contexts in which microfinance in India—or anywhere else—operates. Nonetheless, their actions are powerful. They help prop up a misleading, racialized understanding of gender, poverty, entrepreneurship, and empowerment that provides cover for the gendered extraction that MFIS carry out, shielding these financial companies from scrutiny. Because of these actors' peculiar combination of activism, apathy, and distance, MFIS in India and elsewhere can make women borrowers pay and feel, without a trace of irony, that they are doing good.

7. IMPACT REVISITED

The microfinancial chains explored in previous chapters lay out a structure of gendered financial extraction in which women borrowers, through relational work with one another and with MFI workers, create profit for growing financial institutions in India and, especially, for those at the top of those institutions. Yet the unavoidable topic of impact remains. Does commercial microfinance improve the positions of vulnerable women and their families? How might a critical perspective on gendered extraction help us address the question of impact in a different way from the existing literature? In this chapter, I examine the class trajectories of key stakeholders in the gendered microfinancial chains I have explored in previous chapters—clients, MFI workers, MFI leaders, and MFI professionals living in the US—in order to advance an intersectional understanding of impact. I show how privileges along lines of class, gender, caste, and geography help to preserve and advance the social, cultural, and economic capital of those in the upper echelons of the chain. In contrast, at the base of the chain, disadvantages along those same lines of difference mean that even successful clients achieve, at most, a tenuous stability. In the middle of the chain, MFI professionals often find that employment in the industry can lead them toward middle-class status, even though they do encounter significant barriers to advancement within MFIS. When we consider that MFI professionals are part of a large global workforce of service workers, a group that typically provides services to the wealthy while reinforcing their own positions of subordination, this finding is particularly surprising.[1] MFI workers, who serve marginalized groups rather than wealthy ones, enjoy a real chance at mobility. This advantage distances them from their clients.

When we examine India's microfinance industry with an eye on complex inequality, we advance a concept of class[2] that helps us grasp the dynamics of inequality that structure millennial India. This chapter forges a conception of class difference in millennial India grounded in individuals' livelihoods, marriages, occupational histories, and possibilities for class mobility in different parts of India's commercial microfinance chain.[3] My conception of class difference builds upon Rina Agarwala's relational conception of the informal economy.[4] Agarwala argues that the informal economy, far from being separate from formal economies of production, undergirds the expansion of capitalism in India by supplying the requirements for the reproduction of the working classes employed in formal enterprises. "Informal economies," Agarwala argues, "are an integral and crucial peg in the continuing project of global capitalism."[5] Urban microfinance borrowers, then, are both subordinate within the Indian economy and absolutely crucial to the growth of the current system.

Extending this analysis, I have shown in this book that gendered livelihoods of microfinance clients fuel the expansion of the microfinance industry. I further suggest in this chapter that the highly contingent, flexible strategies through which microfinance clients survive actually subsidize the middle-class trajectories of MFI workers, while supporting—both financially and ideologically—the benevolent protectionist masculinity of MFI leaders.[6] Despite this reliance on clients, both workers and leaders believe that they are helping their clients out of generosity.

An intersectional understanding of class and gender crucially advances an impoverished conception of impact that continues to plague the existing literature on microfinance and other similar development interventions. A focus on impact measures how microfinance has worked as a policy tool or development intervention, obscuring its complex inner workings and value chains. Reviews of microfinance's effects draw from instrumental views of policy, quantitative measures, and before-and-after comparisons across individuals.[7] Even studies that are ultimately critical of microfinance conceive of impact narrowly, thinking of short-term income enhancement. While I have countered this approach to microfinance throughout this book, choosing instead to unpack its inner workings, I now propose a broader, more context-specific understanding of impact that considers not only clients but also actors all along the Indian microfinancial chain I have uncovered in this book.

I have constructed biographies from interviews with clients, MFI workers in India, and MFI professionals in the US and from secondary materials about the lives of prominent MFI leaders. Leaning upon the classic sociological insight of C. Wright Mills—that biography and history constitute one another—I present biographies of individuals from each of the groups I studied.[8] I show that individuals with intersecting forms of gender, caste, class, and geographic privilege are able to convert their work in microfinance into better opportunities. In contrast, although clients are able to incorporate microfinance into their livelihoods, in a best-case scenario they can leverage it to create a cushion from extreme vulnerability. An analysis of biographies across the gendered financial chain helps us understand the material conditions under which microfinance clients carry out the labor of taking and repaying high-interest loans. They contextualize the gendered culture and praxis of microfinance, rooted in class divisions. When women at the bottom repay their loans on time, they ensure their loan officer maintains his job and enhances the institution's reputation. Timely repayment, even under adverse circumstances, then generates goodwill from donors and financial supporters alike, while shoring up the entrepreneurial reputations of MFI industry leaders and the global development experiences of US-based professionals. I begin with the class worlds of professionals abroad and then move from the top of the chain down.

Indian Microfinance as an Experience: US-Based MFI Professionals

In chapter 2, I mentioned that in the early 2000s, American college students moved to India to see how they could help build India's nascent for-profit microfinance industry. Many of these individuals were inspired by the early successes of Vikram Akula's Swayam Krushi Sangh (SKS). Akula, himself a US-born and educated son of an upper-middle-class doctor, pioneered profitable microfinance in India, eventually spearheading the industry's first public offering in 2008. The promise of a form of development that could be both beneficial and profitable attracted many ambitious, well-intentioned students to the industry. I interviewed four US-based professionals with experience in Indian microfinance who shared their biographies. Here, I introduce Aakash, a financial professional who started out his lucrative career at the height of India's early experiment with for-profit microfinance in the early 2000s.

Armed with an undergraduate business degree and a year of experience at a top financial investment firm, Aakash, who had spent his childhood in India, saw a job posting for a position in San Francisco that interested him. The company was working on commercializing India's microfinance sector, harnessing the power of private investment capital to alleviate poverty. Having felt unfulfilled expanding profits for the world's richest companies, Aakash was attracted to the idea of helping funnel venture funds and other forms of financial capital to Indian MFIs who were transforming from nonprofit NGOS to commercial entities. He soon found himself in a Bengaluru office full of bright, ambitious international colleagues in their 20s with business backgrounds. During his years working for a company I will call GlobalCorp, he worked directly with MFIs who had clients mainly in rural India. He examined MFI operations, spoke with clients about their experiences, conducted due diligence checks on the company's internal policies and procedures and then helped MFIs gain access to foreign equity markets. This work felt more fulfilling to him, even though he observed areas he felt needed improvement. He reflected, "It was a young and a fast growing and evolving space. And so you're always thinking about what's going well, what's not going well, what could be improved, etcetera. I think that's always an issue, but I think for the most part working in the microfinance space in India was certainly more personally fulfilling than working at GlobalCorp."

For Aakash, involvement with the microfinance industry helped him forge a socially responsible path in the business world while continuing to advance his career. In so doing, he leveraged the geographic advantages of his connections to the US and his education. Seeking further expertise in the area of global development, Aakash applied for a graduate degree from a top US university, where he shored up his analytical skills to continue working in profit-oriented development work, this time focusing on the impact investment space, a commercial space for investment capital focused on making a positive social impact.[9] Since then, his expertise and skills have helped him become increasingly influential in the sector.

Aakash's story helps us understand how a social agent with geographic, gender, and educational privilege can become an influential actor in microfinance chains, despite remaining at an arm's-length distance from the everyday relational work of leveraging gendered value from clients. From his perspective, the trajectory is natural, with one step setting up the next. Yet, from the very beginning, his advantages put him at the helm of the most dramatic transformations in the Indian microfinance industry, helping to make decisions about which companies would be able to access foreign equity markets and on what terms. Driven by a sense of social responsibility and the conviction that capital markets have an important role to play in poverty alleviation, Aakash helps cement a set of financial and institutional arrangements that continue to structure the Indian microfinance industry. In terms of the model of microfinancial chains, Aakash remains on the outer periphery, producing data, knowledge, and funding that then strengthen capital-oriented solutions to poverty in India.

Doing Good and Building the Nation: The Strategic Work of Microfinance Leadership

Although Aakash may enjoy the privilege of being influential while remaining more or less behind the scenes and remote from public view, MFI leaders face praise and blame in equal measure and represent both their companies and the sector as a whole. MFI leaders come from elite class and educational backgrounds and have often spent time abroad. In public accounts, they are often constructed as generous people who gave up more lucrative careers to lead microfinance companies. They are also almost exclusively men. High-profile women have always been involved in the leadership of MFIs, but I found none who had achieved the public visibility of the dozen or so men who constitute the core leadership of the industry. Rather, women increasingly predominate as one moves from the top of an MFI organization to the bottom, where the targeted clients are women. The high status of MFI leaders allows them to rework the concept of class to suit the neoliberal imagination of millennial India. In their public statements, poverty is a result not of marginalization but of lack of access to good financial services. Serving the poor from their privileged positions, therefore, they echo discourses of nation-building that evoke Gandhi and Nehru, the most prominent patriarchs of contemporary India, further legitimating their industry and its practices.

The biographies of the industry's most charismatic leaders are available in newspapers and books. Most have been celebrated in the Indian media. I synthesized secondary sources about six leaders who have been prominent in the public eye for this chapter and here highlight a single one to illuminate the career trajectories of privileged men in the industry. I found several distinct life trajectories among the MFI leaders whose biographies I studied. They come from various careers before microfinance, including banking, education, NGO work, or information technology. These early careers shaped the internal cultures of the organizations they created, and eventually the interactions between various leaders shaped the industry as a whole.

What they shared, however, were privileged upbringings in terms of caste and class,[10] elite educational credentials, and an orientation toward serving the underserved or unserved. Here, I focus on Vijay Mahajan, considered by many as the "high priest"[11] of microfinance and a mentor to many.

In a 2018 article in India's *Business Standard*, part of a series profiling important business leaders, journalist Anjuli Bhargava delved into Vijay Mahajan's personal history.[12] Engaging a common narrative about privileged men who take up social causes, Bhargava highlights the extent to which systemic inequality bothered Mahajan from a young age in Kolkata, where devastating poverty was evident all around him. While attending the Indian Institute of Technology, in Delhi, he found his studies infused with social consciousness.[13] Still, he joined the corporate sector and worked for Phillips as a marketing executive until 1979, when he enrolled in India's premiere management institution, IIM-Ahmedabad. Mahajan's IIM coursework was also imbued with a social element, thanks to the similarly minded Ravi J. Matthai, the director at the time. After earning a PhD at IIM, Mahajan started work in the rural development sector, beginning in the poor eastern state of Bihar. His first institution, PRADAN, established in 1981, promoted livelihoods and community institutions.

After a fellowship at Princeton's Woodrow Wilson School in the late 1980s, Mahajan secured funding from the Ford Foundation to study the Grameen Bank's programs in Bangladesh, Thailand, and Indonesia and, later, to study US banking institutions, such as ShoreBank in Chicago. He also participated in studies for the World Bank in collaboration with established development organizations in India such as SEWA, the Self-Employed Women's Association in Gujarat. During those crucial years in the early 1990s, he helped produce new knowledge about the importance of the rural nonfarm sector for India's most marginalized.[14] Later, he coauthored a crucial study for the international community that exposed, seemingly for the first time, the grip of informal debt on the lives of India's rural poor.[15]

Mahajan established BASIX, India's first commercial microfinance institution, in 1996, together with copromotors whom he knew from various prestigious institutions in India. BASIX aimed to promote livelihoods among the poorest. Its structure reflected Mahajan's conviction, gained through his travels and experiences, that microfinance in India required a profit orientation. His first loan, of 80 lakhs of rupees, taken from Indian business magnate Ratan Tata, was repaid within a year, thereby vetting not only the idea of commercial microfinance but also Mahajan's own business savvy. From there, BASIX grew, and competitors entered the market.

During the 2010 crisis, Mahajan put himself at the forefront. From 2009, he chaired the Microfinance Institutions Network (MFIN) and appealed to the Reserve Bank on behalf of commercial microfinance (see chapter 2).[16] In 2011, emulating Gandhi, he took a *padayatra*, or a journey by foot, across five thousand kilometers in the twelve Indian states most affected by the crisis, seeking to understand the suffering of clients and the ways the industry might regain their trust.[17] My interviewees recalled seeing Mahajan on TV during the crisis apologizing for the damage that MFI companies had caused. For his sincerity and self-reflection, as well as his dogged leadership, he remained highly regarded in microfinance circles, despite his contradictory positions. Unlike most MFI leaders in the public eye, Mahajan was openly critical of microfinance, even when he led the industry. In a 2010 article in the magazine *Global South Development*, Mahajan suggests that instead of loans and self-employment, the poor require reliable wages, savings, and insurance products, and when they do wish to become entrepreneurs, they need appropriate training to do it. He challenged the idea that microcredit institutions should necessarily be financially sustaining.[18] These objections to the sector's philosophies and operations, however, did not keep him from continuing to participate in the industry.

In 2018, Mahajan became the new CEO and secretary of the Rajiv Gandhi Foundation, one of India's premiere development foundations. His class and caste privilege thus provided a resource through which he could forge a career that changed the landscape of Indian finance. Despite the industry's many ups and downs, Mahajan's reputation as a good, sincere man who sacrificed his privilege for others remained intact, even as he expressed both critical words and persistent support regarding microfinance. Commitment to alleviating inequality and serving the poor provided him a moral, political, and institutional platform, and a strategic position that MFI workers can rarely, if ever, access.

Mahajan's biography, like those of other MFI leaders I analyzed, reveals how class and caste-privileged men were able to leverage their social and economic capital to assume positions at the top of India's microfinance industry, all the while cultivating a benevolent protectionist masculinity that expresses concern for the poor. Mahajan's actions counter a hegemonic masculinity oriented toward material success, now dominant in India, recalling instead older masculine ideals nurtured in the decades immediately following independence and epitomized by Gandhi's sacrifices: living a life of service, eschewing opportunity for accumulating wealth, advocating for the marginalized, and finally, serving the nation.

Articles about Mahajan and other MFI leaders also draw upon the trope of the talented Indian technocrat whose brilliance leads him to leave India but who returns to serve the underprivileged, sacrificing his privileged life and harnessing technical knowledge heroically to address social injustices. This trope has enjoyed prominence in the Indian imagination since at least the early 2000s, epitomized in the 2004 film *Swades*.[19] The message is that these accomplished, privileged men left lives of luxury to set up financial services for struggling women. The public narrative of another MFI leader, Samit Ghosh of Ujjivan, is particularly influenced by this set of understandings. Mahajan and others who have traveled widely and spent time in elite US educational institutions also enjoy the benefit of this trope, which valorizes their actions as part of service for the nation. Although Mahajan and other men who stepped into MFI leadership were, by all accounts, motivated by altruistic aims, the suggestion that they gave up their privileges to lead their organizations is unconvincing. Rather, MFI leaders, including Mahajan, gained prominence because their ventures came to fruition at the right historical moment. Mahajan and other leaders share privileged educational backgrounds and strong positions in the labor market, quite apart from their investments in microfinance. Nonetheless, the public perception of sacrifice in service of the nation allows MFI leaders to forge a state-like ethos of benevolent protectionism, shored up by the gendered organization of MFIs themselves and the close cooperation of the industry with state-run financial inclusion programs (see chapters 1 and 2).

MFI Employees Moving Up

Sohini Kar has observed high levels of turnover for field-workers due to the relatively low pay and grueling, emotionally draining character of the work.[20] In the companies I studied in south India, however, I found that in the most profitable MFIs, field-workers used entry-level jobs in the industry to climb a possible ladder out of precarity. MFI work presented the chance of a long-term stable job and upward mobility. Ultimately, however, frontline workers encountered a class ceiling, where their class background prevented advancement into the upper ranks of the organization. Although I interviewed forty-five frontline MFI workers, I focus here on one MFI professional I was able to keep in contact with over the course of several years, whom I call Velan. His story traces a path of possible upward mobility that exists in the industry, albeit with limits. Velan's success, as well as the constraints he encountered along the way, expose the centrality of class and caste in shaping the possibilities for rising to the top within the stratified industry.

When I met Velan at a crowded intersection in a gentrifying neighborhood near the center of Bengaluru, I gazed longingly at the commonplace Café Coffee Day across the street, a site much acknowledged for its association with global, middle-class India. But when I suggested we talk there, Velan insisted we sit on a bench in a park across the street. As I would come to know, Velan would never spend a rupee unnecessarily, nor did he want anyone else to. As a career microfinance worker and father of two, he presented a biography that traced a historical shift in the opportunities available to a subset of individuals from poor rural backgrounds.

Velan grew up in an orphanage because his parents were too poor to take care of him. With the help of a Christian mission, he became the first in his family to receive a degree, completing an undergraduate commerce degree in 1999. But after graduating, he struggled to find a job. Eventually, he found work as a security guard, a position he felt was beneath a college graduate. He then started a small shop in Krishnagiri, selling cigarettes and miscellaneous household items. He found this job equally oppressive. "For one-and-a-half years, I was running that shop, and no person to give rest to me [sic]," he explained. "From five in the morning to eight o'clock at night, I had to be there. Very boring. Sitting, sitting, sitting. And I cannot go out for any interval too. Very, very difficult."

Once he decided to close the shop, Velan found work in the government sector, with his area's Integrated Rural Development Program (IRDP). In the early 2000s, he earned 750 rupees (about fifteen dollars) a month. In his new role, he was to organize women into groups to take loans. For months, the work felt pointless. Prospective clients had little interest. But at some point, which he described as "a flash in the newspaper," demands for the loans took off, and almost overnight he had more demand than he and the other fieldworkers could handle. This initial experience with a self-help group earned Velan status as well as extensive contacts within the NGO world, but he was still earning very little money. By this time, he was married and eager to earn more. When a friend living in Bengaluru informed him that an NGO was looking for help on an SHG project involving a survey of a slum area, he pursued it. Velan and his wife moved from rural Tamil Nadu to Bengaluru for the job.

The salary of eight thousand rupees (about four hundred dollars) a month to conduct a survey of slum neighborhoods where the NGO operated was the ticket to a stable livelihood. Soon thereafter, Velan connected with the then-nascent commercial MFI I call Sowbagya, now one of India's largest. A chance meeting turned into a job interview, and his experience with organizing poor women into groups for loans, as well as his passion for working with marginalized communities, got him a job. He had some reservations about what he considered a morally ambiguous "finance company, but," he explained, "at that time, my commitment was there. I needed a job. There was no other way. I know this skill only. That is why I joined." Upon joining, Velan felt valued in the company. As he put it, "They respected me. They treated me well. They honored my skills."

Velan was one of Sowbagya's first employees, and he was involved with testing some of its foundational principles. His work helped to answer key strategic questions: What kinds of loan products are appropriate for group loans in urban areas? How much loan capacity can clients bear? Although the work was interesting and his skills were used and expanded, Velan also had reservations about Sowbagya's business practices. He found the company "aggressive in business, [whether] in the field, in forming groups, risk-taking, and branch opening." This culture of aggressiveness led to everyday stress: constant deadlines, targets for disbursing funds, and extreme pressure on employees to make borrowers repay. These demands posed conflicts for Velan, who believed that eradicating poverty while making a profit was impossible. Still, the everyday work of microfinance was more interesting and more rewarding than virtually any job he could do, and the opportunities at Sowbagya were too good to turn down. Working with Sowbagya, Velan learned English, increased his income as he moved into better paid positions, and in the process gained confidence. Within the first year, he became familiar with most slums and lower-middle-class neighborhoods within thirty kilometers of Bengaluru. He went on to become one of the first branch managers in the organization and stayed on at Sowbayga for six years.

When I first connected with Velan in 2012, he was no longer working for Sowbagya but was involved in grassroots mobilization, this time for an organization seeking to organize nonunionized workers and connect them with basic services in the city. Soon after this meeting, however, I learned that Velan had joined another MFI, this one geared toward providing loans to small and midrange enterprises rather than groups or individuals. Once again, Velan's familiarity with poor and working-class communities in and around Bengaluru had become an asset to a rapidly growing company, which was starting to base its product designs and strategies on his recommendations. This job provided a rare chance for Velan to get out of microfinance and into business financing, where he learned a new set of skills, became familiar with industrial areas of the city, and learned about the day-to-day challenges of running various small businesses. In contrast with the MFI sector, these small industrial businesses were mostly run by men. Rather than discussing the costs of education and groceries, he discussed the cost of equipment and supplies. In this position, he was required to report defaults and could not cover them up. Local regulations required his firm to file lawsuits against borrowers in default for more than 90 days. As a result, he became familiar with local and municipal courts. Given limited state capacity, little ever came of these lawsuits. Nonetheless, he dealt with many defaulters with poor accounts.

In 2016, Velan transitioned to another rung of his career, this time with a direct-sales association that brokered traditional loans between banking partners and individuals from a wide range of class backgrounds. This job was better work under less grueling circumstances, and it signaled that Velan had finally left microfinance, having successfully parlayed his skills into other areas of the financial services industry. This new role made him feel a bit out of his league:

> You can't ever get a meeting with them [potential clients] because they have so many offers from other banks too. It's a new experience for me, working with that level of people. People my level or lower, I can go like a street dog in every lane and meet the targets. But this level is difficult for me. It's a new experience, a new kind of people.

Despite his doubts about meeting his targets, Velan was clearly at ease with his middle-class status. We met at a restaurant (though not at Café Coffee Day). His dress was sharp and tidy; he owned a home and was preparing to send his eldest child to college. Yet he still marveled at money people wasted in fancy neighborhoods, like the one we were in.

Velan's career trajectory from acute rural poverty to a stable position among Bengaluru's middle classes would have been impossible without the NGO sector and, more specifically, the for-profit microfinance sector. In India, in the crucible of late capitalism, organizing poor and working-class women into groups that will take loans and repay them over and over again has become a valuable skill that affords long-term opportunities. Without the growth of the microfinance industry, a person like Velan would have been unlikely to gain a foothold in India's urban middle class. For women, too, a job with an MFI organization offers a path to a stable livelihood, despite difficulties women face when working in the field. Women, who make up about 30 percent of the microfinance workforce (less among field-workers), must navigate the industry alongside gendered expectations to lead domestic lives oriented toward children and, often, a stigma against women working in jobs that require them to work or travel extensively in public-facing contexts. The women I spoke to had thus made significant sacrifices, both in their careers and in their personal lives, to work in microfinance field operations. Yet none of the women I met had worked her way up the ladder beyond the industry's first rung or two. Women instead remained on a sticky floor (see chapter 2).

CLASS CEILINGS: "THEY THROW US AWAY"

Commercial microfinance is based on the notion that commercial products must directly serve customers and so must put customer needs first. For-profit lenders aim to "do well by doing good," regarding the poor not as targeted beneficiaries but as clients with specific needs, priorities, and motivations to be met by the market. By that logic, the workers who understand clients best could certainly provide a rich source of information for MFI leaders and might be rewarded with upward mobility within the company. But narratives from my interviews with long-term microfinance workers suggest that the industry presents a distinct class ceiling for workers. Those from marginalized backgrounds can climb the ladder but will never reach corporate leadership.

Friedman, Laurison, and Miles coined the term *class ceiling* to describe the durability of class structures in contemporary Britain. There, they found, even upwardly mobile individuals able to enter the ranks of elite professions were unable to acquire the social, cultural, and economic capital equivalent to their peers from privileged backgrounds.[21] Borrowing this term for analysis of India, I find upwardly mobile MFI workers exercising only limited influence over strategic decisions, which prevents the industry from incorporating the firsthand experiences of those who know clients best. Ironically, the very working-class cultural capital that won these workers their jobs keeps them from rising to lead microfinance organizations.

Velan's narrative of his role at Sowbagya, and the way he left the company, hints at the class ceiling. Sowbagya hired him in 2005 on the basis of his experience organizing women into self-help groups in his home village during early, state-led efforts to promote rural development through microcredit. Having performed vital and strategic field activities for Sowbagya, Velan was rewarded with promotions and opportunities for training. Once he became a branch manager, however, he had nowhere to go. "I do not know [office] politics," he lamented. "I am a poor village agriculturalist. There was so much tension in the field, and the same job and the same challenges. So, I decided—enough." He moved on to a position elsewhere.

Abraham articulated more clearly the frustration of gaining experience but remaining marginalized in his organization, Samudra. Like Velan, Abraham had come from a poor rural background and had gained an education against the odds, becoming the first in his family to attend college. In Madurai, Tamil Nadu, he had completed a postgraduate degree in rural development science, a qualification I encountered among many MFI workers. Before entering the microfinance industry, Abraham had worked for organizations in varied parts of India, on issues ranging from female infanticide to child malnourishment, often in remote tribal areas. Despite his background as a social worker, his work was primarily to keep accounts, a skill he learned on the job from an experienced accountant. When his father passed away, he returned to his village in Tamil Nadu to support his mother and worked at a local hotel.

In landing a job in the microfinance industry in Bengaluru, Abraham sought employment with Samudra, instead of a large company like Sowbagya. Samudra was a newer, more aggressive firm that promised more rapid mobility. He was hired as a branch manager, quickly rose through the ranks, and within four years had become an assistant division manager, the position he held when we met. Still, Abraham felt the company denied him raises and promotions. "They treat us like slaves [*adimaigal*]," he complained.

> Everyone [above us] is getting profit, but the staff are not getting any profit. . . . I have experience that no one is using. I have talent. I want to grow and be in a director position, a leader. I have a hundred talents in each of my five fingers, but no one bothers about us. They are disregarding us. They are using us and throwing us [away]. They are fond of white [skin] color. They simply throw us [away]. I do not know foreign culture. This is my bad luck. I want to use myself, but no one is willing.

Here Abraham points to pervasive racism and caste discrimination in the upper ranks of his organization. His reference to "foreign culture" suggests an awareness that the organization's elites privilege contact with the West and consider it necessary cultural capital for entering a leadership position.

In Vikram Akula's memoir, *A Fistful of Rice*, the former CEO of SKS provides insight into the reasons that experienced field staff like Velan and Abraham seldom move into higher-level, strategic positions. As Akula explains, area managers were badly needed at SKS during its most rapid period of growth, but he chose not to promote staff members who had come through the ranks:

> The conventional thinking in microfinance was to bring in managers with ten or more years of work experience, then train them for six months or more. But bringing in such experienced staff was costly, and seasoned people sometimes come with baggage—stubbornly conventional thinking about how things should be done, based on their "experience." . . . Rather than hiring older, more experienced recruits, I decided to go in the opposite direction . . . [and] hire[d] four recent management graduates, the Indian equivalent of MBAS. . . . I had reasons of my own for believing that relatively inexperienced young people could do such high-level work. "Just because they're young doesn't mean they can't do it," I told my colleague. "I was young at DDS, too, but I just needed some guidance and trust."

With an institutional imperative for efficiency, Akula hired the equivalent of fresh MBAS for upper-level management, ignoring "conventional" thinking and putting "experience" in scare quotes. This approach, while perhaps successful in the short term, likely failed to reward long-term employees with the upward mobility they thought they deserved, while bringing in staff from highly privileged positions with their various blind spots. Akula's decisions in that moment may also have set a precedent in other parts of the industry as it became more profit oriented during the mid-2000s.

Companies may thus have turned away from the legions of NGO workers with immediate experience in marginalized communities to focus instead on fresh blood with top educational credentials. The presumption behind this reasoning is that those who work their way up the ranks lack a perspective that can serve clients or the company at higher levels. Instead, the reasoning goes, those from privileged backgrounds with elite educations will, with a little training, have a desirable perspective. Such reasoning may indeed have constructed a class ceiling for MFI staff, separating the field staff from the more strategic work of upper management.

Clients Getting By

Many SHGs target the rural poor, but commercial MFIS must largely avoid lending to the poorest. Regulations put in place after the 2010 crisis ensure that MFIS target women who can declare a minimum income of at least three thousand rupees and have basic amenities, such as furniture, a house with walls at least six feet high, and a roof of aluminum or asbestos. MFI clients can have a maximum of two loans out at a time, but informal loans are never counted. MFIs verify all these details through extensive interactions before disbursing funds (see chapter 3). These minimum criteria situate MFI clients within India's complex hierarchies of class, caste, and location. Neither poor nor wealthy, MFI clients are economically active women living in areas where access to health care, clean water, and sanitation are everyday challenges. For most, access to these amenities, rather than access to loans, would most directly benefit their quality of life.

The following two biographies of reliable MFI clients who have attended training and paid their loans on time offer a snapshot of possible microfinancial impacts. After many years, these clients continue to need and to use high-interest MFI loans and find their usage embedded in the social and affective ties that structure their everyday lives. Their continued usage of loans justifies the continued expansion of the microfinance industry.

GIRIJA: WORKING AGAINST TRAUMA, FORGING A PATH

Girija lived in a dense neighborhood close to the center of Bengaluru in a well-appointed flat on the main road, just a short walk from the site of Sowbagya's meetings. The adjacent neighborhood was crowded with small concrete houses lacking permanent roofs, but across a bridge spanning a river of open sewage, the road widened and was flanked by three new buildings. Girija's house was on the ground floor with a carport containing a shiny red Hyundai belonging to the owner of the flat. Inside, Girija's home had a sofa, a TV, a fridge, a water filter, a modular kitchen, and new cream tiles identical to those in upper-middle-class homes in other parts of the city. The house looked as if it might even have a private bathroom, a rarity in the neighborhood. But as we discussed her past, Girija's smiling, welcoming countenance and comfortable surroundings started to appear superficial.

Girija had grown up in the same community but as an orphan. Her mother had run away with another man when she was still a young child, and her father, a drunkard, abandoned her, despite having had a good position in a bank. She stayed with a grandmother and finished tenth grade, a significant accomplishment under the circumstances. Her grandmother had little to give her but kept a small plot of land in Girija's name and built a simple house. Before she died, her grandmother authorized a written statement in front of the police that the house belonged to Girija, as she did not wish Girija to live in a rented house. Girija's brother and father, however, never respected her rights to the plot. Family members fought constantly, and

Girija suffered chronic abuse from those who claimed the property. To shame and intimidate her, relatives compared her to her mother, who had run away. When I asked whether her marriage had been arranged or a love match, Girija replied that it had to be arranged. If she had married for love, her family would have "beaten [her] black and blue."

Marriage changed Girija's fortunes for the better. Her husband was understanding, and she could move out of her abusive environment into another home. For years, the couple struggled financially, largely because of medical expenses. She used her first Sowbagya loan, six years before our interview, to pay off an emergency room visit that was followed by three days in intensive care after giving birth to a stillborn child. Her husband had held odd jobs, ranging from cleaning toilets to painting houses, until he finally could hold down a well-paid position as an administrative assistant for a local company. They have since moved into better housing and live what she called a life with "standard" (using the English word).

Although she no longer needed Sowbagya loans, Girija felt the loans had helped her and her husband through tough times. With unstable health, she had been unable to work regularly, although she implied that she might have done domestic work in the past. At the time of our interview, Girija was focused on raising her two children in a stable home and providing them with a good education, as different from her own traumatic past as possible. Her mother, she said, wished to reconcile with her and even lived nearby with children from her most recent marriage, but Girija did not wish to be in touch with her. Girija's open sharing of her life story revealed an upward mobility still fraught with ill health, uncertainty, and the lasting effects of childhood trauma caused by her intersecting gender and class identities. Her account thus offers us a portrait not only of class diversity within slum neighborhoods but also of the extreme vulnerability that can lie just beneath the surface. Girija has been an MFI customer for six years and has experienced the positive impact of loans providing a cushion for her medical vulnerability. But the mobility she has experienced comes from her husband's improved position, which could be tenuous and easily undermined by circumstances outside her control.

RATNA: WORKER-ORGANIZER EMBEDDED IN COMMUNITY

Ratna led a microfinance group in a dense neighborhood in the Anna Nagar section of Chennai. She had hosted one of Kanchan's trainings and was enthusiastic about Shaktisri's teachings and their potential to benefit her. Relative to other group members, Ratna was spunky and outspoken. Everyone clearly respected her. Ratna had dreams for the future similar to many women I spoke to: she wished to own a home and have her children study well and get good jobs. Rather than wishing for her daughter to marry well, she reported needing to set up her daughter with a good business. Unlike many MFI clients I interviewed, Ratna believed in the promise of microenterprise for women and wished to promote it in her community.

Ratna's husband worked for a local candy company, loading and unloading wrappers for chocolate rolls. He was paid on a piece rate, per sack he unloaded, but at his employer the day's total earnings were shared among workers. His pay varied from as little as three hundred rupees to as much as two thousand rupees in a day. Because the palettes on which the wrappers were stored were so large and heavy, they required five people working together to unload and move them. As Ratna explained, "He struggles. He does not wear a tie and sit in an A/C room. He slogs. We cannot eat three meals a day comfortably. So I also have to join him and work. . . . I cannot sit in the home on the pretext that he has gone out to earn for our livelihood."

As a well-connected member of the community, Ratna made her living through a combination of informal work and organizing around various state and commercial products meant to target communities like hers. Her main income, she reported, came from commissions for facilitating and finalizing land deals, a huge source of profit and dispossession in neoliberal India. Several microfinance clients I interviewed played informal roles in the large, speculative economy around real estate, where marginally more privileged members of a community leveraged those privileges to set up land deals.[22] As a group leader, Ratna also mobilized her community around diverse financial products, including commercial microfinance. The women, led by Ratna, worked together in self-help groups and rotating credit associations. She thus carried out what I detail in chapter 4 as social work, crucial volunteering that channels knowledge, state and private funds, and other resources earmarked for marginalized women and children toward her own working-class community.

Ratna's position in her community stemmed from years of organizing, in addition to other privileges related to class, caste, or political party. From her position, she could leverage detailed knowledge of her community for land deals, microfinance, self-help groups, and perhaps other activities targeting marginalized groups. Through these resources, she viewed herself as a provider. "Whenever anyone is in need of money, for school fees, for instance, we draw five thousand rupees [from our credit association] and give it to them, charging one hundred rupees in interest," she explained. "We adjust [to help others]." Ratna believed that the entrepreneurial trainings she was receiving from Kanchan could be useful if community members would band together, on a cooperative basis, and open a shop or other type of business. Unfortunately, the training was directed to individuals who might start small businesses and provided little guidance for starting a cooperative.

As with many clients I met, Ratna found the products and services directed to her working at cross-purposes with her own vision of a possible future. In contrast to Girija, she was yet to experience real upward mobility, despite years organizing in her community and working in whatever informal capacities she could. Her husband's continued employment in the most labor-intensive end of the informal economy meant few options for moving her family ahead. She pinned her hopes on microenterprise but continued to harbor a cooperative, community-centric vision of a microentrepreneurial business, a vision fundamentally different from the individually driven entrepreneurship promoted in Shaktisri's trainings.

MAKING A LIVING AND MOVING UP IN URBAN INDIA: A GENDER AND CLASS ANALYSIS

Although Girija and Ratna's biographies cannot represent India's tens of millions of microfinance clients, their stories give us a sense of the class variation among women microfinance borrowers in urban India. For microfinance clients like Girija and Ratna, relationships with husbands, children, neighbors, and a range of family members shape livelihoods, aspirations, and trajectories of class and residential mobility. More specifically, their husbands' jobs play a significant role in setting up their economic conditions, and loans do not alter women's structural economic dependence on men because they do not enhance women's positions in the labor markets or improve their entitlements to property. While Girija was experiencing upward mobility at the time of our interview, others, like Ratna, face more uncertain futures and pin their hopes to their own resourcefulness and creative strategies.

Girija, who is younger and a mother to young children, appears to have experienced significant upward mobility, but the violence from her past, as well as her proximity to relatives who previously abused her, means she retains a sense of uncertainty. Will Girija and her husband be able to continue renting their comfortable flat? Will they ever attain homeownership? Girija's narrative also hints at the ways in which class and the strictures of respectable femininity may have permanently damaged any future relationship with her mother. Girija and other clients I spoke to (see Vijaya in chapter 4) also mention major medical events, largely stemming from poor access to health care and physically punishing occupations. Loans helped cover medical expenses but had to be repaid with high rates of interest.[23] Perhaps the most entrepreneurial among these clients, Ratna, was determined to create a promising future. She relied upon community connections to realize her goals, carefully cultivating what Pierre Bourdieu calls social capital—dense interconnections to people with varying levels of social power—to make a livelihood for her family.[24]

Considering client biographies with an intersectional perspective pivots a discussion of the impact of microfinance toward a more realistic assessment of how loans enter into women's livelihoods and that of their families. While loans can provide financial cushions and an avenue of hope in an economy that devalues the labor of marginalized women, any mobility they are able to derive while taking loans is tentative. Analysis of client biographies contextualizes loans in ways that narrow impact evaluations cannot and reveals how histories of trauma, family negotiations over property, reproductive health access, and social capital all influence how loans get articulated on the ground. It is not just that women are making microfinance fit, as scholars have argued about microfinance in other contexts, but rather that loans land in clients' families in diverse ways, and thus their real impact cannot easily be generalized or reduced to a measurable index. A fuller understanding of how loans articulate with the complex inequalities that marginalized women face provides us with a more realistic understanding of both MFI loans and self-help loans, allowing for the development of policies and programs that can support the situated lives of clients.

Conclusion

This chapter revisits the pervasive topic of impact within the microfinance and development literature and suggests an altogether different approach: an examination of the class trajectories of the actors involved in the industry at various links in the hierarchical chain, always in conjunction with considerations of caste, gender, and geography, among other relevant intersectional factors. Extrapolating from C. Wright Mills's understanding of biography as history, I examined the biographies of transnational MFI workers, MFI leaders, frontline workers, and clients. I show that while those actors in the upper echelons of India's commercial microfinancial chain, especially men, shore up their positions of privilege through sustained engagement in the industry, these outcomes can be quite different for women and men coming into the industry from non-elite backgrounds.[25] In contrast, clients experience a more ambivalent impact, as loans extract significant value from women's everyday lives without shoring up their entitlements to work or property. In between these two ends of the microfinancial chain, frontline workers, especially men, who otherwise may have limited prospects for employment and career development, find rare opportunities for mobility within the industry and, as in the case of Velan, manage to improve their lives. Still, as I showed by introducing Abraham's interview, caste and class discrimination keeps even long-term employees out of strategic upper-tier positions. It is likely, rather, that elite workers are recruited directly into these positions. When viewed together, this industry-wide view of impact with an eye to gender, caste, and geography highlights the extent to which such inequalities are not only perpetuated by the industry but required for their smooth functioning.

An intersectional and industry-wide understanding of impact injects political sensibilities into an economistic concept that has been used to justify narrow assessments of programs oriented toward women's empowerment and financial inclusion. This nuanced, historically grounded approach requires engagement with the real conditions of the labor market, the hetero-patriarchal construction of families, and varied levels of access to sanitation, medical care, education, and property. It rests upon the relational, chains-oriented approach championed throughout this book to bring to fruition an understanding of microfinance's impact that accounts for actually existing conditions of gendered and class-based power.

CONCLUSION

As I write this conclusion, it has become clear that the microfinance sector in India has again faced crisis, this time due to the ravages of COVID-19. Once again, the sector is likely to improve. Prior to the lockdown, the Indian microfinance sector had enjoyed a 30 percent surge, and their outstanding loan portfolio touched 232,000 crores of rupees (approximately $31 billion USD).[1] The old patterns of scaling up and overlending that precipitated the 2010 crisis had made a comeback, and the industry was bracing for another crisis in the Northeast, one of the newest areas for expansion.[2] Nonetheless, clients across the country continued repaying in the early days of the March lockdown. By May, however, repayments declined, and as much 70 percent of clients were requesting moratoriums as their income streams dried up.[3] Yet, the industry remained optimistic. In an *Economic Times* column by Manoj Joseph Nambiar, the new head of the industry consortium MFIN, he expressed optimism that the industry would thrive, thanks to the reliability, pluck, and loyalty of their large base of women customers, like Rekha Devi of Madhya Pradesh, who traveled alone to her local branch office to repay her loan installment on the first day of the lockdown on March 25.[4] But clients like Rekha Devi were not the only ones that would save the industry through the COVID crisis. In the following months, the industry appealed to the Reserve Bank to cut the industry some slack—they requested a moratorium and access to special funds designed to increase liquidity during the crisis.[5] Amid the gloom of the crisis, investors remained optimistic about the sector and continued to invest, keeping both debt and equity levels positive for the industry.[6] By July, shored up by the relatively resilient rural sector, the industry looked poised to retain its market share, albeit with some consolidation.[7] Furthermore, the small finance banks, the special class of organizations that were previously MFIS but now offer a greater range of services, were shaping up to be employment engines in a time of high unemployment. COVID required more loan officers and frontline staff to aid in collection, and the organizations with the financial wherewithal to handle it were hiring in large numbers.[8]

The ups and downs of India's commercial microfinance industry in the context of the COVID-19 crisis highlight the themes I have underlined throughout this book: a reliance on gendered structures of vulnerability and obligation, the persistent support of state policies and financial investors, and perhaps most importantly, an ability for power brokers within the industry to tweak the rules in order to sustain themselves, all in the name of serving the vulnerable. While interest rates have declined as MFIS have become more efficient, they still exceed 20 percent, despite what Nambiar boasts is a "99% plus" repayment rate that would be the envy of any other sector. But interest rates alone do not explain the methods through which financial companies extract value from a vulnerable client base of women. In this book, I have gone beyond the critique of the interest rates that MFIS charge and have examined instead how the structure, ideology, and positioning of the MFI industry deepens social inequalities, especially along lines of gender and class, while relying upon them for smooth functioning.

MFIs Rely Upon Class and Gender Inequality for Smooth Functioning

The commercial MFI industry, like its state-led counterpart, relies upon specific understandings of gender, class, and caste to balance the competing imperatives of profit and efficiency. Nambiar invoked the loyalty and sense of responsibility of client Rekha Devi as evidence of the need and virtue of MFI women clients, even during the pain of the lockdown. In this opinion piece, as in most journalistic coverage of the industry, the figure of the microfinance borrower, a woman, stands in for a diverse section of the Indian citizenry that is marginalized on the basis of class and caste and can be saved by the reliability of this woman and others like her. Rekha Devi's business, her relationships with other women, and her propensity to save in order to take care for her family members would ultimately save the microfinance sector as well.

I have argued in this book that in order to understand this set of assumptions, we must conceptualize microfinance as an extractive industry, one that extracts financial and symbolic value from marginalized women to individuals and groups in more privileged social locations, primarily men. The financial value that microfinance extracts is made possible by the extraordinary lengths to which economically constrained, socially vulnerable women will go in order to get by. Leveraging inequalities within their communities, groups of women composed of more and less vulnerable women take loans together and accumulate enmeshed social and economic obligations to one another in order to meet their families' basic needs, especially in relation to medical and educational expenses. This level of commitment to their loans, in itself a form of unpaid gendered labor that holds India's gendered financial ecosystem together, is required because of the diminishing avenues that exist for marginalized women to enhance their entitlements to either the labor market or to property, two improvements that would allow women to live more secure lives. Relationships between loan officers and clients are also squeezed to extract repayment and creditworthiness, requiring loan officers to find inventive ways to cover up defaults, prevent nonpayment, and encourage repeat business, whatever the circumstances the clients find themselves in.

But MFIS do not sustain themselves on financial value alone. I have shown that powerful actors also require the extraction of symbolic value from women borrowers. In particular, stories of entrepreneurial success overcoming hardship, stories of MFIs assisting customers in their times of need, and stories of upward mobility from women clients assist MFIs in establishing their legitimacy as organizations engaged in a social mission. These stories, as I have shown particularly in relation to training, must be profoundly decontextualized if they are to serve the aim of shoring up the legitimacy of MFIS. They must focus on a woman's individual story while denying the multiple factors that play into a family's changing fortunes, which are always tenuous for borrowers' families. The extracted stories carry symbolic value for the industry if and only if they make it appear that the loans or the training were the primary factors that made the difference. Frontline MFI workers must constantly be engaged in the work of identifying and recording potential stories of clients to share with their corporate offices in order to continue to uplift the public image of MFIS. Their continued ability to effectively convey symbolic value to a broad audience, both in India and abroad, allows for sustained patterns of exploitative financial extraction to escape scrutiny.

When we turn our analytical gaze to internal MFI operations, we find gendered and class inequalities reproduced even more starkly, as the logics of corporate masculinity that privilege scale, profit, and efficiency trump considerations of fairness and a commitment to justly serving customers what they really need. While the financial system "delivers power and prestige impersonally"[9] into the hands of a few privileged men who make decisions on behalf of the whole industry, women workers who join MFIS encounter a sticky floor in which their deep understanding of customer needs and priorities is undervalued. Women MFI workers, especially those with children, find few paths to promotion or advancement and thus limited options to establish thriving careers. Such practices are particularly ironic for an industry that aims to serve marginalized women. But MFIS' explicit focus on efficiency and profit maximization requires women workers and clients alike to restrict their focus to child-rearing and homemaking while men focus on breadwinning. MFIS understand women as liabilities to their organizations, especially if they are mothers. As a result, the insights that women MFI workers bring into their client-facing work are excluded from MFI corporate culture. Instead, caste and class-privileged men make economic and political decisions that drive forward the financial profits of the firms they promote and run.

Synthesizing perspectives from feminist commodity chains, actor-oriented sociology, and relational work allows us to understand not just whether MFIS are good or bad but *how they work*. I have shown that the gender, class, and, more implicitly, caste divisions that persist in millennial India are not only unchallenged by microfinance but are also required for smooth functioning. As actors pursue their own situated interests in their own specific arenas of the industry, whether in lending, training, investing, or program design, they aim to balance the twin imperatives of profit and legitimacy. Essential relational work, both among clients and between clients and workers, smooths the day-to-day labor of recruitment, disbursement, and collection, while a highly visible but nonessential relational work by remote microfinance professionals and peer-to-peer lenders abroad heightens the legitimacy of microfinance as an enterprise. All the while, the unpaid and underpaid labor of marginalized women produces high repayment rates at high interest rates and performs deference and care to those higher up. These dynamics further cement the ideal of a hetero-patriarchal household composed of a caretaking woman and a breadwinning man, while disincentivizing any effort to improve women's entitlements to labor markets or property. Relational work, whether essential or nonessential, is itself embedded within the context of structural inequality and helps to shore up the relationships required for effective extraction to take place.

The fuller picture of this gender and class extraction, however, cannot be understood by focusing on the actions of commercial financial entities alone. As I have argued throughout the book, the invisibilized state gives sanction, policy support, funding, and mandates that set up this industry and promote it, a set of dynamics that, as introduced at the start of this chapter, has become visible once again during the COVID-19 crisis.

The Invisibilized State

When I started this project, I largely believed what was previously dubbed "the microfinance schism"[10] in the literature: that there was for-profit commercial microfinance on one hand and nonprofit microfinance on the other, and that the for-profit flavor was exploitative while the other was not (or at least less so). Throughout my research with MFIS, an analogous presumption pervaded all programming: that MFIS were more efficient than state programs and served the people better than state programs. Higher-up interviewees sometimes mentioned specific government policies or the Reserve Bank, but their narratives still obscured the role of the state in promoting and expanding India's commercial microfinance sector. The "extractive industry" framing I advance in this book exposes the importance of factors such as national regulations, price controls, the balance between public and private ownership, and the amount of competition in Indian microfinance. These are all factors that are central to policy conversations about other extractive industries, such as minerals or natural gas. In the case of microfinance, this framework helps us see how regulations affect MFIS; how the state, through its inadequate policy provisions in other areas, such as education and health care, creates a demand for MFI services; and, finally, how the state's past and current policies affect competition and the organizational landscape.

When we understand microfinance as an industry, we start to see how important national regulations are in setting up the conditions under which microfinance operates. Although I had anticipated the story of commercial microfinance in India to be primarily one of foreign influence (local-global), I found instead a story of an invisibilized state. The Indian state, after decades of failed policies geared toward the unbanked majority, turned to private financial institutions that operate on the principles of efficiency, scale, and profit to "include" millions of unbanked women. This turn occurred within the context of a large-scale liberalization of banking that reversed decades of active expansion on the part of the nationalized banking sector. The key ideas behind that turn were likely influenced by global trends: microfinance initiatives were gaining prominence around the globe from the 1990s onward. But the explanation of the specific shape and character of India's microfinance industry can be found in the story of national and state-level banking policies. These policies not only included the establishment of the National Agricultural Bank (NABARD) and the dramatic rollout of SHGs around the country but also the nonregulation of new commercial institutions at first. Later, the Reserve Bank funneled key priority sector funds from mainstream banks mandated to lend to marginalized groups to MFIS. Structurally, the Indian state set up the commercial microfinance industry to expand the availability of debt to the most vulnerable and used disadvantaged rural and, later, urban women to advance that goal. In so doing, the state abdicated its responsibility to provide fair financial services to those who need it most. In lieu of fulfilling that responsibility, the state set up a new corporate structure to manage poverty through the creation of a gendered financial ecosystem.

When we understand the state workings in this way, the microfinance schism is rendered moot. Yes, it may be that SHG loans are less exploitative and, relatively speaking, more desirable than commercial MFI loans, as recent research has suggested,[11] but the bigger picture is that both of these kinds of loans produce a saturated financial environment that excludes those who need the most help. This gendered financial ecosystem, structured by hierarchical chains, extracts value from slightly better-off women who can draw upon their familial and social resources to repay expensive loans.

The MFI industry has expanded not because it improves the lives of its clients, although it may in many circumstances, but because it *works*. I have argued that it works because of its reliance on existing inequalities, as touched on above, but it also works because the state cushions it, promotes it, and ensures that it can continue to function efficiently, whatever crises may come. These cushions do not prevent future crises of overlending, as the near crisis in pre-COVID 2020 makes clear, but it does protect the most privileged in the microfinancial chains I have identified: the leaders of the industry and, to a lesser extent, the employees. Although one of the original arguments for privatizing microfinance was that a private company would be more beholden to a client's real needs and desires, the state-led character of commercial microfinance ensures that neither the sense of entitlement provided by state services nor the sense of customer choice provided in consumer markets applies. The livelihoods, entitlements, and well-being of women clients of microfinance who hold up the industry are the last priority for the state, who simply wish to include, even if that inclusion is adverse or predatory.[12]

When we get closer to the ground, we find that in women clients' everyday lives, the state and the services of private MFIS are inseparable. When loan officers recruit, vet, disburse, and successfully collect loans, they cocreate creditworthiness in order to meet state mandates. Loan officers may skirt official rules to participate in this cocreation, but even the character of trust and relationality built between clients and loan officers has emerged from procedures that the state put in place after the crisis of 2010. The very texture of MFI interactions with clients borrows from, while rubbing against, state-led self-help group programs. MFIS try to promote solidarity among clients, respectful and supportive relationships between clients and staff, and an ethos of self-determination, all features borrowed from state programs, but always with small changes that make a big difference: more loan products, higher interest rates, limited training or services, and a shallower, profit-oriented engagement with clients' real situated lives. For clients, they are simply an array of financial products. And clients do not necessarily have the luxury of choosing between them according to their merits. They choose the loans they take out of necessity and a paucity of other options.

Although MFIS present success stories that make it appear as if their loans alone have transformed women's lives, I have shown that these outcomes are always already embedded in state-provided services and policies. When Selvi, for example, gets presented as a successful graduate of an entrepreneurial training program, we learn at closer examination that she has been a serial entrepreneur who has leveraged state programs in order to get her equipment and is waiting for state-provided power in order to get the machine running. While the MFI-provided training program may have given her an extra boost of confidence, it is the larger infrastructure of programming geared to support women with her particular combination of advantage and disadvantage that allows her to be a success. MFI group leaders, as I showed, are relatively advantaged women who corral both state and private programs to help their communities, sometimes with private aims of gain in mind. In all of these arenas, explicit policies, implicit ideologies, and histories of state services toward marginalized women are evident.

This analysis of the invisibilized state corrects a tendency in some corners of the microfinance literature to overstate the influence of global norms and institutions in shaping the everyday dynamics of financialization. While global norms and institutions are indeed important, when the core ideas of microfinance, gendered empowerment, and financial inclusion became salient in India, they were articulated primarily through state programs that then determined the specifics of their subsequent expansion. Actors in the global North, however, continue to play an important, if peripheral, role in microfinance's public image. As I showed in the case of US-based MFI professionals and Kiva.org lenders, the assumptions and engagements of development actors in the global North serve to further obscure the real social and political conditions under which microfinance expands, sheltering the industry from sustained scrutiny.

Gendered Extraction, Not Women's Empowerment

The multilayered analysis of microfinance I have provided here shows that microfinance, far from being a women's empowerment initiative, facilitates value extraction from poor women, who produce value through their underpaid informal labor, their unpaid community labor, and their ability to deftly navigate a complex and unfair gendered financial ecosystem. The picture that emerges suggests that the neoliberal, financialized iteration of women's empowerment that microfinance represents disempowers particularly non-poor, working-class women by locking them more tightly into informal labor markets and the hetero-patriarchal household. By incorporating the social and relational work of microfinance into women's existing productive, reproductive, and community labor obligations, microfinance—whether state led or commercial—limits the potential for women to thrive economically and sustain a life free of structural and physical violence.

Yet official discourse and reporting on microfinance has come to erase gender altogether, even as programs and services designed to sustain marginalized women have declined. In official state discourse, the language of "financial inclusion," "excluded groups," and "priority sector" de-genders what is fundamentally a gendered development intervention. The erasure of gender from official microfinance discourse means that, as with many development discourses dating back to colonialism, women in microfinance are no longer subjects of their own history. The actual voices and experiences of women borrowers figure negligibly into the policies and practices of MFIS. Thus, microfinance works through women to support the impoverished prospects of breadwinning men. Women borrowers must support men whom they are married to, raise children, repay, and take out more loans. Furthermore, they also support other men who are usually not part of their communities: men working for MFIS who experience upward mobility when jobs are scarce, men higher up in MFIs who consolidate their profits and high social status, and men in government who support MFIs rather than providing the basic social services they require. When women continue to take out loans year after year, they can be viewed as creditworthy and successful, regardless of whether they are able to acquire skills and tools to counter the conditions of marginalization they face in their own lives.

This is a fundamental transformation of what the earliest version of microfinance—small-scale microcredit—aimed to be. At the dawn of the microcredit movement, the intention was to build women's capabilities, not only through loans but also through analysis that would lift up their experiences and counter the structural conditions of their marginalization. There are still versions of this increasingly rare variety of microcredit that exist throughout India and around the world, but they are not financially sustainable and they do not scale. For such organizations, repayment with low interest rates is important, but it is not the goal.[13] The goal is the transformation of women's vulnerability and the improvement of their entitlements within their communities and within society at large. Such a model requires intensive supports and responds to local community needs and failures. It is neither lucrative nor charitable. Rather, it is about client learning and application, repairing structural violence, and forging livable futures. It requires funding and decentralized management. And most importantly, it is no substitute for what clients really need scaled up: access to education, health care, and a minimum standard of living that ensures basic access to food and shelter.[14]

But the logic of scaling microfinance up—the fundamental imperative driving state and local programming—does not allow for extra supports, failures, or adaptation. It operates on the logic of coverage and inclusion rather than repair and transformation. The success of microfinance and other large-scale efforts to bank the unbanked for profit has come through a drive for efficiency and scale that has steamrolled the situated needs and desires of the very women it aims to serve. Financialization jet-powered this process of scaling up, took the core idea of microcredit, and transformed it into a neoliberal tool of gendered exploitation, stripping it of the contexts in which it emerged and turning it into a modular solution controlled by the most powerful and privileged actors in societies around the world. This situation requires not only a wholescale reevaluation of what financial inclusion is and who it serves but also how its success is measured and who gets to do the measuring. This requires transforming banking regulations and policies that prop up MFIs and their privileged leaders while also taking a hard look at the sector. Since this book has focused on the sector itself, I focus my comments on changing course within the sector, recognizing how well established it is today.

Changing Course in Gender and Microfinance

Given the resilience of the sector and its deep networked connections within vulnerable communities, I do not suggest abolition of the industry but rather a thorough reexamination of principles through which companies within the sector operate and the logics through which they understand clients. The identification of key mechanisms of gender and class inequality mean that many of these practices, if actively reversed or transformed, could potentially change the course of microfinance in India and around the world. In parallel, if new policies shore up women's entitlements to property and basic services, the demand for microfinance could decline enough to make the industry truly accountable. Several specific recommendations emerge from the analysis I have offered here. If implemented together, these changes could move the state toward programming that values women not only as mothers and care providers but also as workers and subjects of property.

In millennial India, women of all class backgrounds wish to establish social identities that involve paid work outside their homes, even if is not their primary identity. But in 2018, India faced a historic level of unemployment, with the highest rate—10.8 percent—reported for urban women.[15] The women I interviewed almost all wished to be engaged in paid work, often referred to as "doing something" rather than "sitting at home." Not all women I spoke with necessarily wished to be known as workers or entrepreneurs, but most did desire the respect and salary of a proper job, a goal that was unimaginable for many.

An exchange with Halima, a Kanchan MFI client I introduced in chapter 6, stands out in this regard. Halima had just explained to me that she had no real reason to take the loan for business purposes because the money she made from embroidery was too paltry a sum to be worth the time and effort. Mainly, she was taking it in order to be able to take a much larger loan in the future that might let her work at her husband's shop. She waited patiently until I had asked all my questions before revealing her real interest in speaking with me that day: Did I work for Kanchan? And did I know whether they were hiring? When I said that I did not work for the MFI and did not know if they were hiring, she was visibly disappointed but also made me assure her that if any opportunity came up, I would let her know right away. Halima was a young mother with a young child but was eager for a chance to work. She regarded MFI work as good work. As I have mentioned in my ethnographic accounts throughout the book, there were many instances in which women specifically inquired about what opportunities I could provide for them with regard to employment or a real business opportunity that would succeed. I was usually embarrassed to say that I did not have any real leads for them.

While national-level gender policy has promoted education and health care for women to some extent within the framework of women's empowerment, what has been left off the agenda has been attention to women as salaried workers. A 2015 World Bank study suggests that the declining workforce participation rate for women in India since 2012 can be explained in part by the fact that there are more women than ever who wish to participate in the paid labor force in India, but there hasn't been a proportional increase in jobs that are considered appropriate for women.[16] National and state-level policy can actively incentivize organizations to hire women from all backgrounds and provide financial incentives if needed to help retain them over time. Such policies would shore up the economy and work toward transforming a system in which men must appear to be breadwinners while women must appear to be care providers.

Within the industry, significant steps can be taken to make MFI engagements with women clients more suited to their short and long-term interests. In all the urban Indian neighborhoods where I conducted fieldwork with clients, there were women clients interested in being employed with an MFI, like Halima. The women working at MFIs that I spoke with were outstanding at their jobs and expressed pride in their positions, despite tremendous personal and professional sacrifices. Thus, MFIs must take active steps to recruit and hire women, providing support with maternity and childcare. Recent research has shown that training programs geared toward retaining women in their jobs, as well as employer-sponsored childcare, can strongly improve worker retention and reduce turnover for firms in India.[17] My ethnographic work further suggests that having more women MFI workers in the lives of women clients provides inspiration for social, physical, and class mobility. Once again, attentiveness to how gender and class intersect and inform understandings of femininity and work help us to better envision a more inclusive future for India's financial inclusion trajectory.

Relatedly, MFIs can and should take action to break both the class ceiling and the glass ceiling for a chance at systemic transformation. As I reflect upon the experiences of poverty and casteism that many entry-level employees experience in their MFI careers, it becomes clear that advancing men and women within the organization to the upper echelons of MFIS could provide a radically new policy perspective within the industry. An MFI workforce that is more diverse at every level of the industry would go a long way toward ensuring that MFI policies can be fair for clients and equitable for India's development goals overall. This is not to say that the specialized knowledge of financial industry insiders is irrelevant but rather that these forms of knowledge have skewed the social orientation of the industry and enriched those who already sit at the top of India's class structure.[18] MFIS, unlike other financial companies, provide a radical set of opportunities because they are geared toward serving the poor and working classes of India and other global South countries. Can they rise to the ethical task of serving them where they actually are, putting the situated needs and desires of borrowers ahead of imperatives to increase profit and scale up?

I offer these recommendations because, despite many bumps in the road, it is my view that the commercial microfinance industry has become entrenched in India's urban working-class communities. Women coming of age in urban India today understand their role as partly about loan taking and its many unpaid responsibilities. Debt in itself, however, does not provide a sustainable livelihood, even if it may, in the short term, stem the acute deprivations of poverty. If a gendered understanding of financial inclusion and its pitfalls does not infuse the future of microfinance in India and elsewhere, then the industry will continue to serve as an engine for inequality, oppression, and marginalization rather than for livelihoods, repair, and transformation.

Financialization in the Particular: A Ground-Up View

This book advances the study of financialization by demonstrating how, with regard to microfinance, financialization deepens social inequalities. While systemic, firm-level, and everyday studies of financialization all recognize that the multi-scalar phenomenon relies upon and perpetuates social inequalities,[19] it is left to scholars to investigate exactly how and where these inequalities aid in the smooth functioning of dominant institutions. Studying microfinance helps us see how poverty alleviation has become a financial product that extracts, even as it appears to provide. Here, I have leveraged ethnography and interviews to show that the financialization of poverty is not only occurring in policies, algorithms, and in the halls of power at global institutions. It also unfolds as a lived reality, experienced by elite and nonelite social actors in specific times and places.

So, how are the dynamic conditions of financialization experienced by the social groups I studied?

For women borrowers, financialization is experienced as wraparound debt. Women clients, if they are lucky with adequate family supports, learn to navigate a hazardous and saturated financial ecosystem that requires them to take out high-interest debt to meet the requirements for basic human thriving: medical needs, education, and maintaining a stable residence. They accept the loans from every direction—from the state, from commercial MFIS, from traditional banks if they can get it, from relatives, and from moneylenders. While clients juggle the varied repayment schedules, interest rates, terms, and expectations of these loans, they must sustain themselves and their families and appear grateful while doing it. Pinning their hopes on the education and betterment of their children, a woman borrower must set aside aspirations for her own education and upward mobility in order to serve her family and the financial institutions she owes. If she is lucky enough to be married to a man who is upwardly mobile, a rarity in an economy that relies heavily on an informal employment with no protections and high unemployment rates, she may be able to realize her modest hopes.

For MFI workers who are men, financialization means access to a stable job with a real shot at upward mobility. The work of recruiting women, making them creditworthy, and retaining them as long-term customers has become a viable livelihood in India, as in many parts of the world. The men I interviewed and observed who work at the front lines of MFIS, out of all the actors I observed who participate in microfinancial chains, are best able to fulfill personal aspirations for stability and, sometimes, upward mobility, albeit within limits. That this pathway exists primarily for men within a corporate institution structured by masculine dominance is not a coincidence. Rather, their success, even more than the dubious success of women clients, sustains the legitimacy of the sector as these workers construct durable relationships of trust between a client base of marginalized women and a profit-oriented financial institution.

Those at the top of the industry are financialization's winners. They experience enhanced wealth, status, and reputation by managing relationships between investors and policy makers and ensuring that their institutions grow in a durable fashion, even when faced with crisis. They collude with one another and with the state in order to maintain the dominance of the industry within the space of India's banking sector and benefit from regulations that channel critical sources of capital, earmarked for serving the marginalized masses, toward their institutions. While their individual intentions may be altruistic and service oriented, the lack of a critical perspective on financialization, gender, or poverty means that the institutions they build in the wake of financialization advance their own positions without engaging in the work of social transformation.

For remote microfinancial actors, most of whom likely enjoy lifestyles that are possible due largely to financialization, the promise of credit to faraway racialized women holds the promise of salvation for global inequalities. It creates the possibility that any kind of debt, in the hands of a capable woman, can alleviate poverty and save the world. Not only does this perspective perpetuate false and inaccurate understandings of women in poverty around the world, it also obscures the real relationships and circumstances that get women in India and other parts of the global South to pay back on time, almost every time.

An ethnography of financialization in relation to microfinance situates and particularizes the diverse social effects of this global political economic shift to reveal that underpaid and unpaid gendered work, particularly at the base of microfinancial chains, is still required to produce value for financial products. This finding invites us to rethink how gender, labor, and power figure into the logics, practices, institutions, and algorithms of financialization at multiple scales. Only once we uncover the specific mechanisms through which financialization supports and perpetuates inequality—political, programmatic, interactive, and organizational—can we start to reorient, reverse, and counter the proliferation of structural violence and inequality that financialization leaves in its wake.

As a young-looking Indian-American woman and mother, researching the microfinance industry in south India required me to draw upon many cross-cutting identities. I had to observe and interview clients, workers, and leaders with very divergent social locations in India. Access at every stage was difficult and contested. Each program, company, and individual I contacted for research presented me with a new set of complicated social interactions. In all these interactions, I had to balance my status as a dominant-caste, foreign-born Indian woman scholar (a set of identities that opened some doors but not others) with my quest for as comprehensive an understanding of commercial microfinance as possible, knowing that any research in such a vast industry would be partial.

As with any ethnography that interfaces with a formal organization, I needed the permission and buy-in of the company to observe official interactions and to interview employees. I found that permission was easy to obtain with organizations like Sowbagya and Bhavishya but not so easy in many others, and I was refused by many organizations. My position and identity in relation to interviewees was also a significant factor for either gaining access in the first place or navigating interactions when I did gain access. For interviews with the upper echelons of the industry, I was not important enough when I began this project in 2012. I gained access to those interviewees only after studying the topic for years and leveraging contacts in the US. In contrast, for microfinance clients in slum neighborhoods and MFI employees, I was perhaps too important, and my presence at times changed the course of a training or a set of exchanges at a meeting, and I explore those dynamics below. At all times, I was also conscious of the fact that the industry had recently undergone a crisis and had been a subject of much negative media attention. Thus, only those companies who were most confident about their practices agreed to my continued involvement in their organizations.

My initial entry into the Indian microfinance industry was facilitated through the US-based organization I call Prosperity International, which was rolling out the entrepreneurial training program Shaktisri with their corporate partners, Kanchan, a small but growing MFI. My initial contacts in New York City led to my introduction to Prosperity's head office in Bengaluru, and I started working with upper-level staff there to set up my research plan. Initial fieldwork in New York helped me understand the low priority of the entrepreneurial programs within the organization as a whole. These initial observations set up my access to training sites in Tamil Nadu and Bengaluru.

I conducted fieldwork in Tamil Nadu first, where I engaged Bagya, a retired administrative assistant and Chennai local as a research assistant. Bagya agreed to help me conduct interviews in Tamil. I understand Tamil and can speak to some extent, allowing me to nudge the interviews in the directions I wanted and interject at times. In Chennai, Coimbatore, and towns surrounding Coimbatore, Bagya and I conducted some of my most memorable fieldwork on training, shadowing the talented trainers who had a much harder job than I had initially imagined. I forged strong connections with the trainers in Tamil Nadu, those I call Rajiv and Nandini in the book. Rajiv was new to the organization and regarded my visit as a privilege and a personal compliment to him. Although his interview was not as revealing as others, his style of embodying technocratic upwardly mobile masculinity in training sessions helped me start to think about microfinance itself as a project that actually required class and gender difference/inequality in order to be successful. Nandini was also particularly welcoming and arranged visits to specific clients she had worked with for me to understand the positive impacts of the Shaktisri program. The individuals she selected helped me understand how her vision of client success, which was much more specific to the clients' interests and situation, departed in important ways from how the head office of Kanchan understood success for clients. Nonetheless, Nandini's success stories were eagerly appropriated for publicizing Shaktisri's programs. Nandini's interview was lengthy and candid, coming after a series of interactions. Her articulation of compassionate, educated femininity that was constantly trying to be relevant to the women she was serving also strongly influenced my understanding of how trainers and other upper-level staff leverage gendered performances to do their jobs.

After fieldwork in Tamil Nadu, I proceeded to Bengaluru, where I had planned to spend the bulk of my fieldwork studying the Prosperity-Kanchan partnership. Soon after my arrival in Bengaluru, I was invited to observe a grueling six-day training for trainers, or TOT session, in which all Shaktisri trainers gathered. There, I had the opportunity to observe firsthand the dynamics between Prosperity and Kanchan and to understand how the training itself stood in a grey zone between NGO work oriented toward service and a corporate social responsibility (CSR) project that was primarily oriented toward good PR for Kanchan. It became clear that despite the rhetoric that heavily valued client experiences and engagement (the trainer was a woman who usually trained NGO workers), the actual program leaders, such as Maya, were primarily interested in ensuring that the program was financially sustainable and made Kanchan look as caring as possible. Most of my observations and field notes from those packed six days did not make it into this book, but the perspective I gained from those long exhausting days helped me understand the centrality of class differences within the organization, as well as the extent to which local geography and personnel mattered to how people experienced the job.

During the TOT, participants were fairly frank with me about their exhaustion. They complained readily about all the unanswered questions they had and the unsatisfactory answers they had received. Thus, just by being there, I could witness the program's internal dynamics, which helped me understand how contested the program was as a whole for Kanchan, Prosperity's microfinance partner. I also came to understand how important the regional backgrounds of the field staff were. Although I knew the staff from Tamil Nadu and Bengaluru well by that point, those from Kerala, where Shaktisri had the most outreach, were new to me. I made many efforts to shadow those trainers and interview them, both at the TOT session and in Kerala, but I was unable to gain access to that group of trainers. From my observations at the TOT sessions, however, I guessed that these workers related to clients somewhat differently than Rajiv, Nandini, Ranjan, and other trainers I had met. Pradeep, for example, one of the most successful trainers, had been a labor organizer for decades and sang famous political songs to get buy-in from the rural communities for Shaktisri programming. His embodied presence was neither that of an NGO worker nor an upwardly mobile professional but another kind of benevolent masculinity that is specific to the context of Kerala, with its long history of labor organizing and its leftist political culture. Another man from Kerala, Kumar, similar to Rajiv in his more typical upwardly mobile self-presentation, was unusually combative. Despite being a new employee, Kumar expressed criticism of the program more openly than other trainers. He questioned the appropriateness of the program, suggesting that perhaps it had been imported from the US or Latin

America, and pushed back against some of the more tiresome requirements of his job. Maya and others in upper management did not appreciate this style. I did not see this kind of bold style from other trainers or MFI employees, and I wondered whether in Kerala's political culture, Kumar's bold style was more common.

Soon after the TOT, I started conducting more extensive fieldwork and interviews in Bengaluru, first with the Shaktisri program and later with Sowbagya and other MFI workers I met outside the purview of their firms. I hired Mamatha to help me with Kannada language interviews. Mamatha was a career NGO worker with significant experience in poor and working-class communities in and around Bengaluru, where she grew up. Mamatha and I navigated training sessions, center meetings, and individual and group client interviews in the months that followed. I found the Shaktisri program granted Mamatha and I significant access to many trainings early in my fieldwork, but as the weeks wore on, trainers took my calls less frequently and were increasingly selective about which trainings they invited me to. No doubt, my presence proved burdensome for them. They had to coordinate with me over the phone each time they conducted a training to help me get to obscure locations. Neighborhoods in Bengaluru slums were difficult to reach and often required an escort from the main road. These were not roads that cars could traverse. Usually, the homes we congregated in had no addresses or streets by which to identify them. Sometimes, even the identifying landmarks for the meeting place were unhelpful because, for example, there were many statues of Ambedkar, perhaps the foremost Dalit activist and Indian freedom fighter, in the same area.

Coordinating my presence with that of a training also proved more difficult than I expected. Sometimes, I would arrive at the designated place, but none of the clients had gathered as planned. Other times, despite my insistence that the training go on at the appointed time even if I was running late (usually due to traffic or coordination with Mamatha), the trainers would wait for me, delaying the start of the session. My late arrival understandably made clients irritable. Other times, clients did not seem to mind at all that we were late. Regardless of when we arrived, when Mamatha or Bagya and I were present, trainers made every effort to put on the best possible training they could. This expectation to perform for visitors was also understandably tiresome for them. After a few months, without ever directly declining, they stopped allowing me to accompany them, claiming that they had no trainings scheduled.

In Karnataka and Tamil Nadu alike, I was an object of curiosity, suspicion, and respect for clients, whom I invariably met through an initial introduction from the companies they took loans from. Many assumed that I was connected to the company in some way and were eager to make a good impression. My research assistants, Mamatha and Bagya, supported by me, would go to great lengths at the beginning of each interview to say that we had no connection with the company. The opening disclaimers would say, "This is Smitha and I am [Mamatha or Bagya]. We are not connected with [the company] in any way. Smitha is a professor who lives in the US, and she is doing a study about microfinance and microfinance training. She wants to know your perspective, but she will not share this information with anyone at [the company] or any other customers in this area. Please speak honestly and freely because this is just for her information. She will be writing a book based on your interview." Sometimes, the client would repeat this back to us to clarify and ask a question or two, usually asking whether I actually lived in the US. During the interview, however, I would use eye contact, smiles, and body language to set the research participant at ease and build up a rapport, sometimes interjecting an additional question or echoing the client's response to signal understanding. This was usually effective, and most clients had questions of me during and after the interview.

Despite the vast gulf between myself and the clients I was interviewing in terms of privilege, unexpected interconnections built solidarity. In one interview with a client I call Ishwari in the book, she mentioned that she migrated from Tamil Nadu to Bengaluru. I interjected (in Tamil, even though the interview was being conducted in Kannada) to ask where she was from. And we discovered that she comes from the same town my grandparents live in, and she knew exactly where my grandparents' house was on the main road. This connection made her more forthcoming in the rest of the interview, and she said repeatedly that she felt so happy that she knew where my grandparents lived. In another interview, an informal interview in which I went to meet clients in a neighborhood without Mamatha, I met a Tamil-speaking client, Ammu, who excitedly brought me to her home and peppered me with questions about my life. In the best Tamil I could muster, I responded to her questions. She was most interested to know whether I had had an arranged marriage or had married for love. When she learned that I had chosen my own husband, she was impressed. Her expression in Tamil was something akin to, "Way to go, madam! A love marriage, pretty good!" Her playful, teasing, admiring tone stayed with me for a long time. This fact about me seemed to impress her more than my qualifications or my place of residence.

In semi-urban contexts, clients complimented my humility in sitting with them on the floor in the heat for long hours, which they hadn't expected from someone who lived in the US. They seemed to find me more trustworthy as a result. In these instances and others, my identities as a (South Indian) mother with a young child, who traveled a long distance for work, and who was also educated, and thus perhaps able to help them with something, influenced how they viewed me, as did my simple cotton clothing and purposely basic self-presentation. Depending on the person and context, one or more of these identities would be salient to them, and I could never predict which. The clients who regarded me with suspicion usually did not agree to speak with me in a formal interview, and those that did were curt in their responses to my questions. But those that did take the time to speak to me often found ways to connect with me that I did not expect.

Working in MFIs was a different matter from connecting with women in client neighborhoods. As most of these employees were men, many of the identity-based areas where I found solidarity with clients did not apply. The men who were branch staff or loan officers found it difficult to place me. As a result, interviews with that group tended to be shorter and less introspective. I had richer exchanges with branch staff, trainers, and loan officers who were women. They were excited about my interest in their work, and they were happy to share their experiences and opinions, both in the workplace and with clients in the field. As a result of this difference, I have richer stories, especially of difficulties or nonpayment from women compared to men. While the women were, in general, eager to share what their lives were like, the men were careful to make sure that their words did not paint the company in a bad light. Men working at Sowbagya were on the whole unwilling to criticize their company, although previous employees such as Velan and Arathi had a bit more of a critical perspective at times.

With MFI leaders, I pivoted from "studying down" with clients or "studying across" with at least higher-up workers to "studying up," trying to interview public figures and businessmen who did not have any reason to make time for me. MFI leaders were extremely busy men with full calendars. Through a colleague in the Boston area, Kim Wilson, previously a microfinance professional in India, I gained access to a host of upper-level contacts in the industry who ended up transforming my understanding of the industry. In interviews, leaders' narratives led to revelations that corrected my understandings of how Indian MFIs were actually funded and regulated. Only then, quite late in the research process, did I come to understand the importance of the Indian state in an industry that claimed to be driven by market principles. When I finally did make contact with these leaders, I was extremely well informed and was able to ask more detailed questions than I would have if I had met them when I started the fieldwork in 2012. Some of these interviews were remarkably candid and lengthy, as the men I interviewed enjoyed the opportunity to think about their careers in the way I was asking them to do so. Others were business-like, cordial, and brief, mostly reiterating corporate talking points. Even these brief interviews were hugely informative, helping me understand the rhetoric through which MFIS articulate their own purpose and vision. In one case, a CEO set up a whole host of interviews within the company for me at the upper levels of the company and set up field visits as well. Even though these were arranged for me, these interviews helped me better understand what MFIS do at the corporate level of leadership.

Remarkably, interviews at this level seldom touched explicitly upon issues of gender. For most corporate-level interviewees, MFIS are competitive businesses that must make a profit and sustain themselves and their reputations. There was little reflection of how their own organizations may be reinforcing or alleviating gendered inequality. Some of their comments showed me they regarded me as an equal and an insider, sharing their perspective and class privilege, while others viewed me with caution, as a journalist who may decide to represent their companies in a critical light. Because of these dynamics, I know that I gained access to companies that were more confident in their internal procedures and processes than others.

The dynamics that I saw in the bulk of my India research were in many ways previewed during the time at Prosperity preceding my research. On one hand, for those in the organization promoting client education at Prosperity, my interest in their programs was a gift. My research could potentially be used to elevate the low status of client education programming in the company, a fact I came to understand very slowly. Training was viewed as the counterweight to profit orientation—a practice that could save the company's image when it faced scrutiny. They believed that perhaps my examination of training in India would help them expand the program, which was struggling in terms of profitability. But when I produced the memo I promised at the end of my research, providing several concrete suggestions to improve the program so that it would speak more directly to the situated needs of clients, there was no interest in further engagement. The response was simply that I had not seen the whole program and therefore did not understand how great the impact of it was. It is here that I came to understand what I call "distortions of distance" in chapter 6—the presumption that one's programs are for the good of the clients, even if no one realizes it yet.

The final stage of my research was with Kiva lenders and the Kiva.org website. Using social media, I snowball sampled sixty-five online surveys and interviewed a subset of those who took the survey over the phone. While my sample certainly contained an overrepresentation of respondents with a connection to Wellesley College, I found a significant diversity of views among my interviewees, allowing me to understand varied ways in which lenders used the platform and understood it. I systematically collected data directly from the website with the assistance of a computer program designed by my colleague, Eni Mustafaraj, to understand what sorts of loans visitors to the website preferred, which helped me better understand the preferences of lenders. I had realized that financial flows did not directly link Kiva.org to the organizations in India that I studied, but I could not deny that there were discursive and ideological influences that connected these two spaces nonetheless. Compared to the intensive fieldwork and in-person interviews, my work with Kiva lenders was straightforward, and I mostly interviewed "across," as most people I interviewed understood my position as a professor and identified as middle- or upper-class individuals living in the US.

Throughout the book, I took care to give pseudonyms to all the companies and individuals I worked with (with the exception of Kiva.org, since I did not directly study company employees and they have an open access website that invites research). I also have altered the names of places and identifying details in order to make the specifics of different companies' programs and personnel harder to identify for any industry insiders who read this book. Having taken these measures, I hope that both my critique and my admiration for the people who work in the Indian MFI space comes through, as it is through their openness and desire for engagement that I have been able to produce this book. These are difficult jobs in difficult times and, for the most part, under circumstances where everyone is doing the best they can. I hope that nuance and empathy comes through in my representations of those individuals, groups, and institutions I have portrayed in this book.

INTRODUCTION

1 All names in this study are pseudonyms. In some cases, identifying details about companies and individuals have been altered to preserve confidentiality. This incident took place on June 6, 2012.

2 A common outfit in India, worn by women, consisting of a long, fitted tunic and pants.

3 See Graves, "Landscapes of Predation, Landscapes of Neglect"; Gallmeyer and Roberts, "Payday Lenders and Economically Distressed Communities."

4 See the World Bank's Universal Financial Access portal: https://ufa.worldbank.org /en/country-progress/india, accessed November 5, 2019.

5 Anand and Thampi, "Recent Trends in Wealth Inequality in India," 59; Jayadev, Motiram, and Vakulabharanam, "Patterns of Wealth Disparities in India during the Liberalisation Era."

6 Agrawal, "Inequality in India."

7 Detailed in-country analysis suggests that, although poverty has been reduced, inequality has increased since liberalization, and signs of rising unemployment have been visible since the early 2000s. See Mazumdar and Sarkar, *Globalization, Labor Markets, and Inequality in India*. Since that time, the spike in Indian unemployment may have been due in part to new economic indicators. See *Economic Times*, "Is the Job Scene in India Bad?" Unemployment for urban women, at 10.8 percent, is the highest. Scholarship from the early 2000s suggests that, for young urban men, unemployment has been a huge issue for decades, despite a lack of data from official statistical sources. See Jeffrey, *Timepass*.

8 Arunachalam, *The Journey of Indian Micro-Finance*; Wichterich, "The Other Financial Crisis"; Mader, "Rise and Fall of Microfinance in India," *Strategic Change* 22, nos. 1–2: 47–66.

9 This change was about the priority sector lending rule and occurred in 2005. I explain these transformations in detail in chapter 1.

10 Rao, "Reforms with a Female Face."

11 Early studies by economists forged a connection between microfinance, women's empowerment, and poverty alleviation in South Asia that subsequent research sought to support or reject. Drawing from surveys and case studies of the state-

sponsored Grameen Bank and Bangladesh Rural Advancement Committee (BRAC), a few key studies suggested that when small loans were offered to groups of women, these borrowers could leverage their social ties to one another to guarantee the loan. Not only were women borrowers likely to repay, but small loans could elevate their economic and social positions. See Hashemi, Schuler, and Riley, "Rural Credit Programs and Women's Empowerment in Bangladesh"; Kamal, "Poverty Alleviation and Women Empowerment in South Asia." These findings have since been discredited. See Roodman, *Due Diligence*. Other early studies of microfinance in Bangladesh found the impact to be negative or mixed. See Kabeer, "Conflicts over Credit"; Goetz and Gupta, "Who Takes the Credit?"

12 For an early study in Bangladesh on women microfinance workers, see Goetz, *Women Development Workers*.

13 Karim, *Microfinance and Its Discontents*; Paprocki, "'Selling Our Own Skin'"; Brett, "'We Sacrifice and Eat Less'"; Ganle, Afriyie, and Segbefia, "Microcredit."

14 Sanyal, *Credit to Capabilities*.

15 Kabeer, "Is Microfinance a 'Magic Bullet' for Women's Empowerment?"; Moodie, "Enter Microcredit"; Goodman, "Borrowing Money, Exchanging Relationships."

16 Karim, *Microfinance and Its Discontents*.

17 Roy, *Poverty Capital*.

18 Misturelli and Heffernan, "What Is Poverty?" For a more complete discussion on the distinction between the two scales at which the financialization of poverty operates, see Mader, *The Political Economy of Microfinance*, 78–120.

19 Kar, *Financializing Poverty*.

20 I thank one of the anonymous reviewers of this manuscript for this phrase.

21 In sociology, the first occurrence of this term that I found was Bulmer, "Sociological Models of the Mining Community." More recent studies in various parts of the world corroborate Bulmer's early usage. Used more as a descriptive, rather than as an analytical category, the term has been used to analyze rural/urban interdependence, labor exploitation, and the disadvantage that resource-rich countries and areas within countries face. See, for example, Davidson and Haan, "Gender, Political Ideology, and Climate Change Beliefs in an Extractive Industry Community"; Weber, "Extractive Industries and Rural-Urban Economic Interdependence"; Freudenburg, "Addictive Economies: Extractive Industries and Vulnerable Localities in a Changing World Economy."

22 For an overview of the essentialized understandings of women that foster the "untapped resource" perspective, particularly in the 2012 World Development Report, see Chant, "Women, Girls and World Poverty." For further exploration of this and other similar constructions in development discourses, see Calkin, "'Tapping' Women for Post-Crisis Capitalism"; Andersson and Hatakka, "Victim, Mother, or Untapped Resource?"

23 Dunaway, *Gendered Commodity Chains*.

24 Bair, *Frontiers of Commodity Chain Research*; Gereffi and Korzeniewicz, *Commodity Chains and Global Capitalism*; Bair, "Global Capitalism and Commodity Chains."

25 Porter, *Competitive Advantage*.

26 Porter's model comes from a more recent variant of commodity chains analysis, known as the global value chain (GVC) model. Unlike the earlier version of commodity chains theorizing, which emphasized structural global inequalities, Porter and others in this tradition tend to pivot away from the macrocontext, focusing on intermediate actors and improvements in efficiency. For more details about this distinction, see Bair, "Global Capitalism and Commodity Chains." Here, I meld both approaches to examine microfinance, acknowledging the dominance of efficiency-focused GVC models like Porter's and making an effort to "bring back" the structural grounding of earlier approaches.

27 Figure I.2 is based on an earlier conception of microfinancial chains, which I developed with Erin Beck. See Beck and Radhakrishnan, "Tracing Microfinancial Value Chains."

28 This perspective is backed by significant research in feminist studies of political economy. See, for example, Girón, "Women and Financialization"; Weber, "Global Politics of Microfinancing Poverty in Asia"; Roberts, "Gender, Financial Deepening and the Production of Embodied Finance."

29 Mosse and Lewis, "Encountering Order and Disjuncture"; Mosse and Lewis, "Theoretical Approaches to Brokerage and Translation in Development"; Swidler and Watkins, "'Teach a Man to Fish.'"

30 Long, "From Paradigm Lost to Paradigm Regained?," 14.

31 Goodman, "Borrowing Money, Exchanging Relationships"; Sen and Majumder, "Narratives of Risk and Poor Rural Women's (Dis)-Engagements with Microcredit-Based Developments in Eastern India"; Kar, "Relative Indemnity."

32 See Zelizer, *The Purchase of Intimacy*, 154–55.

33 Agarwala, "An Economic Sociology of Informal Work."

34 Kar, *Financializing Poverty*, 122–23.

35 The data probably underestimate the number of workers who come into the industry because a family member received a loan. A managing director of another large MFI stated in an interview that 40 percent of the field staff in his organization had mothers who were customers.

36 Kar, "Recovering Debts."

37 Roberts, "Gender, Financial Deepening and the Production of Embodied Finance."

CHAPTER 1. THE INVISIBLE STATE OF GENDER AND CREDIT

1 In my follow-up research in 2016, financial literacy programs were pushing banking more strongly and so covered the use of ATMs, which are often confusing for MFI clients. From MFI officials and trainers, I heard stories of problems for clients. Some women would pay the ATM guard to carry out transactions, believing a fee was required. Forgetting or misplacing the PIN was another frequent problem. Some clients would write the PIN on the card cover and then find their cards and bank accounts stolen. For all these reasons, banking appeared still to be on the far end of the spectrum of convenience.

2 The restriction has to do with a regulatory distinction. Because MFIS are classified as "nonbanking financial companies" or NFBCS, they are not regulated as banks are and thus do not have the fiduciary requirements of a bank that accepts savings. Although this makes sense from a regulatory standpoint, it reveals that MFIS have never really been considered anti-poverty agents in India. If clients cannot save the money they earn from their livelihoods, then it is impossible for them to experience any kind of social mobility.

3 Young, "Gender, Mobility, and the Financialisation of Development"; Harper, "The Commercialization of Microfinance"; Sanyal, *Credit to Capabilities*.

4 Carswell, De Neve, and Ponnarasu, "Good Debts, Bad Debts."

5 Shah, Rao, and Shankar, "Rural Credit in 20th Century India."

6 From H. W. Wolff's 1893 book, *People's Banks, A Record of Social and Economic Success*. Qtd. in Turnell, "The Rise and Fall of Cooperative Credit in Colonial Burma," 2.

7 Nair, "Caste as a Self-Regulatory Club."

8 Mader, *The Political Economy of Microfinance*, 45–46.

9 Shah, Rao, and Shankar, "Rural Credit in 20th Century India."

10 Turnell, "The Rise and Fall of Cooperative Credit in Colonial Burma."

11 Shah, Rao, and Shankar, "Rural Credit in 20th Century India," 1353.

12 Swaminathan, "Village Level Implementation of Irdp."

13 Burgess, Pande, and Wong, "Banking for the Poor."

14 Burgess and Pande, "Do Rural Banks Matter?"

15 Harper, Iyer, and Rosser, *Whose Sustainability Counts?*, 30–31.

16 Inclusion can be not only adverse, as Marcus Taylor has claimed, but also predatory, as Keeanga-Yamahtta Taylor has claimed in a recent analysis of finance and Black homeownership. See Marcus Taylor, "The Antimonies of 'Financial Inclusion'"; and Keeanga-Yamahtta Taylor, *Race for Profit*.

17 In writings and everyday conversation in the industry, this institution goes by its well-known acronym, NABARD.

18 See Harper, Iyer, and Rosser, *Whose Sustainability Counts?*, 30.

19 Boserup, *Women's Role in Economic Development*; Moser, *Gender Planning and Development*.

20 Sen, Grown, and DAWN, *Development, Crises, and Alternative Visions*.

21 In contemporary parlance, there is little distinction between microcredit and microfinance, but the strict distinction is that microcredit is small-scale and not necessarily linked to banks that sell lending products that require bundling and repackaging risk for financial gain.

22 Sanyal, *Credit to Capabilities*; Sanyal, Rao, and Prabhakar, "How Women Talk in Indian Democracy."

23 Karunakaran, *Women, Microfinance, and the State in Neo-Liberal India*.

24 There is evidence, however, that self-help group federations have been used to great effect in mobilizing women around group farming, especially in Kerala where institutions are strong. See Agarwal, "Does Group Farming Empower Rural Women?" This suggests that the organizational structures of self-help groups can, with the right policies, be leveraged to support rural livelihoods.

25 Arunachalam, *The Journey of Indian Micro-Finance*, 42–46, 514–19.

26 Deininger and Liu, "Longer-Term Economic Impacts of Self-Help Groups in India," 5.

27 Deininger and Liu, "Longer-Term Economic Impacts of Self-Help Groups in India," 5.

28 Srinivasan, *Microfinance India*, 47, 60.

29 Arunachalam, *The Journey of Indian Micro-Finance*, 70–71.

30 Wichterich, "The Other Financial Crisis," 407.

31 Sane and Thomas, "Regulating Microfinance Institutions," 61. Also see Khan, "Report of the Internal Group to Examine Issues Relating to Rural Credit and Microfinance"; Reserve Bank of India, "Lending to Priority Sector."

32 Cited in Reserve Bank of India, "Report of the Internal Group to Examine Issues Relating to Rural Credit and Microfinance."

33 MIX Microfinance, "Mix Microfinance World: How Has the Growth of Indian Microfinance Been Funded?"

34 Rao, "Reforms with a Female Face."

35 This was true in both local and global contexts. To understand the global context, see Roy, "Subjects of Risk." Cross-national understandings of gender and repayment are analyzed and challenged in D'Espallier, Guérin, and Mersland, "Women and Repayment in Microfinance"; Boehe and Cruz, "Gender and Microfinance Performance."

36 For a popular text full of these tropes, see Kristof and WuDunn, *Half the Sky*.

37 Srinivasan, *Microfinance India*, 47–48.

38 Wachtel, "30 Suicides in India Linked to Uber-Aggressive Microfinance Organizations"; Kinetz, "Ap Impact."

39 Srinivasan, *Microfinance India*, 48; Arunachalam, *The Journey of Indian Micro-Finance*, 160–69.

40 Kar, *Financializing Poverty*, 72–73.

41 Anonymized interview by author, June 26, 2016.

42 Original text of letters and proposed code of conduct in Arunachalam, *The Journey of Indian Micro-Finance*, 554–60.

43 For the argument about enhanced state regulations, see Reddy, "Microfinance Industry in India." For broader arguments about the need for specific regulation that the industry has not pursued, as well as a critique of the limits of self-regulation, see Sane and Thomas, "Regulating Microfinance Institutions."

44 Wichterich, "The Other Financial Crisis."

45 For a classic critique of the benevolent patriarch paradigm built into neoclassical economics, which continues to pervade development policies, see Kabeer, "Benevolent Dictators, Maternal Altruists and Patriarchal Contracts."

CHAPTER 2. MEN AND WOMEN OF THE MFI

See Kanter, *Men and Women of the Corporation*. The reference to this work in my title sustains a key argument of this book: that the MFI is, like other corporations, a gendered organization in which men and women are hierarchically sorted and organized, often stereotypically, according to gendered roles. As in Kanter's study, the men and women I analyze often conform to organizational logics but also subvert or creatively transform them.

1 Key works that examine the state include Brush, *Gender and Governance*; MacKinnon, "Feminism, Marxism, Method and the State"; Fraser, "After the Family Wage." For the world of finance, see McDowell, *Capital Culture*; Ho, *Liquidated*; and Salzinger, "Re-Marking Men."

2 Acker, "Hierarchies, Jobs, Bodies."

3 Duerst-Lahti and Kelly 1995, 12, qtd. in Brush, *Gender and Governance*, 34.

4 See Kanter, *Men and Women of the Corporation*. Also see Wajcman, *Managing Like a Man*; and McDowell, *Capital Culture*.

5 Sohini Kar has explored the insurance products baked into microfinance loans in case of death. See Kar, *Financializing Poverty*, 167–98.

6 Kar, *Financializing Poverty*, 168.

7 Evidence suggests that the private schools to which working-class Indians send their children, at great hardship and personal expense, often fail to transmit the skills and dispositions that make a person employable in millennial India. See Mathew, "Aspiring and Aspiration Shaming." As the industry for private schooling has ballooned, partly because of new demand created through the availability of microfinance, government schools have become increasingly crippled, worsening the educational quality for children who lack access to microfinance loans.

8 Brush, *Gender and Governance*, 66.

9 Brush, *Gender and Governance*, 75.

10 But men from marginalized backgrounds seldom rose above a mid-level position, a phenomenon I explore in chapter 7.

11 Agrawal, "Are There Glass-Ceiling and Sticky-Floor Effects in India?"

12 I wrote about these expectations in my previous work on women IT professionals. See Radhakrishnan, "Professional Women, Good Families." Similar priorities have been found in research on women in lower-middle-class families. See Vijayakumar, "'I'll Be Like Water'"; Gilbertson, *Within the Limits*.

13 In a recent interview, Samit Ghosh, of Ujjivan, reflected upon the underrepresentation of women at his company and in the industry and acknowledged that women do indeed tend to be more successful at connecting with clients than men. See Miller, *Breaking Barriers*.

14 I have adapted this term from Connell's work in financial companies. See Connell, "Organized Powers," 92.

15 Connell, "Inside the Glass Tower."

16 Some women leaders in the industry include Usha Thorat, Girija Srinivasan, Bindu Ananth, and Vinatha Reddy. All these women have continued to have careers in microfinance but without continuing as CEOS, despite having founded important organizations around the country. Brief articles by some of these women pioneers are included in Harper, Sharma, and Arya, *Crests and Troughs*.

17 Sa-Dhan, "The Bharat Microfinance Report 2018," 35 (part 2).

18 Wajcman, *Managing Like a Man*; Faulkner, "Doing Gender in Engineering Workplace Cultures"; Kanter, *Men and Women of the Corporation*; Connell, "Inside the Glass Tower."

1 D'Espallier, Guérin, and Mersland, "Women and Repayment in Microfinance."

2 A significant feminist literature deals with this issue. The classic critique of "women" as a universal category in development can be found in Mohanty, "Under Western Eyes." For an understanding of the ways neoliberal finance policies perpetuate masculinist norms, see Griffin, "Gendering Global Finance."

3 See Karim, *Microfinance and Its Discontents*, 84–85.

4 See chapters 2 and 5 of Karunakaran, *Women, Microfinance, and the State in Neo-Liberal India.*

5 Kar, *Financializing Poverty*, 107–38.

6 Kar, "Recovering Debts."

7 As I and others have observed, taking out an MFI loan also requires a male kin guarantor. See Kar, "Relative Indemnity."

8 Zelizer, *The Purchase of Intimacy*; Bandelj, "Relational Work and Economic Sociology."

9 Zelizer, *The Purchase of Intimacy*, qtd. in Bandelj, "Relational Work and Economic Sociology."

10 Relational work has been used to understand the economic dimensions inherent in intimate relationships that appear to be noneconomic or outside the realm of a designated economic relationship. Examples include relatives, childcare providers and children, married or romantically involved partners, and, more recently, egg donors and recipients and collaborating colleagues in organizations. See Bandelj, "Relational Work and Economic Sociology"; Haylett, "One Woman Helping Another"; Zelizer, "Intimacy in Economic Organizations."

11 The relationships between women in groups also promote relational work that sustains commercial microfinance. I touch upon this process in chapter 6. For more on the forms of sociality that microfinance produces among women, see Schuster, "The Social Unit of Debt." See also Davidson and Sanyal, "Associational Participation and Network Expansion."

12 For details about the industry's response to these accusations, stemming from an official government report by the Society for the Elimination of Rural Poverty (SERP), see Mader, *The Political Economy of Microfinance*, 160–94.

13 During her fieldwork, Kar, "Recovering Debts," 489, recognized the rise of regulation related to previously unregulated emotional labor. I observed this regulated environment during my fieldwork.

14 Chit funds, the most frequent institutional arrangement under which such scams appear to have taken place, are, like MFIs, regulated as nonbanking financial institutions (NBFCS) but are accountable to other state agencies as well. They present a downside to widespread initiatives for financial inclusion: opportunity for fraud, which then leads ordinary people to (rightly) distrust financial institutions. See Deb, "The Chit (Cheat!) Fund Saga in India." For a broader understanding of public perceptions, see Anitha and Natarajan, "Public Awareness and Reforms Expected about Various Scams in India That Nurtures Business Environment."

15 The routinized service interactions in microfinance resemble what has been identified in fast-food restaurants, but they are also significantly more complicated

because of the long duration of the interactions involved in loan-taking and repayment. See Leidner, *Fast Food, Fast Talk*.

16 Stephen Young has observed this practice in an even more widespread way during his fieldwork in Andhra Pradesh in the early 2000s, when norms for behavior were likely more open-ended. See Young, "Gender, Mobility, and the Financialisation of Development." Kar also notes that practices of care during a time of unregulated emotional labor included loan officers calling clients *didi*, or elder sister. More recently, however, terms of address have become an explicit part of managing relationships with clients. See Kar, *Financializing Poverty*.

17 Notably, with Kanchan's microfinance operation smaller and newer than its competitors, the company's program was less extensive than others I saw.

18 In her study of the fast-food industry, Leidner, *Fast Food, Fast Talk*, shows that routinization of social interactions fulfills similar aims. Here, however, regulating interactions allows clients and workers to forge long-term relationships.

19 For a fuller discussion of this state-like form of governance, see chapter 2.

20 The Grameen Bank's "sixteen decisions" constituted the backbone of the organization's social program, meant to be taken up with the loan, especially in its early days. For more details, see Rahman, *Women and Microcredit in Rural Bangladesh*, 89–90.

CHAPTER 4. SOCIAL WORK

1 A complete discussion of relational work appears in chapter 3 as well as in the introduction. See Zelizer, *The Purchase of Intimacy*. Also see Bandelj, "Relational Work and Economic Sociology," 175–201. Here, I hew more closely to the original notion of relational work, in which informal social relations are analyzed for the economic exchanges they produce. This is in contrast with the previous chapter, in which I identify the fundamentally economic relationship between the loan officer and client to be laden with social relations, trust, and intimacy, built up over time.

2 See Moser, *Gender Planning and Development*, 34–36.

3 Holvoet, "The Impact of Microfinance on Decision-Making Agency," 75–102.

4 Kar has developed the notion of credit-work as "domesticated" labor related to microfinance that has been helpful in my thinking. Here, I propose that this labor is even broader and related to spheres beyond credit. See Kar, *Financializing Poverty*, 122–23.

5 Other helpful accounts of women's volunteer work in social and economic spheres include Daniels, "Good Times and Good Works," 363–74; and Kusimba, "'It Is Easy for Women to Ask!,'" 246–59. In the parallel context of microfinance in Paraguay, relationships between women have also shown to be extremely significant. See Schuster, "The Social Unit of Debt," 563–78.

6 South Indian steamed dumplings, usually eaten with a savory stew. These are commonly sold on the streets in Bengaluru and Chennai.

7 Zulfiqar, "Financializing the Poor," 476–98.

8 Agarwal, *A Field of One's Own*.

9   Karim found that moneylenders in rural Bangladesh were actually strengthened as microfinance became more saturated and more women needed loans to pay off MFIS. See Karim, *Microfinance and Its Discontents*.

10 Kar's research in West Bengal also found that a male kin guarantor was required for MFI loans. See Kar, "Relative Indemnity," 302–19.

CHAPTER 5. EMPOWERMENT, DECLINED

1   This dance form, familiar to elites, is commonly viewed on television and in movies, especially in South India, and has become a popular hobby for middle-class girls in urban areas in recent decades. It was difficult to discern whether the audience of clients recognized or understood the dance form, although the filmmakers assumed that the form would be familiar to "Indian" audiences.

2   Mader, *The Political Economy of Microfinance*, 81–84. The official industry report continues to feature such stories as well. See Sa-Dhan, "The Bharat Microfinance Report 2018," 18–19.

3   I observed the prevalence of these trainings throughout my research, but there is a limited scholarly literature about such trainings. Client training is one kind of educational program that falls under "Other development services" in the industry's annual report. See Sa-Dhan, "The Bharat Microfinance Report 2018," 74–75. These official reports do not report on trainings for clients in the commercial MFI sector.

4   Moeller, *The Gender Effect*, 71–73.

5   Sharma, *Logics of Empowerment*.

6   Sangtin Writers Collective and Nagar, *Playing with Fire*.

7   Radhakrishnan, "'Low Profile' or Entrepreneurial?"

8   I would later learn that this statement was misleading because the study was carried out by a volunteer group of college students, not in a systematic way. In chapter 7, I show that this 75 percent figure was shared in the US as well.

9   See, for example, Acker, "Gender, Capitalism, and Globalization." Ethnographic studies that deal specifically with constructions of motherhood in the context of neoliberal capitalism include Lee, *Gender and the South China Miracle*; Lynch, *Juki Girls, Good Girls*; Salzinger, *Genders in Production*.

10 Radhakrishnan and Solari, "Empowered Women, Failed Patriarchs."

11 Kar, *Financializing Poverty*.

12 The literature on neoliberal subjectivities has been largely restricted to analyses of the US, the UK, and Europe. See, for example, Rose, *Powers of Freedom*. But the notion of "entrepreneurial subjectivities," pertaining more to women in global South contexts has become more influential, including in the context of microfinance. See Altan-Olcay, "The Entrepreneurial Woman in Development Programs."

13 Fernando, "Disciplining the Mother."

14 Young, "Gender, Mobility, and the Financialisation of Development."

15 Altan-Olcay, "The Entrepreneurial Woman in Development Programs."

16 A gold loan is a financial product offered by banks and nonbanking financial companies all over India. A consumer (usually a woman) receives a loan in exchange

for gold jewelry, which the bank holds as collateral. This is a formalized, less exploitative form of informal pawnbroker "pledges" that also exist in parallel. From my observation, gold loans are utilized by all classes of society, due to the ubiquity of gold jewelry in the lives of Indian women.

17 Elyachar, *Markets of Dispossession.*

18 Goodman, "Borrowing Money, Exchanging Relationships." For other studies that emphasize women's own visions for their communities in the context of Indian microfinance, see Moodie, "Enter Microcredit." Also see Sen and Majumder, "Narratives of Risk."

19 In my later interview with soft-spoken Prashanth, I found that he shared Maya's view that most clients were not ready for the world-class empowerment training he was offering. In sessions where the women seemed interested, I observed that he was animated and engaging, but when clients expressed disinterest he gave up quietly.

20 In a previous paper, I showed how MFI leaders and trainers construct clients as too poor to be suitable for entrepreneurship. See Radhakrishnan, "'Low Profile' or Entrepreneurial?"

21 See Karim's discussion of Jahanara the moneylender in Karim, *Microfinance and Its Discontents*, 105–10.

CHAPTER 6. DISTORTIONS OF DISTANCE

1 Long, "From Paradigm Lost to Paradigm Regained?," 3–24; Mosse and Lewis, "Theoretical Approaches to Brokerage and Translation in Development," 1–26.

2 Roy, *Poverty Capital.*

3 See the discussion of Danone in chapter 3 of Karim, *Microfinance and Its Discontents*, 67–68. Also see chapter 1.

4 Mader, *The Political Economy of Microfinance*, 334.

5 Schwittay, *New Media and International Development*, 81.

6 Schwittay, *New Media and International Development*, 80–100.

7 Mohanty, "Under Western Eyes," 72.

8 Mohanty, "Under Western Eyes," 80.

9 Moeller, *The Gender Effect.*

10 Roy, *Poverty Capital*, 12–15.

11 Shain, "The Girl Effect," 1–11; Malkki, *The Need to Help*, 12–13.

12 Roy, *Poverty Capital*, 33.

13 Roy, *Poverty Capital*, 33.

14 See Spivak, "Can the Subaltern Speak?," 66–111.

15 Mani, "Contentious Traditions," 88–126; Chatterjee, "The Nationalist Resolution of the Women's Question," 233–53.

16 Said, *Orientalism*; Mohanty, *Feminism without Borders.*

17 Carr et al., "Kiva's Flat, Flat World," 1–15.

18 Several interviewees mentioned this article. Narang, "Web-Based Microfinancing."

19 Charity Navigator is part of the movement to shift away from charity to social responsibility, as it is itself an organization that uses organizational data to ensure to lenders that charity money is being spent responsibly.

20 See Eyben, "The Power of the Gift," *IDS*, 88–98; Hattori, "The Moral Politics of Foreign Aid," 229–47; Kowalski, "The Gift," 189–205.

21 For details on the Matter to a Million campaign, which is currently ongoing at the time of this writing, see https://www.kiva.org/blog/matter-to-a-million-the -groundbreaking-partnership-that-created-over-20m-in-impact, accessed November 15, 2019.

22 Roodman, "Kiva Is Not Quite What It Seems."

23 Harper, "The Commercialization of Microfinance," 49–64; Harper, Iyer, and Rosser, *Whose Sustainability Counts?*

24 Sen and Majumder, "Narratives of Risk," 121–41; Ehlers and Main, "Women and the False Promise of Microenterprise," 424–40.

25 Khader, "Why Are Poor Women Poor?"

CHAPTER 7. IMPACT REVISITED

1 A rich literature on service work suggests that those working in service industries involving emotional labor primarily provide direct service to wealthy clients, a set of interactions that reinforces the subordinate status of the workers. See Romero, *Maid in the U.S.A.*; Ray and Qayum, *Cultures of Servitude*; Hoang, *Dealing in Desire*; and Kang, *The Managed Hand*.

2 The concept of class itself has been highly contested in India, forged through British conceptions that anchored the meaning of class in relations of production. For a discussion of competing understandings of class in contemporary India, see Deshpande, *Contemporary India*. Also see Chandavarkar, "The Making of the Working Class," 177–96; and Sanchez and Strumpell, "Anthropological and Historical Perspectives." As Sanchez and Strumpell suggest, the concept of class in India has lost its conceptual clarity and utility in recent years, and, where it has been engaged, scholars have also rehearsed colonial tropes that emphasize caste, violence, and subservience.

3 For a discussion of the ways microfinancial chains provide a more thorough, structural understanding of microfinance, see Beck and Radhakrishnan, "Tracing Microfinancial Value Chains," 116–42.

4 See Agarwala, "An Economic Sociology of Informal Work," 315–42. Agarwala finds that examinations of informal work in India have been sociologically impoverished, overlooking the extent to which the informal economy supports and subsidizes capitalism.

5 Agarwala, "An Economic Sociology of Informal Work," 315–42.

6 See chapter 2 for a full discussion of benevolent protectionism.

7 Reviews of existing evidence on microfinance's effects reflect this view. See Duvendack and Palmer-Jones, "High Noon for Microfinance Impact Evaluation," 1864–80; Hickel, "The Microfinance Delusion"; Roodman, *Due Diligence*. For a

more detailed overview of this approach, see Beck, "Repopulating Development," 19–32.

8 Although I focus on a single biography when possible, for some groups I draw in a second biography to better establish the context for my analytical points. My approach to biography draws from Mills, "The Promise," 3–24.

9 Impact investing depends upon interlocutors like Aakash to interpret what counts as social impact in order to justify the existence of the field itself. See Barman, *Caring Capitalism*.

10 An exception to this is Vikram Akula, who writes in his book that his father was considered lower caste back in India and overcame those barriers to eventually build an affluent life in the United States.

11 Rajshekhar, "MFI Basix Boss."

12 Bhargava, "Why Vijay Mahajan's Political Career Never Took Off."

13 Mahajan went to college in the early 1970s, a time when India's national policies were focused on poverty alleviation and the country was in the middle of a political crisis. This environment likely made a socially conscious engineering education possible.

14 Harper, Iyer, and Rosser, *Whose Sustainability Counts?*, 17.

15 Harper, Iyer, and Rosser, *Whose Sustainability Counts?*, 23.

16 Arunachalam, *The Journey of Indian Micro-Finance*, 194–96.

17 Rajshekhar, "MFI Basix Boss."

18 Bhusal, "Myths of Microfinace," 15.

19 Banerjee, *Gender, Nation and Popular Film in India*, 126.

20 Kar, "Recovering Debts," 480–93.

21 See Friedman, Laurison, and Miles, "Breaking the 'Class' Ceiling?," 259–89.

22 Michael Levien discusses extensively the role of middlemen and land brokers in Levien, "Social Capital as Obstacle to Development," 77–92. Anecdotally, my interviews with microfinance clients like Ratna suggest that, at least in urban areas, women may also be involved in smaller deals, leveraging their community influence.

23 In rural India, health crises systematically push even comfortable families into poverty. See Krishna, *One Illness Away*, 69–95.

24 See Bourdieu, "Forms of Capital," 241–58.

25 For a more extensive treatment of the differential treatment of women within MFIS, see chapter 2.

CONCLUSION

1 Ray, "Microfinance Sector Surges about 30% in Fiscal FY20."

2 Ray, "Microfinance Troubles Back in Focus."

3 Ray, "Rising Stress."

4 Nambiar, "Will Microfinance Survive the Covid-19 Crisis?"

5 *Economic Times*, "RBI's Liquidity Scheme Will Prevent Distressed NBFCs from Defaulting."

6   Ray, "Investors Raise Stakes in India's Microfinance Sector."
7   "Collection Efficiency of Micro-Finance Institutions Improve in June."
8   Ray, "Bandhan Bank, Small Finance Banks Emerge as Job Creators amid Coronavirus Pandemic."
9   Connell, "Inside the Glass Tower," 77.
10 Morduch, "The Microfinance Schism."
11 Carswell, De Neve, and Ponnarasu, "Good Debts, Bad Debts."
12 Taylor, "The Antimonies of 'Financial Inclusion'"; Taylor, *Race for Profit*.
13 The organization Rang De features these types of small-scale, low-interest projects with extra supports.
14 While most client households I interacted with report net incomes of anywhere from 15,000 to 50,000 rupees per month, an emergency surgery due to an occupational injury, such as the one reported by Jayanthi in chapter 4, costs 250,000 rupees. School fees were reported to cost 10,000 rupees. Any kind of construction work on homes costs a minimum of 100,000.
15 See *Economic Times*, "Is the Job Scene in India Bad?"
16 Chatterjee, Murgai, and Rama, "Job Opportunities along the Rural-Urban Gradation."
17 For a study of employer-sponsored childcare in India, see Pedulla and Ranganathan, "Are All Children Created Equal?" For a study of the positive impact of in-house training aimed at retaining women workers, see Ranganathan, "Train Them to Retain Them."
18 In Vikram Akula's reflection on his time with SKS, he admitted that the stakeholders they had were not socially minded enough but tended not to see workers or investors in terms of the class-specific experiences they brought to the workforce. See Bellman, "What India's Microloan Meltdown Taught One Entrepreneur."
19 Natascha van der Zwan, "Making Sense of Financialization."

Acker, Joan. "Gender, Capitalism, and Globalization." *Critical Sociology* 30, no. 1 (2004): 17–41.

Acker, Joan. "Hierarchies, Jobs, Bodies: A Theory of Gendered Organizations." *Gender and Society* 4, no. 2 (1990): 139–58.

Agarwal, Bina. *A Field of One's Own: Gender and Land Rights in South Asia.* Vol. 58. Cambridge: Cambridge University Press, 1994.

Agarwal, Bina. "Does Group Farming Empower Rural Women? Lessons from India's Experiments." *Journal of Peasant Studies* 27, no. 4 (2019): 1–32.

Agarwala, Rina. "An Economic Sociology of Informal Work: The Case of India." *Research in the Sociology of Work* 18 (2009): 315–42.

Agrawal, Nisha. "Inequality in India: What's the Real Story?" In *India Economic Summit.* World Economic Forum, October 10, 2016. https://www.weforum.org/agenda /2016/10/inequality-in-india-oxfam-explainer/.

Agrawal, Tushar. "Are There Glass-Ceiling and Sticky-Floor Effects in India? An Empirical Examination." *Oxford Development Studies* 41, no. 3 (2013): 322–42.

Altan-Olcay, Özlem. "The Entrepreneurial Woman in Development Programs: Thinking through Class Differences." *Social Politics: International Studies in Gender, State and Society* 23, no. 3 (2016): 389–414.

Anand, Ishan, and Anjana Thampi. "Recent Trends in Wealth Inequality in India." *Economic and Political Weekly* 51, no. 50 (2016): 59–67.

Andersson, Annika, and Mathias Hatakka. "Victim, Mother, or Untapped Resource? Discourse Analysis of the Construction of Women in Ict Policies." *Information Technologies and International Development* 13 (2017): 72–86.

Anitha, J., and Nikitha Natarajan. "Public Awareness and Reforms Expected about Various Scams in India That Nurture Business Environment." *Abhigyan* 33, no. 3 (2015).

Arunachalam, Ramesh S. *The Journey of Indian Micro-Finance: Lessons for the Future.* Chennai: Aapti Publications, 2011.

Bair, Jennifer, ed. *Frontiers of Commodity Chain Research.* Palo Alto, CA: Stanford University Press, 2009.

Bair, Jennifer. "Global Capitalism and Commodity Chains: Looking Back, Going Forward." *Competition and Change* 9, no. 2 (2005): 153–80.

Bandelj, Nina. "Relational Work and Economic Sociology." *Politics and Society* 40, no. 2 (2012): 175–201.

Banerjee, Sikata. *Gender, Nation and Popular Film in India: Globalizing Muscular Nationalism*. Vol. 117. Abingdon, UK: Routledge, 2017.

Barman, Emily. *Caring Capitalism: The Meaning and Measure of Social Value*. Cambridge: Cambridge University Press, 2016.

Beck, Erin. "Repopulating Development: An Agent-Based Approach to Studying Development Interventions." *World Development* 80, no. 1 (2016): 19–32.

Beck, Erin, and Smitha Radhakrishnan. "Tracing Microfinancial Value Chains: Beyond the Impasse of Debt and Development." *Sociology of Development* 3, no. 2 (2017): 116–42.

Bellman, Eric. "What India's Microloan Meltdown Taught One Entrepreneur: Vikram Akula Speaks about What Went Wrong in 2010 and What's Next." *Wall Street Journal*, June 9, 2015.

Bhargava, Anjuli. "Why Vijay Mahajan's Political Career Never Took Off." *Business Standard*, October 13, 2018.

Bhusal, Manoj Kr. "Myths of Microfinace." *Global South Development Magazine*, October–December 2010, 12–28.

Boehe, Dirk Michael, and Luciano Barin Cruz. "Gender and Microfinance Performance: Why Does the Institutional Context Matter?" *World Development* 47 (July 2013): 121–35.

Boserup, Ester. *Women's Role in Economic Development*. London: Allen and Unwin, 1970.

Bourdieu, Pierre. "Forms of Capital." In *Handbook of Theory and Research for the Sociology of Education*, edited by J. G. Richardson, 241–58. New York: Greenwood Press, 1995.

Brett, John A. "'We Sacrifice and Eat Less': The Structural Complexities of Microfinance Participation." *Human Organization* 65, no. 2 (2006): 8–19.

Brush, Lisa D. *Gender and Governance*. Lanham, MD: Alta Mira Press, 2003.

Bulmer, M. I. A. "Sociological Models of the Mining Community." *Sociological Review* 23, no. 1 (1975): 61–92.

Burgess, Robin, and Rohini Pande. "Do Rural Banks Matter? Evidence from the Indian Social Banking Experiment." *American Economic Review* 95, no. 3 (2005): 780–95.

Burgess, Robin, Rohini Pande, and Grace Wong. "Banking for the Poor: Evidence from India." *Journal of the European Economic Association* 3, nos. 2–3 (2005): 268–78.

Calkin, Sydney. "'Tapping' Women for Post-Crisis Capitalism." *International Feminist Journal of Politics* 17, no. 4 (2015): 611–29.

Carr, John, Elizabeth Dickinson, Sara L. McKinnon, and Karma R. Chávez. "Kiva's Flat, Flat World: Ten Years of Microcredit in Cyberspace." *Globalizations* (2015): 1–15.

Carswell, Grace, Geert De Neve, and Subramanian Ponnarasu. "Good Debts, Bad Debts: Microcredit and Managing Debt in Rural South India." *Journal of Agrarian Change* 1, no. 1 (2020): 1–21.

Chandavarkar, Rajnarayan. "The Making of the Working Class: E. P. Thompson and Indian History." *History Workshop Journal* 43, no. 1 (1997): 177–96.

Chant, Sylvia. "Women, Girls and World Poverty: Empowerment, Equality or Essentialism?" *International Development Planning Review* 38, no. 1 (2016): 1–24.

Chatterjee, Partha. "The Nationalist Resolution of the Women's Question." In *Recasting Women: Essays in Indian Colonial History*, edited by Kumkum Sangari and Sudesh Vaid, 233–53. New Brunswick, NJ: Rutgers University Press, 1990.

Chatterjee, Urmila, Rinku Murgai, and Martin Rama. "Job Opportunities along the Rural-Urban Gradation and Female Labor Force Participation in India." Policy Research Working Paper 7412. World Bank Group, Poverty Global Practice Group and Office of the Chief Economist, September 2015. http://documents.worldbank.org/curated/en/732961468189870923/pdf/WPS7412.pdf.

Connell, Raewyn. "Inside the Glass Tower: The Contruction of Masculinities in Finance Capital." In *Men, Wage Work and Family*, edited by Paula McDonald and Emma Jeanes, 65–79. New York: Routledge, 2012.

Connell, Raewyn. "Organized Powers: Masculinities, Managers, and Violence." In *Men and Development: Politicizing Masculinities*, edited by Andrea Cornwall, Jerker Edstrom, and Alan Greig, 85–97. London: Zed Books, 2013.

D'Espallier, Bert, Isabelle Guérin, and Roy Mersland. "Women and Repayment in Microfinance: A Global Analysis." *World Development* 39, no. 5 (2011): 758–72.

Daniels, Arlene Kaplan. "Good Times and Good Works: The Place of Sociability in the Work of Women Volunteers." *Social Problems* 32, no. 4 (1985): 363–74.

Davidson, Debra J., and Michael Haan. "Gender, Political Ideology, and Climate Change Beliefs in an Extractive Industry Community." *Population and Environment* 34, no. 2 (December 2012): 217–34.

Davidson, Thomas, and Paromita Sanyal. "Associational Participation and Network Expansion: Microcredit Self-Help Groups and Poor Women's Social Ties in Rural India." *Social Forces* 95, no. 4 (2017): 1695–724.

Deb, Rajat. "The Chit (Cheat!) Fund Saga in India." *Asian Academic Research Journal of Social Sciences and Humanities* 1, no. 12 (2013).

Deininger, Klaus, and Yanyan Liu. "Longer-Term Economic Impacts of Self-Help Groups in India." Policy Research Working Paper 4886. World Bank Development Research Group Sustainable Rural and Urban Development Team, March 2009. http://documents.worldbank.org/curated/en/473751468268776052/pdf/WPS4886.pdf.

Deshpande, Satish. *Contemporary India: A Sociological View*. New Delhi: Viking, 2003.

Dunaway, Wilma. *Gendered Commodity Chains: Seeing Women's Work and Households in Global Production*. Stanford, CA: Stanford University Press, 2014.

Duvendack, Maren, and Richard Palmer-Jones. "High Noon for Microfinance Impact Evaluation: Re-Investigating the Evidence from Bangladesh." *Journal of Development Studies* 48, no. 12 (2012): 1864–80.

Economic Times. "Collection Efficiency of Micro-Finance Institutions Improve in June: Icra." July 21, 2020.

Economic Times. "Is the Job Scene in India Bad? Depends on How You See It, Says Govt." May 31, 2019.

Economic Times. "RBI's Liquidity Scheme Will Prevent Distressed NBFCs from Defaulting: Capri Global Capital." July 2, 2020.

Ehlers, Tracy Bachrach, and Karen Main. "Women and the False Promise of Microenterprise." *Gender and Society* 12, no. 4 (1998): 424–40.

Elyachar, Julia. *Markets of Dispossession: NGOs, Economic Disposession, and the State in Cairo*. Durham, NC: Duke University Press, 2005.

Eyben, Rosalind. "The Power of the Gift and the New Aid Modalities." *IDS Bulletin* 37, no. 6 (2006): 88–98.

Faulkner, Wendy. "Doing Gender in Engineering Workplace Cultures. I. Observations from the Field." *Engineering Studies* 1, no. 1 (2009): 3–18.

Fernando, J. L. "Disciplining the Mother: Micro Credit in Bangladesh." *Ghadar* 1, no. 1 (1997).

Fernando, J. L. "Microcredit and Empowerment of Women: Visibility without Power." In *Microfinance: Perils and Prospects*, edited by Jude L. Fernando, 162–205. London: Routledge, 2006.

Fraser, Nancy. "After the Family Wage: Gender Equity and the Welfare State." *Political Theory* 22, no. 4 (1994): 591–618.

Freudenburg, William R. "Addictive Economies: Extractive Industries and Vulnerable Localities in a Changing World Economy." *Rural Sociology* 57, no. 3 (1992): 305–32.

Friedman, Sam, Daniel Laurison, and Andrew Miles. "Breaking the 'Class' Ceiling? Social Mobility into Britain's Elite Occupations." *Sociological Review* 63, no. 2 (2015): 259–89.

Gallmeyer, Alice, and Wade T. Roberts. "Payday Lenders and Economically Distressed Communities: A Spatial Analysis of Financial Predation." *Social Science Journal* 46, no. 3 (2009): 521–38.

Ganle, John Kuumuori, Kwadwo Afriyie, and Alexander Yao Segbefia. "Microcredit: Empowerment and Disempowerment of Rural Women in Ghana." *World Development* 66, February (2015): 335–45.

Gereffi, Gary, and Miguel Korzeniewicz. *Commodity Chains and Global Capitalism*. Westport, CT: Greenwood, 1994.

Gilbertson, Amanda. *Within the Limits: Moral Boundaries of Class and Gender in Urban India*. New Delhi: Oxford University Press, 2017.

Girón, Alicia. "Women and Financialization: Microcredit, Institutional Investors, and MFIs." *Journal of Economic Issues* 49, no. 2 (2015): 373–96.

Goetz, Anne Marie. *Women Development Workers: Implementing Rural Credit Programmes in Bangladesh*. London: SAGE Publications, 2001.

Goetz, Anne Marie, and Rina Sen Gupta. "Who Takes the Credit? Gender, Power, and Control over Loan Use in Rural Credit Programs in Bangladesh." *World Development* 24, no. 1 (1996): 45–63.

Goodman, Rachael. "Borrowing Money, Exchanging Relationships: Making Microfinance Fit into Local Lives in Kumaon, India." *World Development* 93 (May 2017): 362–73.

Graves, Steven M. "Landscapes of Predation, Landscapes of Neglect: A Location Analysis of Payday Lenders and Banks." *Professional Geographer* 55, no. 3 (2003): 303–17.

Griffin, Penny. "Gendering Global Finance: Crisis, Masculinity, and Responsibility." *Men and Masculinities* 16, no. 1 (2012): 9–34.

Harper, Malcolm. "The Commercialization of Microfinance: Resolution or Extension of Poverty." In *Confronting Microfinance: Undermining Sustainable Development*, edited by Milford Bateman, 49–64. Sterling, VA: Kumarian Press, 2011.

Harper, Malcolm, Lalitha Iyer, and Jane Rosser. *Whose Sustainability Counts? Basix's Long March from Microfinance to Livelihoods*. Sterling, VA: Kumarian Press, 2011.

Harper, Malcolm, Vipin Sharma, and Vibhu Arya, eds. *Crests and Troughs: Microfinance in India*. New Delhi: Access Development Services, 2013.

Hashemi, Syed M., Sidney Ruth Schuler, and Ann P. Riley. "Rural Credit Programs and Women's Empowerment in Bangladesh." *World Development* 24, no. 4 (April 1996): 635–53.

Hattori, Tomohisa. "The Moral Politics of Foreign Aid." *Review of International Studies* 29, no. 2 (2003): 229–47.

Haylett, Jennifer. "One Woman Helping Another: Egg Donation as a Case of Relational Work." *Politics and Society* 40, no. 2 (2012): 223–47.

Hickel, Jason. "The Microfinance Delusion: Who Really Wins?" *Guardian*, June 10, 2015. https://www.theguardian.com/global-development-professionals-network/2015/jun/10/the-microfinance-delusion-who-really-wins.

Ho, Karen. *Liquidated: An Ethnography of Wall Street*. Durham, NC: Duke University Press, 2009.

Hoang, Kimberly Kay. *Dealing in Desire: Asian Ascendancy, Western Decline, and the Hidden Currencies of Global Sex Work*. Berkeley: University of California Press, 2015.

Holvoet, Nathalie. "The Impact of Microfinance on Decision-Making Agency: Evidence from South India." *Development and Change* 36, no. 1 (2005): 75–102.

Jayadev, Arjun, Sripad Motiram, and Vamsi Vakulabharanam. "Patterns of Wealth Disparities in India during the Liberalisation Era." *Economic and Political Weekly* (2007): 3853–63.

Jeffrey, Craig. *Timepass: Youth, Class, and the Politics of Waiting in India*. Stanford, CA: Stanford University Press, 2010.

Kabeer, Naila. "Benevolent Dictators, Maternal Altruists and Patriarchal Contracts: Gender and Household Economics." In *Reversed Realities: Gender Hierarchies in Development Thought*, 95–135. London: Verso, 1994.

Kabeer, Naila. "Conflicts over Credit: Re-Evaluating the Empowerment Potential of Loans to Women in Rural Bangladesh." *World Development* 29, no. 1 (2001): 63–84.

Kabeer, Naila. "Is Microfinance a 'Magic Bullet' for Women's Empowerment? Analysis of Findings from South Asia." *Economic and Political Weekly* 60, nos. 44–45 (2005): 4709–18.

Kamal, Samina. "Poverty Alleviation and Women Empowerment in South Asia: The Dual Benefits of Microcredit." In *South Asia Poverty Alleviation Program*. Islamabad: UN Development Program, 1997.

Kang, Milliann. *The Managed Hand: Race, Gender and the Body in Beauty Service Work*. Berkeley: University of California Press, 2010.

Kanter, Rosabeth Moss. *Men and Women of the Corporation*. New York: Basic Books, 1977.

Kar, Sohini. *Financializing Poverty: Labor and Risk in Indian Microfinance.* South Asia in Motion. Edited by Thomas Blom Hansen. Stanford, CA: Stanford University Press, 2018.

Kar, Sohini. "Recovering Debts: Microfinance Loan Officers and the Work of 'Proxy-Creditors.'" *American Ethnologist* 40, no. 3 (2013): 480–93.

Kar, Sohini. "Relative Indemnity: Risk, Insurance, and Kinship in Indian Microfinance." *Journal of the Royal Anthropological Institute* 23, no. 2 (2017): 302–19.

Karim, Lamia. *Microfinance and Its Discontents: Women in Debt in Bangladesh.* Minneapolis: University of Minnesota Press, 2011.

Karunakaran, Kalpana. *Women, Microfinance, and the State in Neo-Liberal India.* Abingdon, UK: Routledge, 2017.

Khader, Serene J. "Why Are Poor Women Poor?" *New York Times,* September 11, 2019.

Khan, H. R. "Report of the Internal Group to Examine Issues Relating to Rural Credit and Microfinance." Reserve Bank of India Reports, edited by A. V. Sardesai. Mumbai: Reserve Bank of India Cental Office, July 2005.

Kinetz, Erika. "Ap Impact: Lender's Own Probe Links It to Suicides." *Yahoo Finance,* February 24, 2012. https://finance.yahoo.com/news/ap-impact-lenders-own-probe -080122405.html.

Kowalski, Robert. "The Gift: Marcel Mauss and International Aid." *Journal of Comparative Social Welfare* 27, no. 3 (2011): 189–205.

Krishna, Anirudh. *One Illness Away: Why People Become Poor and How They Escape Poverty.* Oxford: Oxford University Press, 2011.

Kristof, Nicholas D., and Sheryl WuDunn. *Half the Sky: Turning Oppression into Opportunity for Women Worldwide.* New York: Vintage, 2010.

Kusimba, Sibel. "'It Is Easy for Women to Ask!': Gender and Digital Finance in Kenya." *Economic Anthropology* 5, no. 2 (2018): 246–59.

Lee, Ching Kwan. *Gender and the South China Miracle.* Berkeley: University of California Press, 2001.

Leidner, Robin. *Fast Food, Fast Talk: Service Work and the Routinization of Everyday Life.* Berkeley: University of California Press, 1993.

Levien, Michael. "Social Capital as Obstacle to Development: Brokering Land, Norms, and Trust in Rural India." *World Development* 74 (October 2015): 77–92.

Long, Norman. "From Paradigm Lost to Paradigm Regained? The Case for an Actor-Oriented Sociology of Development." *Revista Europea de Estudios Latinoamericanos y del Caribe / European Review of Latin American and Caribbean Studies,* no. 49 (1990): 3–24.

Lynch, Caitrin. *Juki Girls, Good Girls: Gender and Cultural Politics in Sri Lanka's Global Garment Industry.* Ithaca, NY: ILR, 2007.

MacKinnon, Catharine. "Feminism, Marxism, Method and the State." *Signs: Journal of Women, Culture, and Society* 7, no. 3 (1982): 515–44.

Maclean, Kate. "Gender, Risk, and Micro-Financial Subjectivities." *Antipode* 45, no. 2 (2013): 455–73.

Mader, Philip. "Financialisation through Microfinance: Civil Society and Market-Building in India." *Asian Studies Review* 38, no. 4 (2014): 601–19.

Mader, Philip. *The Political Economy of Microfinance: Financializing Poverty*. Studies in the Political Economy of Public Policy. Edited by Toby Carroll, M. Ramesh, Darryl S. L. Jarvis, and Paul Cammack. New York: Palgrave Macmillan, 2015.

Malkki, Liisa H. *The Need to Help: The Domestic Arts of International Humanitarianism*. Durham, NC: Duke University Press, 2015.

Mani, Lata. "Contentious Traditions: The Debate on *Sati* in Colonial India." In *Recasting Women: Essays in Indian Colonial History*, edited by Kumkum Sangari and Sudesh Vaid, 88–126. New Brunswick, NJ: Rutgers University Press, 1990.

Mathew, Leya. "Aspiring and Aspiration Shaming: Primary Schooling, English, and Enduring Inequalities in Liberalizing Kerala (India)." *Anthropology and Education Quarterly* 49, no. 1 (2018): 72–88.

Mazumdar, Dipak, and Sandip Sarkar. *Globalization, Labor Markets, and Inequality in India*. Routledge Studies in the Growth Economies of Asia. London: Routledge, 2008.

McDowell, Linda. *Capital Culture: Gender at Work in the City*. Oxford: Blackwell, 1997.

Miller, Karen. *Breaking Barriers: Women Changemakers in Financial Inclusion, Ep. 1 Featuring Samit Ghosh*. Podcast audio. Driving Action for Gender Diversity: Samit Ghosh. Accessed October 8, 2019. https://www.womensworldbanking.org/insights -and-impact/podcast-women-leaders-samit-ghosh/.

Mills, C. Wright. "The Promise." In *The Sociological Imagination*, edited by C. Wright Mills, 3–24. Oxford: Oxford University Press, 1959.

Misturelli, Federica, and Claire Heffernan. "What Is Poverty? A Diachronic Exploration of the Discourse of Poverty from the 1970s to the 2000s." *European Journal of Development Research* 20, no. 4 (2008): 666–84.

"Mix Microfinance World: How Has the Growth of Indian Microfinance Been Funded?" Microfinance MIX, December 2010. Accessed September 7, 2021. https:// www.findevgateway.org/sites/default/files/publications/2019/How%20has%20 the%20growth%20of%20indian%20microfinance%20been%20funded.pdf.

Moeller, Kathryn. *The Gender Effect: Capitalism, Feminism, and the Corporate Politics of Development*. Berkeley: University of California Press, 2018.

Mohanty, Chandra Talpade. *Feminism without Borders: Decolonizing Theory, Practicing Solidarity*. Durham, NC: Duke University Press, 2003.

Mohanty, Chandra Talpade. "Under Western Eyes: Feminist Scholarship and Colonial Discourses." *Feminist Review* 30 (1988): 61–88.

Moodie, Megan. "Enter Microcredit: A New Culture of Women's Empowerment in Rajasthan?" *American Ethnologist* 35, no. 3 (2008): 454–65.

Morduch, Jonathan. "The Microfinance Schism." *World Development* 28, no. 4 (2000): 617–29.

Moser, Carolyn. *Gender Planning and Development: Theory, Practice, and Training*. New York: Routledge, 1993.

Mosse, David, and David Lewis. "Encountering Order and Disjuncture: Contemporary Anthropological Perspectives on the Organization of Development." *Oxford Development Studies* 34, no. 1 (2006): 1–13.

Mosse, David, and David Lewis. "Theoretical Approaches to Brokerage and Translation in Development." In *Development Brokers and Translators: The Ethnography of Aid Agencies*, edited by David Mosse and David Lewis, 1–26. Bloomfield, CT: Kumarian Press, 2006.

Nair, Malavika. "Caste as a Self-Regulatory Club: Evidence from a Private Banking System in Nineteenth Century India." *Journal of Institutional Economics* 12, no. 3 (2016): 677–98.

Nambiar, Manoj Joseph. "Will Microfinance Survive the Covid-19 Crisis? Yes, It Will Thrive." *Economic Times*, 2020.

Narang, Sonia. "Web-Based Microfinancing." *New York Times Magazine*, December 10, 2006.

Paprocki, Kasia. "'Selling Our Own Skin': Social Dispossession through Microcredit in Rural Bangladesh." *Geoforum* 74 (2016): 29–38.

Pedulla, David, and Aruna Ranganathan. "Are All Children Created Equal? Child Gender, Childcare and Female Labor Force Participation in India." Paper presented at the Academy of Management Proceedings, 2017.

Porter, Michael E. *Competitive Advantage: Creating and Sustaining Superior Performance*. New York: Free Press, 1985.

Radhakrishnan, Smitha. *Appropriately Indian: Gender and Culture in a New Transnational Class*. Durham, NC: Duke University Press, 2011.

Radhakrishnan, Smitha. "'Low Profile' or Entrepreneurial? Gender, Class, and Cultural Adaptation in the Global Microfinance Industry." *World Development* 74 (2015): 264–74.

Radhakrishnan, Smitha. "Professional Women, Good Families: Respectable Femininity and the Cultural Politics of a 'New' India." *Qualitative Sociology* 32, no. 2 (2009): 195–212.

Radhakrishnan, Smitha, and Cinzia Solari. "Empowered Women, Failed Patriarchs: Neoliberalism and Global Gender Anxieties." *Sociology Compass* 9, no. 9 (2015): 784–802.

Rahman, Aminur. *Women and Microcredit in Rural Bangladesh: Anthropological Study of the Rhetoric and Realities of Grameen Bank Lending*. Boulder, CO: Westview Press, 1999.

Rajshekhar, M. "MFI Basix Boss, Vijay Mahajan Goes on 12-State Padayatra." *Economic Times*, February 10, 2011.

Ranganathan, Aruna. "Train Them to Retain Them: Work Readiness and the Retention of First-Time Women Workers in India." *Administrative Science Quarterly* 63, no. 4 (2018): 879–909.

Rankin, Katherine. "Governing Development: Neoliberalism, Microcredit, and the Politics of Development." *Economy and Society* 30, no. 1 (2001): 18–37.

Rao, Smriti. "Reforms with a Female Face: Gender, Liberalization, and Economic Policy in Andhra Pradesh, India." *World Development* 36, no. 7 (2008): 1213–32.

Ray, Atmadip. "Bandhan Bank, Small Finance Banks Emerge as Job Creators amid Coronavirus Pandemic." *Economic Times*, June 23, 2020.

Ray, Atmadip. "Investors Raise Stakes in India's Microfinance Sector Despite Stress during Lockdown." *Economic Times*, July 1, 2020.

Ray, Atmadip. "Microfinance Sector Surges about 30% in Fiscal FY20." *Economic Times*, June 19, 2020.

Ray, Atmadip. "Microfinance Troubles Back in Focus: Blame It on Greed Alone!" *Economic Times*, February 12, 2020.

Ray, Atmadip. "Rising Stress: About 70% Micro Loan Borrowers Want Moratorium as Household Cash Flow Depletes." *Economic Times*, May 10, 2020.

Ray, Raka, and Seemin Qayum. *Cultures of Servitude: Modernity, Domesticity, and Class in India*. Stanford, CA: Stanford University Press, 2009.

Reddy, Y. Venugopal. "Microfinance Industry in India: Some Thoughts." *Economic and Political Weekly* 46, no. 41 (October 8, 2011): 46–49.

Reserve Bank of India. "Lending to Priority Sector." In *Reserve Bank of India Guidelines*. Mumbai: Reserve Bank of India, 2006. https://rbidocs.rbi.org.in/rdocs/Content/PDFs/77070.pdf.

Reserve Bank of India. "Report of the Internal Group to Examine Issues Relating to Rural Credit and Microfinance." 2005. https://rbidocs.rbi.org.in/rdocs/PublicationReport/Pdfs/65111.pdf.

Roberts, Adrienne. "Gender, Financial Deepening and the Production of Embodied Finance: Towards a Critical Feminist Analysis." *Global Society* 29, no. 1 (2015): 107–27.

Romero, Mary. *Maid in the U.S.A.* New York: Routledge, 1992.

Roodman, David. *Due Diligence: An Impertinent Inquiry into Microfinance*. Washington, DC: Center for Global Development, Brooking Institution Press, 2012.

Roodman, David. "Kiva Is Not Quite What It Seems." Center for Global Development. October 2, 2009. http://www.cgdev.org/Blog/Kiva-Not-Quite-What-It-Seems.

Rose, Nikolas. *Powers of Freedom: Reframing Political Thought*. Cambridge: Cambridge University Press, 1999.

Roy, Ananya. *Poverty Capital: Microfinance and the Making of Development*. New York: Routledge, 2010.

Roy, Ananya. "Subjects of Risk: Technologies of Gender in the Making of Millennial Modernity." *Public Culture* 24, no. 1 (66) (2012): 131–55.

Sa-Dhan. "The Bharat Microfinance Report 2018." New Delhi: Sa-Dhan, 2018.

Said, Edward. *Orientalism*. New York: Vintage Books, 1978.

Salzinger, Leslie. *Genders in Production: Making Workers in Mexico's Global Factories*. Berkeley: University of California Press, 2003.

Salzinger, Leslie. "Re-Marking Men: Masculinity as a Terrain of the Neoliberal Economy." *Critical Historical Studies* 3, no. 1 (2016): 1–25.

Sanchez, Andrew, and Christian Strumpell. "Anthropological and Historical Perspectives on India's Working Classes." *Modern Asian Studies* 48, no. 5 (2014).

Sane, Renuka, and Susan Thomas. "Regulating Microfinance Institutions." *Economic and Political Weekly* 48, no. 5 (2013): 59–67.

Sangtin Writers Collective and Richa Nagar. *Playing with Fire: Feminist Thought and Activism through Seven Lives in India*. Minneapolis: University of Minnesota Press, 2006.

Sanyal, Paromita. *Credit to Capabilities: A Sociological Study of Microcredit Groups in India*. Cambridge: Cambridge University Press, 2014.

Sanyal, Paromita, Vijayendra Rao, and Umang Prabhakar. "How Women Talk in Indian Democracy." *Qualitative Sociology* 42, no. 1 (2019): 49–70.

Schuster, Caroline E. "The Social Unit of Debt: Gender and Creditworthiness in Paraguayan Microfinance." *American Ethnologist* 41, no. 3 (2014): 563–78.

Schwittay, Anke. *New Media and International Development: Representation and Affect in Microfinance.* Abingdon, UK: Routledge, 2015.

Sen, Debarati, and Sarasij Majumder. "Narratives of Risk and Poor Rural Women's (Dis)-Engagements with Microcredit-Based Developments in Eastern India." *Critique of Anthropology* 35, no. 2 (2015): 121–41.

Sen, Gita, Caren Grown, and DAWN. *Development, Crises, and Alternative Visions: Third World Women's Perspectives.* New Feminist Library. New York: Monthly Review Press, 1987.

Shah, Mihir, Rangu Rao, and P. S. Vijay Shankar. "Rural Credit in 20th Century India: Overview of History and Perspectives." *Economic and Political Weekly* 42, no. 15 (April 14–20, 2007): 1351–64.

Shain, Farzana. "'The Girl Effect': Exploring Narratives of Gendered Impacts and Opportunities in Neoliberal Development." *Sociological Research Online* 18, no. 2 (2013): 1–11.

Sharma, Aradhana. *Logics of Empowerment: Development, Gender and Governance in Neoliberal India.* Minneapolis: University of Minnesota Press, 2008.

Spivak, G. C. "Can the Subaltern Speak?" In *Colonial Discourse and Postcolonial Theory,* edited by P. Williams and L. Chrisman, 66–111. New York: Columbia University Press, 1985.

Srinivasan, N. *Microfinance India: State of the Sector Report 2011.* New Delhi: SAGE Publications, 2011.

Swaminathan, Madhura. "Village Level Implementation of IRDP: Comparison of West Bengal and Tamil Nadu." *Economic and Political Weekly* (1990): A17–A27.

Swidler, Ann, and Susan Cotts Watkins. "'Teach a Man to Fish': The Sustainability Doctrine and Its Social Consquences." *World Development* 37, no. 7 (2009): 1182–96.

Taylor, Keeanga-Yamahtta. *Race for Profit: How Banks and the Real Estate Industry Undermined Black Homeownership.* Chapel Hill: University of North Carolina Press, 2019.

Taylor, Marcus. "The Antimonies of 'Financial Inclusion': Debt, Distress, and the Workings of Indian Microfinance." *Journal of Agrarian Change* 12, no. 4 (2012): 601–10.

Turnell, Sean. "The Rise and Fall of Cooperative Credit in Colonial Burma." Research Papers, Macquarie University, Department of Economics (June 2005). https://ideas.repec.org/p/mac/wpaper/0509.html.

van der Zwan, Natascha. "Making Sense of Financialization." *Socio-Economic Review* 12, no. 1 (2014): 99–129.

Vijayakumar, Gowri. "'I'll Be Like Water' Gender: Class and Flexible Aspirations at the Edge of India's Knowledge Economy." *Gender and Society* 27, no. 6 (2013): 777–98.

Wachtel, Katya. "30 Suicides in India Linked to Uber-Aggressive Microfinance Organizations." *Business Insider,* October 19, 2010.

Wajcman, J. *Managing Like a Man: Women and Men in Corporate Management.* College Park: Pennsylvania State University Press, 1998.

Weber, Bruce A. "Extractive Industries and Rural-Urban Economic Interdependence." In *The Changing American Countryside*, 155–79. Lawrence: University Press of Kansas, 1995.

Weber, Heloise. "Global Politics of Microfinancing Poverty in Asia: The Case of Bangladesh Unpacked." *Asian Studies Review* 38, no. 4 (2014): 544–63.

Wichterich, Christa. "The Other Financial Crisis: Growth and Crash of the Microfinance Sector in India." *Development* 55, no. 3 (2012): 406–12.

Young, Stephen. "Gender, Mobility, and the Financialisation of Development." *Geopolitics* 15, no. 3 (2010): 606–27.

Young, Stephen. "The 'Moral Hazards' of Microfinance: Restructuring Rural Credit in India." *Antipode* 42, no. 1 (2010): 201–23.

Zelizer, Viviana. *The Purchase of Intimacy.* Princeton, NJ: Princeton University Press, 2005.

Zulfiqar, Ghazal. "Financializing the Poor: 'Dead Capital,' Women's Gold and Microfinance in Pakistan." *Economy and Society* 46, nos. 3–4 (2017): 476–98.

Page numbers followed by f indicate figures; page numbers followed by c indicate charts.

Aakash (financial professional), 179–80, 181

Abraham (MFI worker), 189–90, 196

ACCION, 149

Acker, Joan, 49

actor-oriented sociology, 8, 11–12, 200

Aditya (Sowbagya employee), 53, 54

Agarwala, Rina, 178, 229n4

Agrawal, Bina, 110–11

Agriculturalists Loan Act (1884), 29

agriculture, 29, 31, 34, 40, 41, 71, 74, 202, 222n24

Ajit (loan officer), 89–92, 94–95

Akula, Vikram, 153, 179, 189–90, 230n10, 231n18

alcoholism, 40, 110

Altan-Olcay, Özlem, 132–33

altruism, 50, 64, 156–57, 162, 163, 167, 169, 176

Ammu (client), 215

Andhra Pradesh, 36–37, 39, 40–41, 43, 74, 77–78, 132. *See also* Crisis of 2010

Anjali (MFI leader), 38

Anna Nagar (Chennai), 192–93

Anne (Kiva lender), 162, 163

AP crisis. *See* Crisis of 2010

Arathi (former MFI employee), 216

ATMS, 26, 221n1

auditing practices, 78–79, 80–81, 82, 83–84

Bagya (research assistant), 126, 211, 214, 215

Bandelji, Nina, 73

Bangalore. *See* Bengaluru

Bangladesh, 6, 34–35, 71, 132, 146, 149, 219n11

BASIX (MFI), 36, 182

Beck, Erin, 11

benevolent protectionism, 50c, 64; career advancement, 50–51; corporate masculinity, 47–48, 49–50, 50c, 60; emotional labor, 6–7, 12, 53–54, 72–73, 78–80, 88, 90–98, 100–101, 103, 122, 153–54, 184, 225n13, 226n16; ethos of, 182–84; feminine versions of, 58–60, 67–68, 96–97, 126–27, 136, 212, 213; of loan officers, 49, 57, 88, 94, 97; masculine performance of, 49–50, 56–58, 178, 183–84, 213; performing authority and care, 52–54, 94; of female MFI employees, 58, 68, 96–97; women's perceived vulnerability, 54–57, 71–72, 74, 96–98, 117–18, 192, 202

Bengaluru (Bangalore), 1–2, 14, 19–20, 65, 104, 107, 111, 141, 143, 212–13, 215

Bhargava, Anjuli, 182

Bhavishya (MFI), 57, 76, 79–80, 82, 130, 211

BizTalk (Prosperity International), 168, 169, 171–72

Boserup, Esther, 35

Bourdieu, Pierre, 195

BRAC (Bangladesh Rural Advancement Committee), 6, 219n11

bribery, 80, 82

Brush, Lisa D., 49, 50c, 60

building trades, 100, 103, 126

Bulmer, M. I. A., 220n21

cab agencies, 137, 138

Cairo, microfinance in, 139

career advancement: accounts of, 180, 184–87; class ceiling, 184, 188–90, 196, 200, 207–8; corporate resistance to, 65, 67; educational credentials, 117, 137, 140, 180, 186, 189–90; marital status, 61–63; repayment of loans in, 13, 17, 72, 179; sense of social responsibility, 95–96, 180; sticky floor effects, 8, 16, 22, 50, 61, 68–69, 188, 200; women MFI employees, 16, 64–65, 67, 187–88, 200, 224n16

caste: in banking networks, 26, 30, 31; and career advancement, 182–83, 189–90, 196, 230n13; caste discrimination, 189–90, 196, 230n10; class and caste hierarchies of male MFI employees, 56–58; and clients' success, 128; marriage arrangements, 118; mobility, 14; in the practice of governance, 49; privilege of, 182–83, 189–90, 196, 230n13

Center for Global Development, 165

CGAP (Consultative Group for Assistance to the Poor), 149

Chandran (Bhavishya employee), 80

Charity Navigator, 152, 157, 163, 183, 229n19

Chennai, 19–20, 52, 55, 57–58, 65, 77, 192–93

Chettair banking system, 30, 31

children: childcare, 61–63, 125, 137, 144, 192–93, 200, 231n17; education of, 57, 105, 109, 111, 112, 116, 117; marriage of, 109, 192

chit funds, 13–14, 75, 106, 113, 119, 225n14; calling chit funds, 113

Christina (Kiva lender), 156–57, 158

Clara (client education, Prosperity International), 168–73, 174, 175

class: class privilege in microfinance industry, 8, 64–65, 182–83, 230n13; defining, 229n2; gendered performance of, 56–58, 60; job mobility, 61, 67–68; upper-class women in corporate culture, 64; in value chain of Michael Porter, 9–10, 9f, 221n26

class ceiling, 184, 188–90, 196, 200, 207–8

clients, absconding, 78–79, 96–98

Coimbatore, 19, 58, 111, 125

colonial banking system, 28–31

community leadership, 101–5, 107–10, 112, 114–15, 193–94, 203

Connell, Raewyn, 63–64

construction work, 100, 103, 138

cooperative societies, 30–31

cooperative women's NGOs, 36

corporate masculinity, 50c; benevolent protectionism, 47–50, 60; interactions with women borrowers, 55–57, 75–76, 78–80, 79–80, 83–84, 87–89, 91, 94–98, 226n16; public image of MFIs, 49–50, 60, 62–64, 66–67, 200; social capital of class-privileged men, 182–83, 230n13; of women loan officers, 50, 62–63, 66–67, 200

COVID-19, 197–98, 202

Craig (Kiva lender), 161–62, 163

credit associations, 30, 193

creditworthiness of women borrowers, 14, 22, 35–41, 70–71, 73, 75–76, 88–89, 94–95, 97–98, 205, 208–9, 225n7

Crisis of 2010 (Andhra Pradesh crisis), 98; community activism after, 106; corporate culture after, 52, 76; farmer suicides, 41, 74; lending patterns precipitating, 36, 45, 197; loan repayments, 72; privatization of banking system, 27, 28; qualifications for loans after, 190–91; re-imaging of MFIs after, 28; Vijay Mahajan and, 183

CSR (corporate social responsibility initiative), 19, 57, 70, 126, 128–30, 163–64, 172–73, 213

dalits, 128

dance sequences in training films, 125, 126

Darshana (group member), 111–12, 113, 114

David (Kiva lender), 158

debt, 8, 25, 37–38, 41, 47, 110, 133–34, 202. *See also* repayment of loans

Deepa (Sowbagya employee), 64, 65

desire to "do something," 60, 109, 111, 129, 137, 144, 206–7

Devi, Rekha, 197, 198

digital credit bureau, 28

disbursement protocols, 2, 3

doing good, 156–57, 162, 163, 167, 169, 176

domestic labor, 14, 60, 116, 118, 120, 133

double bottom line, 16–17

Dunn, Sheryl Wu, 157

education: career advancement and educational credentials, 117, 180, 182, 186, 189–90; of children, 57, 105, 109, 111, 112, 116, 117; educational background of MFI employees, 51–52, 55–56, 61, 64–65, 117, 137, 140, 144,

180, 182, 186, 189–90; expenses of, 105, 109, 209, 231n14; opportunities for, 35–37, 43, 57, 168–71, 180, 182–84, 224n7, 230n13

Elyachar, Julia, 139

embroidery work, 143–44

emotional labor, 6–7, 12, 53–54, 72–73, 78–80, 88, 90–98, 100–101, 103, 122, 153–54, 184, 225n13, 226n16

empowerment training, 36, 66–67, 124–25, 128–29, 131, 139, 145–47

English language skills, 15, 111, 186

entrepreneurship: BizTalk (Prosperity International), 168, 169, 171–72; films promoting, 125–26, 134, 141; guidance for starting businesses, 144–45, 146, 174, 194; identification of, 143; marketing, 139; of women borrowers, 14, 85–86, 91, 112, 119, 122, 132, 135f, 136–40, 137f, 146–47, 194, 203; working mother identity, 136–40

Excelsior Growth Fund, 149

exploitative financial extraction, 41, 71–72, 199

extraction: of creditworthiness, 14, 22, 35–41, 70–71, 73, 75–76, 88–89, 94–95, 97–98, 205, 209, 225n7; of debt, 8, 25, 37–38, 41, 47, 110, 202; exploitative financial extraction, 13–14, 41, 71–72, 199; extractive (use of term), 7–8, 220n21; inclusion as, 34, 222n16; in microfinancial value chain, 10f, 27; performance of field staff, 55–57, 75–76, 78–80, 83–84, 87–89, 91, 96–98, 226n16; stereotype of Third World women, 151, 153–54, 169; of success stories, 17, 22, 54, 79, 119, 123, 125, 127–28, 137–41, 199, 203, 212; of symbolic value, 145, 147, 199; volunteer labor, 22, 100–101, 103–5, 107, 111, 193–94; women in microfinancial value chain, 10f, 27. See also benevolent protectionism; corporate masculinity; gendered extraction; relational work; repayment of loans; unpaid labor of women

farmers, 29, 41, 74, 222n24

female loan officers, 50, 58–59, 59f, 60–63, 66–67, 95–97, 126–27, 136, 212, 213

feminist commodity chains, 8, 9, 11, 12, 200

Fernando, Jude, 132

field staff: auditing practices, 78–79, 80–81, 82, 83–84; call-and-response dialogue, 86, 91; class ceiling for, 184–86, 188–89; conduct during presentations, 43, 75, 83–84; corporate masculinity, 47–48, 50, 50c, 60, 63–64; educational background, 64, 184, 189; employment history, 184–85; family background of, 184, 185, 186–87, 188, 189; interactions with women borrowers, 55–57, 75–76, 78–80, 79–80, 83–84, 87–89, 91, 226n16; job mobility of, 61, 178, 188, 204–5, 209, 224n10; opinions of training programs, 213–14; organizing women into loan groups, 185; regional background of, 56, 186–87, 213; success stories collected by, 199. See also loan officers; trainers

financial literacy programs, 19, 21, 43, 168, 173, 174; importance of, 120–21, 129, 170; instructional material, 26–28, 38, 126, 133–34; instructional videos, 92, 93, 112, 118, 125–26, 133, 134, 141; Prosperity International (MFI), 170; responsible financial behavior, 133–34; savings and loans options, 26–27, 221n1; training in, 16. See also Vriddhi program

A Fistful of Rice (Akula), 189–90

floating fund, 166

Francesca (Kiva lender), 158, 159–60, 163, 166, 167

Friedman, Sam, 188

gambling, 87, 91, 117

gender: benevolent protectionism and governance of, 49, 57, 58, 60; class privilege in microfinance industry, 8, 64–65; of governance, 49–50, 50c, 60; inequity, 29–30, 32, 43–44, 50, 64–65, 223n45; microfinancial value chains, 9–10, 10f, 27, 221n26; social ties, 73, 91, 96, 98, 180, 225n10, 225n11. See also corporate masculinity

gendered extraction, 10f, 27, 95–96; clients' success stories, 17, 22, 54, 79, 119, 123, 125, 127–28, 137–41, 199, 203, 212; of creditworthiness, 14, 22, 35–41, 70–71, 73, 75–76, 88–89, 94–95, 97–98, 205, 208–9, 225n7; interactions with women borrowers, 55–57, 75–76, 78–80, 83–84, 87–89, 91, 94–98, 226n16; stereotype of Third World poor women, 151, 153–54, 169; volunteer labor, 22, 100–101, 103–5, 107, 111, 193–94 gender of governance: job advancement, 8, 16, 22, 50, 61, 64–69, 187–88, 200; mother-hood in corporate culture, 49–50, 60, 61, 62–63, 68, 133–36, 200; performances of relational work, 49, 58, 66–67, 200, 207

Ghosh, Samit, of Ujjivan, 153, 184, 224n13

ghost lending, 93, 108, 112, 114

gift-giving relationships, 159, 162–63, 164, 166

Girija (MFI client/borrower), 191–92, 194, 294

"giving back," 156–57

global North microfinance, 148–49

global value chain (GVC) model, 9f, 221n26

gold loans, 137, 227n16

Gopal (MFI founder), 38

Gouriamma (group member), 113–14

governance of gender: interactions with women borrowers, 49–50, 55–57, 75, 76, 78–80, 87–89, 91, 96–98

government small-business programs, 2, 4, 138, 139

Grama Valachi (MFI), 38, 77, 129–30

Grameen Bank, 6, 90, 106, 149, 182, 219n11

group leaders, 87; coercion applied by, 111–12, 113; as community leaders, 108–9, 115, 193–94, 203; financial brokering skills of, 106, 108–9, 110, 114–15; home environment of, 101, 104–5, 107–8; social work, 110–12, 193–94

groups: joint liability group model, 34–35; membership qualifications, 101–2, 110, 111–13; organization of, 22, 37, 100–103, 122–23, 185; seating arrangements, 58, 59f, 92, 216; as self-monitoring, 71; self-realization exercises, 134–35, 135f; size of, 138, 140, 141, 143; social work, 100–101, 103, 104–5, 193–94; social work in, 122. See also repayment of loans; SHGS

Half the Sky (Kristof and Dunn), 157

Halima (Kanchan MFI client), 143–44, 206–7

hand loans, 113, 118, 119

health care, access to, 112, 127, 128, 130, 205

Heifer International, 153

Hewlett-Packard, 163–64

home ownership, 86, 118, 187

home repairs, 107, 231n14

hospitality, 80, 81f

household incomes, 14, 16, 27, 44, 231n14

house verification procedures, 84–88

husbands, 111, 123; business ventures with wives, 137; in eligibility criteria, 119; employment of, 14, 86, 87, 91, 133, 192–94; entrepreneurship of, 137, 138; wives' sup-port of, 109, 204–5; women's independence from, 138

hygiene education, 128, 130

II-M-Ahmedabad, 182

impact investing, 180, 187, 230n9

India: agriculture, 29, 31, 34, 71, 202; eco-nomic inequality in, 4–5; establishment of commercial microfinance industry, 202; liberalization in Indian economy, 3–4

indigenous banking institutions, 30, 31

Indira Kranti Patham, 37

informal loans. See gold loans; hand loans; moneylenders; pawnbrokers

instructional material, 26–27, 38, 92–93, 112, 118, 125–26, 130, 133–34, 135f, 141

Integrated Rural Development Program, 31–32, 33

interest rates, 1, 26–27, 36, 41–42, 49, 113, 121, 166

intimate transactions, 12, 88, 100–101, 103, 122, 153–54, 225n10

invisibilized state, 201, 203–4

IRDP (Integrated Rural Development Pro-gram), 185

Ishwari (loan client), 86, 88, 91, 94, 120–22, 215–16

Jagruti (MFI), 77–78

Janaki (Sowbagya loan officer), 61

Janine (Prosperity director), 170–71, 173

Jayanthi (group leader), 104–5, 107, 231n14

jewelry, 91, 110, 119, 121, 227n16

John (head of Bhavishya's CSR division), 57, 70

joint liability group model (Bangladesh), 34–35

Jyoti (MFI employee), 61

Kabeer, Naila, 6

Kalyani (loan client, group leader), 87, 89, 91, 92, 116–17, 122

Kamala (client, construction worker), 126, 141

Kanchan (MFI): after crisis of 2010, 52, 106; CSR (corporate responsibility initiative), 19, 126, 129; fieldwork in, 19, 20, 107; group leaders, 107–10, 111, 112, 114–15; loans from, 109, 110, 113; Maya (director, Kanchan client education program in India), 66–67, 171–74, 214; Prosperity International (MFI) partnership with, 171; TOT (training for trainers), 66, 76, 80, 130–31, 213. *See also* Shaktisri training program

Kannada language, 1, 100, 134, 214, 215

Kanter, Rosabeth Moss, 223–24

Kar, Sohini: on bundled life insurance, 54; on credit work, 14, 71, 226n4; on emotional labor, 225n13, 226n16; on field-workers, 71, 72, 184; on impact of commercial MFIS, 7

Karim, Lamia, 6, 146, 227n9

Karnataka, 15, 19, 52, 100, 215

Karunakaran, Kalpana, 36, 71, 72

Keira (Kiva lender), 164–65

Kelly (Kiva lender), 167

Kerala, 213, 214, 222n24

Khader, Serene, 175

Khushi (character in training video), 133–34

Kiva gift certificates and cards, 159, 162–63, 164, 166

Kiva lenders: altruism of, 148–49, 159, 161, 176, 210; assumptions of, 204; contributions to MFIS, 165–66; corporate lenders, 163–64; guilt, 156–57, 168; images of impoverishment, 161, 163–65, 164f, 176; lender strategies, 159–62, 163; person-to-person linkages with borrowers, 8, 150, 160–62, 164, 167, 210; reactions to ticking clock controversy, 166, 167; satisfaction of, 156–57, 158, 161–62, 164–65, 166, 167; selecting recipients, 158–59, 160f, 161, 163–64; stereotype of Third World poor women, 151, 153–54, 169; surveys of, 157–58, 166; women as, 156–57, 158, 159–60, 163, 166, 167

Kiva loans: description of, 158; gender empowerment, 158; gift certificates and cards, 159, 162–63, 164, 166; gift-giving relationships, 159, 162–63, 164, 166; relationships forged by, 164–65; repayment of, 158; ticking clock controversy, 165–67

Kiva.org, 10f; compared with bad charities, 157–58; donors' impressions of, 156–57;

influence of, 155–56, 162; loan offerings, 152, 155–56, 158, 165–66; marketing techniques, 165–67; perceived altruism, 155–56; political accountability, 151–52; profiles of women borrowers, 151, 153–54, 155–58, 169; surveys of, 157–58, 218; vision of microfinance presented by, 155

Kiva.org website: profile of loan recipients, 158, 160f; selecting a borrower, 158–59, 160f, 161; ticking clock icon, 165–66

Krishnan (Bhavishya), 83–84

Kristof, Nicholas, 157

Kumar (Shaktisri trainer, Kerala), 213–14

Lakshmi (MFI member), 144–45

Land Improvement Loans Act (1883), 29

Latin America: client education programs in, 168–69, 173, 174

Laurison, Daniel, 188

leaf plate-making machine, 136–37, 137f

Levien, Michael, 230n22

life insurance policies, 53–54

loan *melas*, 33

loan officers, 10f; career advancement for, 13, 17, 22, 72, 75, 88–91, 95–96, 179; client interviews, 84–89, 91; clients' expressions of gratitude, 47–48, 70, 73; conduct of, 41, 71, 72, 74–75, 77–78, 84–87, 90; emotional labor of, 6–7, 12, 53–54, 72–73, 78–80, 88, 90–98, 100–101, 103, 122, 153–54, 184, 225n13, 226n16; experiences with nonpayment, 78–79, 95–96; gendered performance, 56–58, 70, 75, 96–98, 213; loan verification procedures, 84–88, 94; orientation training, 89–91; relational work of, 12, 13, 15–16, 71–73, 78, 84–93, 96–97; standardization of client presentations, 83–88; trust relationships with clients, 8, 12–13, 28, 73, 78, 80, 91, 96–98, 157, 216; women as, 50, 58–59, 59f, 60–63, 66–67, 95–97, 126–27, 136, 212, 213; on women's work, 132, 133

loans: for businesses, 137; for child-rearing, 105, 121, 133–34, 231n14; conditions for denial of, 87; disbursement of, 1–2, 28, 32–33, 38–39, 165–66; empowerment training, 36, 66–67, 124–25, 128–29, 131, 139, 145–47; ghost lending, 93, 108, 112, 114; gold loans, 137, 227n16; life insurance policies, 53–54;

loans: for businesses (continued)
  moneylenders, 14, 26–31, 34, 41, 109, 113,
  121, 133, 227n9; multiple sources of, 36, 41,
  87–88, 109, 113, 118, 120–21, 191; pawnbrokers, 91, 110, 121, 137, 227n16; women's
  empowerment as justification for,
  127–28, 157

Mader, Philip, 149, 219n8, 220n18, 222n8,
  225n12, 227n2, 228n4
Mahajan, Vijay, 35–37, 43, 182–84, 230n13
Malegam Report, 42
male kin guarantors, 227n10
male MFI employees: backgrounds of, 56–57,
  70, 180, 182–83, 185–86; career advancement, 13, 17, 22, 61, 72, 75, 88–91, 95–96,
  179, 224n10; caste privilege and career
  advancement, 56–58, 182–83, 189–90, 196,
  230n13; corporate masculinity, 50, 63–64;
  educational background, 61, 180, 182; family
  responsibilities, 62–63; job stability, 209;
  perspectives on their companies, 180, 216;
  preferred by women loan officers, 62–63
Mamatha (research assistant), 53, 89, 104, 140,
  214, 215
marketing, 9f, 10f, 18, 142, 163–66
marriage, 14, 61–63, 119, 132, 137, 192, 215–16
Mary (loan customer), 86, 91, 122
Matter to a Million campaign (Hewlett-
  Packard), 163–64, 164f
Maya (director, Kanchan client education program in India), 66–67, 142–43, 171–74, 214
medical expenses, 53–54, 78, 105, 107, 109,
  191–92, 194–95, 209, 231n14
meetings of borrowers: author's presence at,
  92, 216; discipline of, 91–92, 95; emphasis
  on financial responsibility, 90, 91, 92,
  93, 94; leaders of, 104–5, 107–10, 111, 112,
  114–15, 231n14; loan conditions reviewed
  at, 90–94; orientation at, 89–91; pledge
  rituals, 12, 90, 92; seating arrangements,
  58, 59f, 92, 216
MFI employees: career advancement, 16,
  64–65, 72, 75, 88–91, 95–96, 180, 184,
  187–90; client presentations, 79–80, 83–84,
  83–88, 226n16; educational background,
  51–52, 55–56, 64–65, 117, 137, 140, 144, 180,
  182, 186, 189–90; employment back-

ground, 189; family backgrounds, 186, 189;
gendered performance of, 49, 55–56; job
mobility, 61, 178, 188, 204–5, 209, 224n10;
job satisfaction, 16, 47–48, 53–55, 75, 78,
186, 207–8, 231n17; rural backgrounds of,
56; women borrowers' support of male
workers, 204–5. *See also* field staff; loan
officers; trainers
MFIN (Microfinance Institutions Network),
183, 197
MFI professionals in the United States,
150–51, 169–70
MFIS, 1, 10f; accounting practices, 80–84;
clients' success stories, 17, 22, 54, 79, 119,
123, 125, 127–28, 137–41, 199, 203, 212; commercial MFIS, 7, 13–14, 153, 202; competition for clients, 36–37, 39–40, 187; consent
for research interactions, 211; corporate
culture of, 16, 38–39, 47–48, 50–52, 60–63,
68, 133–36, 151–52, 186, 189, 200; corporate
masculinity, 49–50, 60, 62–64, 66–67, 200;
criticism of, 41, 78, 183, 186, 189, 213–14;
CSR (corporate responsibility initiative),
19, 57, 126, 128, 129, 130, 172–73, 213; hiring
practices, 189–90, 197–98; impact of
COVID-19 on, 197–98, 202; investments in,
4, 36, 37–39, 41; job mobility, 61, 224n10;
life insurance policies, 53–54; Malegam
Report influence on, 42; Microfinance
Institutions Network (MFIN), 42–43;
monitoring of client interactions, 27, 76;
national banking policies, 201–2; as NFBCS
(nonbanking financial companies), 38,
222n2, 225n14; regulation of, 28, 36–37;
scams, 75, 225n14; state support for, 6, 8,
26–27, 201–2. *See also* Crisis of 2010; Kiva
headings; SHGS; training programs; individual headings (e.g., Sowbayga [MFI])
microcredit programs, 36, 222n21, 231n13
Microfinance Institutions Network (MFIN),
42–43
microfinance schism, 201, 202
microfinancial value chains, 9, 10f, 27,
177–179, 209–210
Miles, Andrew, 188
Mills, C. Wright, 179, 195
minimalist training model (Bhavishya
[MFI]), 130

Moeller, Katherine, 128
Mohanty, Chandra, 151, 154
moneylenders, 14, 26–31, 34, 41, 109, 113, 121, 133, 227n9
money management. *See* financial literacy programs
Moser, Caroline, 101
motherhood: childcare, 61–63, 125, 137, 144, 192–93, 200, 231n17; construction of, 132; in corporate culture, 49–50, 60, 61, 62–63, 68, 133–36, 200; gender of governance, 49–50, 60; household responsibilities of, 39–40, 102, 109, 132–33, 204–5; stay-at-home mothers, 14, 143, 147; in training program modules, 124, 134–36; working mother identity, 124–25, 127, 133–41, 143, 146, 200
multiple loans, 36, 41, 87–88, 109, 113, 118, 120–21, 191
Mustafaraj, Eni, 218

NABARD (National Agricultural Bank), 34, 71, 202
Nadia (loan officer), 61, 95–96
Nagar, Richa, 129
Nair, Malavika, 30
Nalini (loan customer), 87, 89, 117–18, 122
Nambiar, Manoj Joseph, 197, 198
Nandini (Shaktisri trainer), 58–59, 59f, 60, 126–27, 136, 212, 213
Narayan (MFI leader), 42–43
Naren (Sowbagya loan officer), 53, 54, 61
National Agricultural Bank (NABARD), 34, 71, 202
neighborhood advocacy, 101–3
NFBCS (nonbanking financial companies), 38, 222n2, 225n14
Nike Corporation, 128
nonpayment of loans, 1–2, 41, 42, 78–79, 95–96, 101, 187

Padmavathi (loan client), 140–41
Parvathy (loan client), 141–42
patriarchalism, 43–44, 64, 121, 200–201, 223n45
pawnbrokers, 91, 110, 121, 137, 227n16
peer-to-peer platforms. *See* Kiva.org
pledge rituals, 12, 90, 92

Porter, Michael: classic value chain of, 9–10, 9f, 221n26
postal banking system, 27, 29–30
PRADAN, 182
Pradeep (Shaktisri trainer), 213
Prashanth (Shaktisri trainer), 140, 228n19
priority sector lending requirement, 28, 31–32
property ownership, 109, 110–11, 118, 191–92, 200
Prosperity International (MFI): BizTalk, 168, 169, 171–72; client advocacy, 168–73, 174, 175; client education initiatives at, 19, 153, 168–69, 170–74, 175; commercial MFIS in India, 153; CSR programming, 172–73; donor priorities of, 173; evaluations of client training, 131–32, 227n8; Indian microfinance industry, 153; low-income microfinance market, 170; New York office, 19, 168; research interviews at, 217–18. *See also* Kanchan (MFI); Shaktisri training program
public image of MFIS: after 2010 crisis, 28, 41–43; corporate culture, 16, 38–39, 50–52, 60–63, 68, 133–36, 151–52, 186, 189, 200; corporate masculinity, 49–50, 60, 62–64, 66–67, 200; as ethical, 151–52; as legitimate, 74, 75, 149, 225n14; performance of authority and care, 47–48, 52–54, 94, 182–84; publicity videos, 136; scams in, 75, 225n14; women's success stories, 17, 22, 79, 119, 123–25, 127–28, 137–41, 199, 203, 212. *See also* Kiva.org

race, representations of, 126, 133–34, 158–59, 189
Radhakrishnan, Smitha (author): access to training sessions, 214; clients' engagement with, 53, 119, 211, 215–16; connections with clients, 215–16; construction of biographies, 179, 195; corporate connections, 212–14; improvements on TOT program suggested by, 217–18; interviews with MFI leaders, 216–17; on Kerala's political culture, 213–14; personal details of, 215–16; proposed improvements to education programs, 174; report to Prosperity International (MFI), 174; research assistants, 53, 89, 104, 126, 140, 211, 214, 215; research techniques, 212

Rajiv (Shaktisri trainer), 55–56, 58, 142, 212, 213
Rajiv Gandhi Foundation, 183
Ramanathan (founder-director of Grama Valachi), 77, 78
Ramya (director of financial literacy program), 26–27, 28
Rang De (microcredit organization), 231n13
Ranjan (Shaktisri trainer), 56–57, 58, 213
Ratna (group leader), 192–94, 195, 230n22
RBI (Reserve Bank of India), 38–39, 42
relational work: articulations of benevolent protectionism, 56–58, 58–60, 126–27, 136, 183–84, 212, 213; auditing practices, 78–79, 80–81, 82, 83–84; boundaries of, 55–56, 57–58, 75, 78, 79–80, 91, 226n16; client relations with loan officer, 78–79, 87, 91–92, 94–98; embedded in structural inequality, 200–201; gendered performances of, 49, 55–56, 58, 66–67, 75, 96–98, 200, 207, 212, 213; interactions with women borrowers, 55–57, 75–76, 78–80, 83–84, 87–89, 91, 96–98, 226n16; in Kiva loans, 159, 162–63, 164, 166; recruitment of borrowers, 1–4, 34, 36–37, 39, 74, 130–31, 187, 207, 209; social ties, 73, 91, 96, 98, 102–3, 180, 225nn10–11; terms of address, 55–56, 79, 226n16; trust relationships with clients, 8, 12–13, 28, 73, 78–80, 91, 96–98, 157, 216; women's financial management roles, 101–3
remote microfinance. See Kiva.org
repayment of loans, 138; absconding clients, 78–79, 96–98; career advancement for loan officers, 13, 17, 72, 75, 95–96, 179; in classic value chain of Michael Porter, 9f; conditions for, 1–2, 12, 74, 90, 92, 216; during COVID-19 lockdowns, 197; crisis of nonpayment, 32, 41, 45, 70–74, 78–79, 96–98, 187; goodwill generated by, 179; of informal loans, 113; interest rates, 1, 26–27, 36, 41–42, 49, 103, 121, 133, 166; in microfinancial value chain, 10f; nonpayment of loans, 1–2, 41, 42, 78–79, 95–98, 101, 187; relational work of, 1–2, 73, 88–89, 95–96; as unpaid gendered labor, 70–72, 199, 200; by women, 13, 25, 40, 71, 74, 179, 197, 219n11

research assistants, 53, 89, 104, 126, 140, 211, 214, 215
Reserve Bank of India (RBI), 21; commercial microfinance, 183; during COVID-19 crisis, 197–98; financial ecosystem, 39; gendered financial extraction, 39; Malegam Committee, 42; MFIS, 41, 197–98, 201, 202; priority sector lending requirements, 31–32, 38; regulatory actions of, 28
Richard (HP employee), 163
Ritu (bank worker), 62–63, 64, 66
Roodman, David, 165, 167
Roy, Ananya, 6, 149, 153
Rs.200 crore Micro Finance Development and Equity Fund, 39
rural areas: agriculture, 29, 31, 34, 40, 41, 71, 74, 202, 222n24; banking services in, 28, 30–31, 32, 34, 39; women in, 34–35, 39–40, 45, 222n24

Said, Edward, 154
Samantha (Prosperity International [MFI] director), 173, 174
Samudra (MFI), 1, 2–3, 189
Sanchez, Andrew, 229n2
Sandhya (Samudra loan officer), 1, 2, 3
Sangtin Collective, 129
Sanjay (Samudra loan officer), 1, 2, 3
Santosh (investment banker, MFI founder), 47–48, 50
Sanyal, Paromita, 6, 36
Saradha chit fund scam, 75
Sarina (MFI employee), 77–78
Satish (Jayanthi's husband), 104–5, 107
savings associations, 106, 110, 113
scams, 75, 225n14
Schwittay, Anke, 153
self-realization exercises, 134–35, 135f
self-sufficiency, 6, 13, 18
Selvi (entrepreneur), 136–40, 137f, 146, 147, 203
SEWA (Self-Employed Women's Association), 182
Shaktisri training program: BizTalk (Prosperity International), 168, 169, 171–72; borrowers as mothers, 124, 127, 134–36; business training, 144–45; children's success, 134, 136; clients' expressions of gratitude, 136–37; as CSR initiative, 129;

effectiveness of, 141, 170; entrepreneurial training program, 19, 66, 125–27, 136–40, 137f, 146–47, 194, 203; films, 125–26, 134, 141; instructional styles, 55–57; Maya (director of client education program in India), 66–67, 171–74, 214; self-evaluation, 134, 135f; self-management module, 125, 134–36, 135f, 140–41, 143; training sessions for trainers, 130–31. *See also* individual headings for trainers (e.g., Rajiv)

Shankari (group organizer), 100–101, 103, 122–23

Shanthi (group leader, community leader), 107–10, 112, 114–15

SHARE, 36

Sharma, Aradhana, 128–29

Sheila (loan customer), 85–86, 91, 112, 119, 122

SHGS (self-help groups): business ventures, 137–38, 139; educational programs of, 26–27, 34–36, 40–41, 45, 137–38; funding of, 37–38; linkage programs, 34–36, 40–41; loans to women, 26–27, 35, 39, 40–41, 202; MFIS, competition with, 36–37, 41, 45; National Agricultural Bank (NABARD), 34, 71, 202; organization of, 28, 34, 36–37, 71, 110, 222n24; social programs, 127–28; state-run programs of, 6, 25, 45

single women, 61, 85–86, 91, 112, 113, 119, 122, 132

SKS Microfinance (Swayam Krushi Sangh), 36, 41, 153, 179, 189–90, 230n10, 231n18

small finance banks, 198

small-scale microcredit, 205, 231n13

social impact investing. *See* Kiva.org

social work, 100–101, 103, 104–5, 122, 193–94

Sowbagya (MFI): corporate culture of, 47–48, 117, 129, 186, 188–89; customer benefits, 94; customers' praise of, 140–41; loan approval, 115; loan officers, 95–96, 186–89; loans from, 109, 115, 119, 140–41, 191, 192; monitoring of client interactions, 76; relational work, 75; research access to, 53–54, 211; training programs, 89–94, 115, 128; Vriddhi program, 19–21, 26, 36, 124, 129, 133–34, 136; women employees in, 61, 95–96

standardized letters in Bhavishya training model, 130

sticky floor effects, 8, 16, 22, 50, 61, 68–69, 188, 200

Strumpell, Christine, 229n2

success stories, 17, 22, 54, 79, 119, 123, 125, 127–28, 137–41, 199, 203, 212

suicides, 41, 74

Sundaram (microfinance policy maker), 43–44

Sundari (MFI employee), 61, 95

supertrainers, 130, 131

Suresh (Sowbagya employee), 53, 54

Swades (film), 184

tailoring businesses, 78, 79, 110, 111, 126, 135, 144

talented Indian technocrat: trope of, 184

Tamil language, 1, 90, 93, 100, 134, 212, 215

Tamil Nadu, 52, 55–60, 59f, 77, 126–27, 136, 142, 212–13, 215

Tata, Ratan, 182

Taylor, Keeanga-Yamahtta, 222n16

Taylor, Marcus, 222n16

terms of address, 55–56, 79, 226n16

Third World women, stereotype of, 151, 153–54, 169

ticking clock controversy (Kiva.org), 165–67

time management, 109, 134, 137–38, 139

TOT (training for trainers), 66, 76, 80, 130–31, 213

trainers, 10f, 20f; customer engagement, 55–58, 80, 125, 214; educational background, 55, 56, 189–90; evaluation of, 76, 125–27, 131–32, 143, 227n8; femininity idealized by, 125; gendered performance, 55–56, 75, 213; knowledge of training material, 126; personalities of, 168–70, 213–14; quotas, 16; women as, 36, 58–61, 59f, 67–68, 126–27, 212, 213

training programs, 59f, 81f; audience engagement, 22, 55–58, 125, 126, 136–37, 141–43; clients' responses, 22, 55–58, 89–93, 124–26, 140–43, 147, 228n19; corporate representatives at, 126, 127; CSR (corporate responsibility initiative), 19, 57, 126, 128–30; entrepreneurial training programs, 66, 127, 136–40, 137f, 146–47, 168–69, 171–72, 194, 203; gendered ideals in, 134–36; guidance for starting businesses in, 144–45, 146,

training programs (continued)
174, 194; instructional videos, 92, 93, 112,
118, 125–26, 133–34, 141; loan conditions
reviewed at, 90–94; for new employees,
82–83; primacy of motherhood, 133–36; researcher's presence at, 126, 140–41, 212–13,
214; self-realization exercises, 134–35,
135f; success stories at, 17, 79, 119, 123, 125,
127–28, 137–41, 199, 203, 212; TOT (training
for trainers), 66, 76, 80, 130–31, 213
trust relationships, 8, 12–13, 28, 73, 78, 80, 91,
96–98, 157, 216
Turkey: entrepreneurial training programs
in, 132–33
Turnell, Sean, 30–31

Ujjivan, 153, 184, 224n13
unbanked majority, women as, 201–2
UN Conference on Women (1995), 35
unemployment rates, 4, 105, 107, 206, 219n7
Union Budget (2005–6), 38–39
unpaid labor of women: childcare, 61–63,
125, 137, 144, 192–93, 200, 231n17; financial
management, 71–72, 102–4, 199, 200–201;
as volunteers, 22, 100–101, 103–5, 107, 111,
193–94
urban women, 14, 25, 39–40, 45, 206
Urdu language, 1, 100

value chain of Michael Porter, 9–10, 9f,
221n26
Velan (MFI employee), 75, 184–89, 196, 216
Velugu (state-sponsored program), 37
videos as instructional material, 92, 93, 112,
118, 125–26, 133–34, 141
Vijaya (client), 109–10, 113
Vinay (Sowbagya branch manager), 53,
84–87
Vishadi (character in training video), 133–34
volunteers, women as, 22, 100–101, 103–5, 107,
111, 193–94
Vriddhi program, 19–21, 26, 36, 124, 129,
133–34, 136

wage labor, 101, 132, 143–44
weddings, loans for, 121, 133–34
Wichterich, Christa, 43
William (HP employee), 163–64

Wilson, Kim, 216
women borrowers, 10f, 135f; ambitions of,
60, 85, 137–38, 144–46, 174, 193, 194, 209;
childcare, 61–63, 125, 137, 144, 192–93, 200,
231n17; community connections of, 15,
108–10, 192–94, 195, 230n22; creditworthiness of, 14, 22, 35–41, 70–71, 73, 75–76,
88–89, 94–95, 97–98, 205, 208–9, 225n7;
desire for concrete direction, 144–46, 174,
194; desire for paid work, 60, 109, 111, 129,
137, 144–46, 206–7; educational background of, 8, 61, 64–65, 105, 111, 116–17,
119, 137–38, 140, 144, 191; empowerment
of, 5, 6, 36, 39–40, 66–69, 127–28, 157;
as entrepreneurs, 14, 85–86, 91, 112, 119,
122, 132, 135f, 136–40, 137f, 146–47, 194,
203; extractive value of, 7–8, 27, 88, 207,
220n21, 220n22; histories of trauma, 192,
194, 195; household incomes, 14, 16, 27, 44,
110, 231n14; household responsibilities of,
39–40, 102, 109, 132–33, 204–5; interactions with, 55–57, 75–76, 78–80, 83–84,
87–89, 91, 96–98, 226n16; Kiva.org and,
151, 153–54, 155–58, 169; living conditions,
14, 85, 86, 87, 107–8, 110, 118, 191–92,
205; loan histories, 84–89, 118–19, 140;
loyalty of, 129, 191, 192, 197, 198; marital
status, 14, 61–63, 119, 132, 137, 192, 215–16;
multiple loans, 36, 41, 87–89, 109, 113, 118,
120–21, 191; profile of, 13–15, 70–71, 225n2;
qualifications of, 85–86, 87, 110, 118, 130–32,
190–91; recruitment of, 1–4, 34, 36–37,
39, 74, 130–31, 187, 207, 209; reliability of,
2, 25, 43, 190–91, 197, 198; responses to
training sessions, 22, 55–58, 88–93, 124–26,
140–43, 147, 228n19; retention of, 88–89,
96–98, 209; success stories of, 17, 22, 54,
79, 119, 123, 125, 127–28, 137–41, 199, 203,
212; trust relationships with loan officers,
8, 12–13, 28, 73, 78–80, 91, 96–98, 157, 216;
vulnerability of, 54–57, 71–72, 74, 96–98,
117–18, 120–21, 192, 202; Western profiles
of, 151, 153–54, 155–58, 169–70. See also
group leaders; groups; individual headings
(e.g., Ishwari [loan customer]); individual
interviewees
women in MFIs: advancement of, 8, 16, 22,
50, 61, 64–69, 187–88, 200; as aspirational

figures, 49; benevolent protectionism of, 58, 60, 96–97; career advancement, 16, 61–63, 200, 224n16; childcare responsibilities, 61–63, 200; class-privilege of, 64–65, 67–68; client relations, 49, 58, 66–67, 200, 207; corporate masculinity adopted by, 50, 62–63, 66–67, 200; job satisfaction, 61, 66–67, 207–8, 231n17; as loan officers, 50, 58, 61–63, 66–67, 95–97; Maya (director, Kanchan client education program in India), 66–67, 171–74, 214; recruitment of, 61, 67–68; as trainers, 36, 58–61, 59f, 67–68, 126–27, 212, 213
women's triple burden (Moser), 101
working-class women: class disadvantages, 14; community leadership, 101–5, 107–10, 112, 114–15, 193–94, 203; creditworthiness of, 14, 22, 35–41, 70–71, 73, 75–76, 88–89, 94–95, 97–98, 205, 208–9, 225n7; financial interactions in neighborhoods, 109–10; impact of financial regulations on, 43; in microfinancial value chain, 10f; repayment of loans by, 2; social relationships, 109–10; social work of, 100–101, 103, 104–5, 122, 193–94. *See also* groups
working mother ideal, 124–25, 134–41, 143, 146, 200
World Bank, 37, 128, 149, 182, 207

Young, Stephen, 132, 226n16
Yunus, Mohammad, 6, 90, 106, 149, 182, 219n11

Zelizer, Viviana. *See* relational work